"Mark Dever persuasively covers in this well-written book the basics of reaching the lost with the gosr   ·acti-
cal application."
    —ROBERT E. COLEM   :lism
    and discipleship, (y

"Few men have the heart and s................... to the subject of evangelism as my friend Mark Dever. We will all be better evangelists having read and reflected on the theological truths of this great book."
    —JOHNNY HUNT, pastor, First Baptist Church of Woodstock,
    Georgia

"The author led me to Christ more than a decade ago. He knows whereof he speaks. He's the only Christian I know who once led a college "atheists' group" for evangelistic purposes! This book—filled with practical insights about how to obey the Great Commission—should spur us on, both individually and as churches, to shine like stars in the universe."
    —JOHN FOLMAR, pastor, United Christian Church of Dubai,
    United Arab Emirates

"Our theological lenses vary, but this we all still see the same: the fulfillment of the Christian life and the vocation of the church is to share in God's redeeming work in the world. And whatever your tradition, there is something in this book that will help you understand and do that better. In the thirty years I have known Mark Dever, he has always been studying and practicing what he writes about here. Read, grow, and go!"
    —DAVID R. THOMAS, senior pastor, Centenary,
    A United Methodist Congregation, Lexington, Kentucky

"Mark's deep felt desire to see people come to Christ combined with a rock steady commitment to Biblical evangelism has birthed an important book for our times; a book that everyone who desires to share their faith—faithfully—should read."
    —J. MACK STILES, general secretary, IFES, Dubai; author,
    Speaking of Jesus

THE GOSPEL &
PERSONAL EVANGELISM

Crossway Books by Mark Dever:

The Message of the Old Testament: Promises Made
The Message of the New Testament: Promises Kept
Nine Marks of a Healthy Church (New Expanded Edition)
The Deliberate Church:
Building Your Ministry on the Gospel (co-author)
What Is a Healthy Church?

THE GOSPEL &
PERSONAL EVANGELISM

Mark E. Dever

Foreword by C.J. Mahaney

CROSSWAY BOOKS
WHEATON, ILLINOIS

The Gospel and Personal Evangelism

Copyright © 2007 by Mark Dever

Published by Crossway Books
          a publishing ministry of Good News Publishers
          1300 Crescent Street
          Wheaton, Illinois 60187

Unless otherwise indicated, Scripture quotations are from *The Holy Bible: New International Version.*® Copyright © 1973, 1978, 1984 by International Bible Society. Used by permission of Zondervan Publishing House. All rights reserved.

The "NIV" and "New International Version" trademarks are registered in the United States Patent and Trademark Office by International Bible Society. Use of either trademark requires the permission of International Bible Society.

Cover art direction: Josh Dennis

Cover design: Luke Daab

Cover illustration: Bridgeman Art Gallery

First printing 2007

Printed in the United States of America

Library of Congress Cataloging-in-Publication Data
Dever, Mark.
  The Gospel and Personal Evangelism / Mark E. Dever;
foreword by C.J. Mahaney.
    p. cm.
  ISBN 13: 978-1-58134-846-0 (tpb)
  ISBN 10: 1-58134-799-5
  1. Evangelistic work. 2. Witness bearing (Christianity) I. Title.
BV3790.D4765   2007
248'.5—dc22   2007016748

CH		17	16	15	14	13	12	11	10	09	08	07
15	14	13	12	11	10	9	8	7	6	5	4	3	2	1

With thanks to God
for his faithfulness
in fruit given through evangelism,
now precious friends—John, Karan, Ryan—and in
friends who've taught me about evangelism:

JIM PACKER

WILL METZGER

MACK STILES

and

SEBASTIAN TRAEGER

Contents

Foreword

One of the first things I discovered about my very good friend Mark Dever is that he walks as fast as he talks. It was over ten years ago that I drove from my home church in the suburbs of Washington DC to meet Mark at Capitol Hill Baptist Church, where he serves as senior pastor. It was a pleasant day, so Mark suggested we walk the short distance from his church's historic building to a nearby Subway restaurant. Even though I usually walk at a brisk pace myself, I had trouble keeping up with Mark.

Moments before entering the fast-food establishment, Mark explained that he ate there often, not because of the fine cuisine, but for the purpose of sharing the gospel. Inside, he greeted the owners—a Muslim couple from India—by name and engaged them in friendly conversation.

As we sat down, I began to quiz Mark about his heart for unbelievers and his strategy for sharing the gospel. He told me that he intentionally frequents the same restaurants and businesses so he can develop relationships and hopefully create evangelistic opportunities.

Since that day, I've attempted to follow Mark's example and had the joy of sharing the good news with many people I meet along the seemingly uneventful route of daily life.

If you, like me, have walked through entire days unconcerned and unaware of the lost sinners all around you, or if you desire to share the gospel but are unsure how to build a relationship or start a conversation, *The Gospel and Personal Evangelism* will encourage and equip you. As you read, you will catch Mark's contagious passion to share the gospel of Jesus Christ and receive practical instruction in personal evangelism.

While this book is for all Christians, it is also a gift to pastors. Cultivating evangelism in the local church is one of a pastor's most important responsibilities and difficult challenges. Perhaps *the* most difficult. However, through the pages of *The Gospel and Personal Evangelism,* Mark's wisdom, teaching, and experience will support you in this vital work of ministry.

That's why, for many years now, I've been pestering Mark to write this book. It's so that by the grace of God, church members and pastors and you and I will notice those we once ignored. It's so that we will befriend sinners who are without hope and without God. It's so that we will share with them the good news of Jesus Christ's substitutionary sacrifice on the cross. It's so that someday those lost souls might turn from their sins and trust in the Savior's death and resurrection on their behalf. And then, there will be some serious rejoicing—on earth and in heaven (Luke 15:10)!

Mark, thank you for writing *The Gospel and Personal Evangelism*. Thank you even more for your compelling example of compassion for the lost and for your faithfulness to proclaim Jesus Christ and him crucified. May there be many gospel conversations and abundant evangelistic fruit as a result of this book.

I'm looking forward to our next lunch together, my friend. Let's walk to Subway.

C.J. Mahaney
Sovereign Grace Ministries

Introduction
An Amazing Story

Let me tell you an amazing story about a person you want to be like. And please hang in there through some of the details. I can't tell stories any other way.

John Harper was born in a Christian home in Glasgow, Scotland, in 1872. When he was about fourteen years old, he became a Christian himself, and from that time on, he began to tell others about Christ. At seventeen years of age, he began to preach, going down the streets of his village and pouring out his soul in passionate pleading for men to be reconciled to God.

After five or six years of toiling on street corners preaching the gospel and working in the mill during the day, Harper was taken in by the Reverend E. A. Carter of Baptist Pioneer Mission in London. This set Harper free to devote his whole time and energy to the work so dear to his heart—evangelism. Soon, in September 1896, Harper started his own church. This church, which he began with just twenty-five members, numbered over five hundred by the time he left thirteen years later. During this time he had been both married and widowed. Before he lost his wife, God blessed Harper with a beautiful little girl named Nana.

Harper's life was an eventful one. He almost drowned several times. When he was two-and-a-half years of age, he fell into a well but was resuscitated by his mother. At the age of twenty-six, he was swept out to sea by a reverse current and barely survived. And at thirty-two he faced death on a leaking ship in the Mediterranean. If anything, these brushes with death simply seemed to confirm John Harper in his zeal for evangelism, which marked him out for the rest of the days of his life.

While pastoring his church in London, Harper continued his fervent and faithful evangelism. In fact, he was such a zealous evangelist that the Moody Church in Chicago asked him to come over to America for a series of meetings. He did, and they went well. A few years later, Moody Church asked him if he would come back again. And so it was that Harper boarded a ship one day with a second-class ticket at Southampton, England, for the voyage to America.

Harper's wife had died just a few years before, and he had with him his only child, Nana, age six. What happened after this we know mainly from two sources. One is Nana, who died in 1986 at the age of eighty. She remembered being woken up by her father a few nights into their journey. It was about midnight, and he said that the ship they were on had struck an iceberg. Harper told Nana that another ship was just about there to rescue them, but, as a precaution, he was going to put her in a lifeboat with an older cousin, who had accompanied them. As for Harper, he would wait until the other ship arrived.

The rest of the story is a tragedy well known. Little Nana and her cousin were saved. But the ship they were on was the *Titanic*. The only way we know what happened to John Harper after is because, in a prayer meeting in Hamilton, Ontario, some months later, a young Scotsman stood up in tears and told the extraordinary story of how he was converted. He explained that he had been on the *Titanic* the night it struck the iceberg. He had clung to a piece of floating debris in the freezing waters. "Suddenly," he said, "a wave brought a man near, John Harper. He, too, was holding a piece of wreckage.

"He called out, 'Man, are you saved?'

"'No, I am not,' I replied.

"He shouted back, 'Believe on the Lord Jesus Christ, and thou shalt be saved.'

"The waves bore [Harper] away, but a little later, he was washed back beside me again. 'Are you saved now?' he called out.

"'No,' I answered. 'Believe on the Lord Jesus Christ and thou shalt be saved.'

"Then losing his hold on the wood, [Harper] sank. And there, alone in the night with two miles of water under me, I trusted Christ as my savior. I am John Harper's last convert."[1]

Now for something completely different—my life story as an evangelist. I am no John Harper. Sometimes I'm a reluctant evangelist. In fact, not only am I sometimes a reluctant evangelist, sometimes I'm no evangelist at all. There have been times of wrestling: "Should I talk to him?" Normally a very forward person, even by American standards, I can get quiet, respectful of the other people's space. Maybe I'm sitting next to someone on an airplane (in which case I've already left that person little space!); maybe it's someone talking to me about some other matter. It may be a family member I've known for years, or a person I've never met before; but, whoever it is, the person becomes for me, at that moment, a witness-stopping, excuse-inspiring spiritual challenge.

If there is a time in the future when God reviews all of our missed evangelistic opportunities, I fear that I could cause more than a minor delay in eternity.

If you are anything like me when it comes to evangelism

(and many people are), then let me encourage you for picking up this little book at all. It is meant to be an encouragement, a clarification, an instruction, a rebuke, and a challenge all rolled up into several short chapters. My prayer is that because of the time you spend reading this book, more people will hear the good news of Jesus Christ.

Isn't it amazing that we have trouble sharing such wonderful news? Who would mind telling a friend that they held a winning lottery ticket? What doctor wouldn't want to tell their patient that the tests came back negative (which, of course, is a good thing)? Who wouldn't be honored by a phone call from the White House saying that the president wanted to meet with him?

So why is it, when we have the best news in the world, that we are so slow to tell it to others? Sometimes our problem may be any one of a long list of excuses. Perhaps we don't know the gospel well enough—or we don't think we do. Maybe we think it's someone else's job, the work of a minister or a missionary. Maybe we just don't really know how to go about it. Or perhaps we *think* we are evangelizing when we really are not.

Let's say that we are faithful with evangelism, but what do we do if the one we are evangelizing gets upset or even gets mad at us? On the other hand, what do we do if it works, if someone "prays the prayer" with us, or at least says that she wants to be a Christian?

And one more question Christians often ask about evangelism: is it okay if I don't really want to evangelize but simply do it out of guilt? I know it's not best, but is it at least okay? These are some of the questions we want to answer. In addition to those, I want to look at a few other questions about sharing the good news: Why don't we evangelize? What is the gospel? Who should evangelize? How should we evangelize? What *isn't* evangelism? What should we do after we evangelize? Why should we evangelize? In sum, we discuss in this book the best news that there has ever been, and how we should share that news.

God has established who and how we should evangelize. God himself is at the heart of the *evangel*—the good news we are spreading. And we should evangelize, ultimately, because of God. All we are doing in this book is connecting some of those dots in our thinking, and, I pray, in our speaking, as well.

Our answers to these questions are not all completely distinct. They weave in and out and one influences the other, but they each provide a separate viewpoint from which to see and understand this great biblical topic of evangelism. To answer these questions, we will look through all the New Testament, from that epicenter of evangelism—the book of Acts—to the Gospels and the letters.

Of course, this little book can't answer all the questions there are about evangelism (because I can't answer all the questions!), but my prayer is that by considering them, you'll find that you can be more understanding and obedient in evangelism. I can't promise you'll become another John Harper (I haven't yet), but we can all become more faithful.

I also pray that as you come to evangelize more, you will help your church to develop a culture of evangelism. What do I mean by a culture of evangelism? I mean an expectation that Christians will share the gospel with others, talk about doing that, pray about it, and regularly plan and work together to help each other evangelize. We want evangelism to be normal—in our own lives and in our churches.

It's to this end I've written this book, and I pray it's to this end you're reading it.

1

Why *Don't* We Evangelize?

A. T. Robertson was a famous Bible teacher and a beloved seminary lecturer. He was also known as a tough professor. At the time, students would stand in class and recite from memory long passages from their assigned books. Sometimes it went well for students; other times it didn't. Once after a particularly poor performance, Dr. Robertson said to a student, "Well, excuse me, brother, but all I can do for you is pray for you and flunk you."[1]

"Flunk" is a word we don't use much anymore. It's a hard, sharp, inflexible kind of word. But it's probably a good word to use to quickly summarize how most of us have done in obeying the call to evangelize. Jesus says to tell all nations the good news, but we haven't. Jesus calls people to be fishers of men, but we prefer to watch. Peter says to always be ready to give a reason for the hope that we have, but we are not. Solomon says he who wins souls is wise, but we flunk.

But if you're anything like me, you're probably not quite so blunt about your failures in evangelism. You've altered your mental records. In fact, even at the time you're not witnessing, you're busy spinning, justifying, rationalizing, and explaining to your conscience why it was really wise and faithful and kind and obedient *not* to share the gospel with a particular person at that time and in that situation.

Throughout the rest of this chapter, we want to consider some of the most common excuses we use to justify our non-evangelism. Generally, those excuses just come into our minds, save us from having certain conversations, and then quickly pass by. In this chapter, we want to slow down our excuses and keep them quiet for just a moment so that we can talk to each of them. Of course, there are thousands more excuses than those listed here, but these are some particularly popular ones. First we'll consider five especially common ones. Then we'll look at a few excuses that are rooted in unbelievers, those who are refusing the gospel news we try to bring. Finally, we'll consider the excuses that are more about ourselves, and we'll see what we can do about them.

Basic Excuse 1: "I don't know their language."

Now, a language barrier is an impressive excuse. And it's got to be about the best one in this chapter. If you're sitting next to people who only speak Chinese or French, you don't have much of an opportunity to share any news with them, let alone news about Christ and their own soul. Of course, you can work to learn another language and so be able to share with many other people. You can keep around Bibles or evangelistic literature in other languages to give away as you have opportunity. But ever since the Tower of Babel, "I don't know" has been one of the most legitimate excuses we could imagine. Paul warns the Corinthians of the uselessness of speaking words that are unintelligible to someone (1 Cor. 14:10–11, 16, 23). After all, the whole point of our using words is to be understood!

Basic Excuse 2: "Evangelism is illegal."

In some places, evangelism *is* illegal. There are countries around the world in which tyrannies of darkness reign. They might be atheistic or Muslim, secular or even "Christian" (in name). But in many countries, sharing the evangelical gospel is forbidden. And it certainly is not to be believed by people who are not already confessing Christians! In such countries, you can usually go out and evangelize—once. It's the second or third time that might be prevented by social pressure, or laws, or jails, or guns. Not many of us reading this book are probably in that position, though.

Basic Excuse 3: "Evangelism could cause problems at work."

Even in countries where evangelism is legally allowed, many of us have jobs for which employers are paying us to get a certain amount of work done, and they have a legitimate expectation. During those work hours, it may be that our evangelism distracts people, or reduces our productivity, or does other things that can cause our employers valid concern. We certainly don't want the sharing of the gospel to bring us or the gospel into disrepute for any reason other than a disagreement with the message itself. We understand that everyone is, by nature, at enmity with God; but we simply don't want to give people other reasons to oppose our evangel. We don't want our evangelism to stand in the way of the *evangel*—the good news.

Basic Excuse 4: "Other things seem more urgent."

There is so much else to do in any given day. We've got to care for our families and plan for our weekend. The job has to be done, and the bills have to be paid. Studies, cooking, cleaning, shopping, returning calls, writing e-mails, reading, praying—I could go on and on about all the good things we need to do. And many of these things are time-sensitive. If I have a misunderstanding with my wife, I need to take care of that immediately. If the baby is crying, I need to get her home now. If the paper is due tomorrow, I've got to get the writing done right away. If we've got no food for tonight, I've got to do some shopping and cooking now. It is legitimate for me to make and fulfill many commitments in life other than evangelism. But do our other commitments sometimes become so numerous—or do we interpret them so—as to leave no time for evangelism? If we are too busy for that, what things are we managing to make time for?

Basic Excuse 5: "I don't know non-Christians."

Isolation from unbelievers may be the most common excuse for a lack of evangelism. This is the excuse of choice for mature Christians. When I'm honestly reflecting on my own life, I see that I have fairly few significant relationships with non-Christians. I'm a pastor. I'm not around non-Christians much as part of my job. I am busy writing sermons, counseling, planning, training other Christians, returning phone calls—even writing a book on evangelism! I'm generally unavailable to people except for my church members during the day or my family in the evening. I'm really absorbed with Christian relationships, and I think that I'm called to be.

But in cases like mine, how does evangelism fit in? If you're a young mother at home with her children, or an older Christian, retired and not easily able to build new relationships, then you, too, know something of this challenge. If you're a new Christian, you've probably been advised (wisely) to build new, significant friendships with Christians. And if you've been a Christian for a while, then you're probably busy with service in the church and spending your time discipling younger Christians. One of the best decisions we can make is to pray and talk with a Christian friend about how we can legitimately fulfill our roles in the church, in our family, and in our job while also getting to know and speak with non-Christians.

Excuses Concerning Them

Another set of excuses has to do with problems you and I think that others will have with our witnessing to them. How many times have I had these more subtle and advanced excuses assemble in my mind as I'm thinking about sharing the gospel with someone? "People don't want to hear." "They won't be interested." "They probably already know the gospel." "It probably won't work. I doubt they'll believe." I don't think about how powerful the gospel is. I get myself in a wrongly hopeless mindset.

Of course, I should consider how faithless all this is. As Paul said to the Corinthians, "Who makes you different from anyone else? What do you have that you did not receive?" (1 Cor. 4:7). Why do we think that *we* would respond to the gospel, but someone else wouldn't? Haven't you found that God saves some of the most unlikely converts? If you aren't sure about this, consider some friends you've seen converted. Consider your own conversion. Jonathan Edwards called one account of the Great Awakening *A Narrative of Surprising Conversions*. Of course, in one sense, all conversions are surprising: enemies are loved, the alienated are adopted, those who should be punished inherit eternal life instead. But it is exactly this radical, surprising nature of conversion that should encourage us in our evangelism. God may save anyone. And the more unlikely it appears, the more glory, we might even reason, he gets to himself when it happens!

The Heart of the Matter: Plan to Stop Not Evangelizing

Here we are getting down closer to the heart of most of our non-evangelism. What's going on with us when we don't evangelize? Let's think about twelve steps we can take: pray, plan, accept, understand, be faithful, risk, prepare, look, love, fear, stop, and consider.

1) **Pray.** I think many times we don't evangelize because we undertake everything in our own power. We attempt to leave God out of it. We forget that it is his will and pleasure for his gospel to be known. He wants sinners saved. Simply put, we don't pray for opportunities to share the gospel, so how surprised should we be when they don't come? If you're not evangelizing because you think you lack opportunities, pray and be amazed as God answers your prayers.

2) **Plan.** As we've already considered, sometimes we don't evangelize because we think, "I'm busy with other good things. Those other things are legitimate ways for me to spend my time. So I just don't have time for evangelism right now. When my health improves . . . after my paper is due . . . when my son is in school . . . when my husband retires . . . when I get that promotion . . . when she's in a better mood, then," we say, "I'll share the gospel with her." To fight such excuse making, we can plan to make time to build relationships or to put ourselves in positions where we know we'll be able to talk with non-Christians. We plan for so many less important things; why not plan for our evangelism?

3) **Accept.** We have to accept that this is our job. We'll consider this more in chapter 3, but for now, let's just acknowledge that sometimes we don't evangelize because we think it's not our job. It's the job of preachers, we think, or someone else who is trained and paid for it. But if we are going to evangelize, we have to realize and admit how we've been dodging our duty and adjust ourselves to accept responsibility for evangelism. We might be the closest Christians to a particular unbeliever. Maybe he has a Christian uncle or aunt, friend, or employee who has been praying for him. Maybe we are the answer to those prayers. We must accept, we may accept, we get to accept the wonderful role that God has for us as evangelists in others' lives!

4) **Understand.** Part of our failure to evangelize comes from a lack of understanding. God uses not so much gifts for evangelism (though there is a biblical gift of evangelism) but the faithfulness of thousands and millions of Christians who would never say evangelism is their gift. Your conclusion that you are not gifted for a particular task does not absolve you of responsibility to obey. You may conclude that evangelism is not your gift, but it is still your duty. Not having the gift of mercy in no way excuses us from being merciful. All Christians are to exercise mercy; some will be particularly gifted to do this in special ways at certain times, but all are to be merciful. So with evangelism. God may unusually bless and own a Peter and a Philip, a Whitefield and a Spurgeon, a Hudson Taylor and an Adoniram Judson, but he calls all of us to share the good news.

5) **Be Faithful.** Perhaps we need to rebalance our allegiances. Maybe we are too polite to be faithful to God in this area. Maybe we are more concerned about people's response than God's glory. Maybe we are more concerned about their feelings than God's. God does not like having his truth suppressed, and that's what the non-Christian is doing (Rom. 1:18). Good manners are no excuse for unfaithfulness to God, but we have, too often, used them so.

6) **Risk.** Related to being faithful is being willing to risk. Let's obey, even when we are not exactly sure of the response. Maybe you don't evangelize sometimes because you're shy. You don't really enjoy talking to others that much, especially about things that may upset them. It seems tiring and dangerous. Maybe you would rather let someone else, someone who seems more comfortable, do the evangelizing. But could you invite unbelievers to a meeting where they will hear the gospel? Can you share with them a useful book or a story from your own life? Can you befriend them so that you may be able more

naturally in the future to share the gospel with them? We must be willing to risk in order to evangelize.

7) **Prepare.** Sometimes we don't evangelize because we think we are unprepared or ill-equipped. Maybe we don't know how to transition the conversation. Or perhaps we think that in our ignorance we'll fail at this and actually do spiritual harm to the person by discrediting the gospel in their eyes. We fear our ignorance. We think that it's up to us to make the gospel seem sensible to them or to answer all their questions. And, so, having inflated these expectations, we decide we can't meet them and so neglect evangelism. Instead, we could prepare ourselves by knowing the gospel, working on our own humility, and studying more. Just as we might plan to have time, so we might prepare to be able to use the opportunity well when it comes.

8) **Look.** Have you ever prayed for something and then been surprised when it comes? I know I have. And I guess that means I really must not have been expecting God to answer that prayer request. It may be the same with my evangelism. Maybe I've prayed for opportunities but then not really looked for them. Perhaps I've been careless when they've come.

The way I've been careless can vary. Sometimes I don't see the opportunities because I'm busy. Evangelism can, after all, be time consuming and inconvenient. Or maybe I'm too tired. Perhaps I've used up all my energy on entertaining myself, or working, or on everything other than this non-Christian whom I could talk to. And therefore I don't even notice the opportunity.

Maybe my neglect of opportunities is more habitual. Maybe I'm lazy, caring more that I not be hassled or hurried than that this person hears the gospel. Maybe, when it comes right down to it, I'm simply selfish. I don't see the opportunities because I'm unwilling to be inconvenienced. I guess that means that I am, finally, apathetic. My blindness to God's provision is voluntary. I don't consider the reality and finality of death, judgment, and hell. So I don't notice the reality of the person and their plight before me. We must not only close our eyes in prayer for opportunities, but we must then open our eyes to see them.

9) **Love.** We are called to love others. We share the gospel because we love people. And we don't share the gospel because we don't love people. Instead, we wrongly fear them. We don't want to cause awkwardness. We want their respect, and after all, we figure, if we try to share the gospel with them, we'll look foolish! And so we are quiet. We protect our pride at the cost of their souls. In the name of not wanting to look weird, we are content to be complicit in their being lost. As one friend said, "I don't want to be the stereotypical Christian on a plane."

That attitude too often characterizes me. My heart is cold to other people. I have a distorted self-love and a deficient love for others. And just to drive this home, as I've been writing this, a non-Christian friend called and wanted to talk to me. We chatted for about thirty minutes, the whole time during which I was impatient to get back to writing this book on evangelism! Aargh! Wretched man that I am! Who shall deliver me from this body of indifference? If we would evangelize more, we must love people more.

10) **Fear.** We should also fear. But our fear should be directed not to man but to God. When we don't share the gospel, we are essentially refusing to live in the fear of the Lord. We are not regarding him or his will as the final and ultimate rule of our actions. To fear God is to love him. When the One who is our all-powerful creator and judge is also our merciful redeemer and savior, then we have found the perfect object for the entire devotion of our heart. And that devotion will lead

us to share this good news about him with others. We should pray that God will grow in us a greater love and fear of him.

11) **Stop.** We should stop blaming God. We should stop excusing ourselves from evangelism on the basis that God is sovereign. We should not conclude from his omnipotence that our obedience is therefore pointless. We should instead read from the Word that God will call a great number to himself from every tribe, tongue, and nation, which will encourage us in evangelism. It encouraged Paul in Corinth when he was discouraged (see Acts 18). Again, if you will realize that conversion always accompanies proclaiming the gospel and the Spirit's work, then you will stop trying to do the Spirit's work, and you will give yourself to proclaiming the gospel. Just because we don't know everything doesn't mean we don't know anything! We can't answer all the questions of how God's sovereignty and human responsibility fit together, but we can certainly believe that they do. It was Paul who wrote one of the clearest biblical passages about God's sovereignty (Romans 9) and then went on to write one of the most pointed biblical passages about man's responsibility in evangelism (Romans 10). He certainly believed both these things to be true. So who are we to blame God for our sinful silence?

12) **Consider.** The writer of Hebrews said, "Consider him who endured such opposition from sinful men, so that you will not grow weary and lose heart" (Heb. 12:3). When we don't sufficiently consider what God has done for us in Christ—the high cost of it, what it means, and what Christ's significance is—we lose the heart to evangelize. Our hearts grow cold, our minds grow smaller (more taken up with passing concerns), and our lips fall silent. Consider that God has loved us as he has. Consider that God is glorified by our telling others of this amazing love of his. And consider that instead of gossiping about God's goodness and the gospel, we engage in a con-

spiracy of silence. We reveal ourselves as being cold to God's glory. If we would be more faithful in evangelism, we should fuel the flame of love toward God within us, and the flame of gratitude and of hope. A fire so enflamed by God will have no trouble igniting our tongue. As Jesus said, "Out of the overflow of the heart the mouth speaks" (Matt. 12:34). How much evangelism do we find flowing out of our mouths? What does that suggest about our love for God?

For that matter, why should we so love God? That brings us to consider what exactly this message is that we want to share. What is it that would so fire our hearts? That's what we want to consider in the next chapter.

2

What Is the Gospel?

My friends know that I enjoy words, so sometimes for Christmas I'll get calendars with interesting stories or word facts. I can't remember on which calendar I read the following account, but I was so struck by it, I made a note of it. I don't know if it's true, but it's a great illustration of the importance of getting your story right.

According to this account, a little over a hundred years ago the editor of an English newspaper opened a copy of his paper—after it was already for sale—only to find in it a most embarrassing, unintentional typographical conflation of two stories, one about a patented pig-killing and sausage-making machine, and the other about a gathering in honor of a local clergyman, the Reverend Doctor Mudge, at which he was presented with a gold-headed cane. A portion of it read as follows:

> Several of Rev. Dr. Mudge's friends called upon him yesterday, and after a conversation the unsuspecting pig was seized by the hind leg, and slid along a beam until he reached the hot-water tank. . . . Thereupon he came forward and said that there were times when the feelings overpowered one, and for that reason he would not attempt to do more than thank those around him for the manner in which such a huge animal was cut into fragments was simply astonishing. The doctor concluded his remarks, when the machine

seized him and, in less time than it takes to write it, the pig was cut into fragments and worked up into a delicious sausage. The occasion will be long remembered by the doctor's friends as one of the most delightful of their lives. The best pieces can be procured for tenpence a pound, and we are sure that those who have sat so long under his ministry will rejoice that he has been treated so handsomely.

Christianity is all about news. It is all about the good news, really the best news the world has ever heard. And yet that news—far more important than the story about the Reverend Doctor Mudge or the sausage machine—is often every bit as scrambled and confused. That which passes for the gospel too often becomes a very thin veneer spread lightly over our culture's values, becoming shaped and formed to its contours rather than to the truth about God. The real story, the real message, becomes lost.

This idea of the good news isn't some later Christian packaging scheme. Jesus Christ talked about the good news, and when he did, he reached back to the language of the prophecies of Isaiah hundreds of years earlier (Isa. 52:7; 61:1). Whatever Jesus may have said in Aramaic, the way the Christians, and even his own disciples, remembered it in Greek was with this word *evangel*—literally, good news.

Well, what exactly *is* this good news? In this chapter, we want to try to set the story straight; we want to get the news right. What is the message that we Christians have to tell? Is it that "I'm okay" or "God is love"? Is it that "Jesus is my friend" or "I should live right"? What is the good news of Jesus Christ?

The Good News Is Not Simply That We Are Okay

You may have heard of the book title of almost forty years ago now, *I'm OK, You're OK.*[1] Some people seem to think that Christianity is fundamentally a religious therapy session, where we sit around trying to help each other feel good about ourselves. The pews are couches. The preacher asks questions. The text to be expounded is your inner self. And yet, when we have finished plumbing our inner depths, why is it that we so often feel empty? Or even dirty? Is there something about us and our lives that is incomplete or even wrong?

I remember hearing one celebrity being interviewed on television after the death of a close friend. Weeping, this celebrity exclaimed, "Why does everyone I love die?" Yes, why indeed. The Bible utterly rejects the idea that we are okay, that the human condition is just fine, that everyone is merely in need of accepting their current condition, their finitude, or their imperfections, or that we simply need to begin to look on the bright side of it.

The Bible teaches that in our first parents, Adam and Eve, we have all been seduced into disobeying God. We are therefore not righteous and on good terms with God. In fact, our sin is so serious that Jesus taught that we need a new birth (John 3), and Paul taught that we need to be created again (1 Corinthians 15). As we find in Ephesians 2, we are *dead* in our sins and transgressions.

You know what transgressions are—they are sins simply represented as going across a boundary. In our day and age, Michel Foucault would live, like the Marquis de Sade before him, in order to transgress boundaries. And so there is some thought that Foucault deliberately sought to infect others with the AIDS virus as he himself contracted it and died through it. The bathhouses of San Francisco became the place where Foucault not only transgressed the boundaries of respect for sexuality but also of respect for life itself. Transgressions. Crossings over the line.

Our transgressions may not seem so blatant and offensive, but they are surely no less deadly for our relationship with God. Paul says in Romans 6:23 that "the wages of sin is death." We understand more of why and how that is the case by turning to the letter of James. James said, "For whoever keeps the whole law and yet stumbles at just one point is guilty of breaking all of it. For he who said, 'Do not commit adultery,' also said, 'Do not murder.' If you do not commit adultery but do commit murder, you have become a lawbreaker" (James 2:10–11).

Notice the seriousness of each sin. The point James is making is that the laws of God are not simply external statutes passed by some congress in heaven that God enforces. The law of God is the expression of God's own character. To break out of this law, to live against it, is to live against God.

If my wife sends me to the store with specific instructions to get a particular item and I come back without having gotten it and with no good excuse (such as "They were out of it" or "I couldn't find it" or "We shouldn't get this"), but simply having decided not to get it, that will reflect on our relationship.

The Bible presents God not simply as our creator but as our jealous lover. He wants us—every part of us. For us to think that we can disregard him sometimes, to set aside his ways when it suits us, is to show that we haven't understood the nature of the relationship at all. So, you see, we can't claim to be believers and yet knowingly, repeatedly, happily break God's law.

But this is our state. We have crossed over the bounds that God has rightly set for our lives. We have contradicted him in both the letter and the spirit of his instructions to us. And so we not only feel guilt, but we actually are guilty before God. We are not only conflicted in ourselves; we are actually in conflict with God. We break God's laws again and again. And we do this because we are, says Ephesians 2, dead in our sins and transgressions.

Now all of this may seem to be too grim to have much at all to do with anything called "the good news." But there is no doubt that an accurate understanding of where we are now is essential to getting to where we need to be. One of the early stages of becoming a Christian is, I think, realizing that our problems aren't fundamentally that we have messed up our own lives, or have simply failed to reach our full potential, but that we have sinned against God. And so it begins to dawn on us that we are rightly the objects of God's wrath and his judgment, and that we deserve death, separation from God, and spiritual alienation from him now and even forever.

This is what the theologians call depravity. It is the death that deserves death.

Do you see the reason that all of these wrongs are so tragic? These sins are committed against a perfect, holy, loving God. And they are committed by creatures made in his image.

True Christianity is realistic about the dark side of our world, our life, our nature, our heart. But true Christianity is not finally pessimistic or morally indifferent, encouraging us to merely settle in and accept the cold, hard truth. No. The news that we, as Christians, have to bring is so great, so tremendous, not only because our depravity is so pervasive and our sin so widespread, but also because God's plans for us are so different, so wonderful.

And when we begin to realize it, we become thankful for the fact that Christianity is not finally about anesthetizing us to life's pain, or even about waking us up to it and teaching us to live with it. It is about teaching us to live with a transforming longing, with a growing faith, with a sure and certain hope of what's to come.

The Good News Is Not Simply That God Is Love

Other times we may hear the gospel simply represented as the message that God is love. Now, this one is sort of like the Oklahoma newspaper headline that read, "Cold Weather Causes Temperatures to Drop." It's not that it's not true; it's just that it's so obvious that something is missing or left out.

That "God is love" is certainly true. It's even in the Bible! "God is love" (1 John 4:8). But there is a danger in simply saying so as if it is self-evident.

Maybe we get a little sense of what this love is when, as parents, we tell our children that, for some good reason about which we are aware, they can't do something they want to do. And what is an oft-heard response? "If you really *loved* me, you'd *let* me." Now that's just plain wrong! But it's a falsehood that can be as subtle as it is significant. Love doesn't always let. Indeed, sometimes love prevents, and sometimes love punishes.

If we say that God is love, what are we thinking that his love must look like?

And furthermore, is love all that the Bible says that God is? Doesn't the Bible say that God is a Spirit? How does a Spirit love? Doesn't the Bible say that God is holy? How does a Holy Spirit love? Doesn't the Bible say that God is unique, that there is none other like him? How does the only perfect Holy Spirit in the universe love? How can you know if he doesn't tell you? Can you surmise it, figure it out, assume it from your own experience, or chart out how it would be from your own heart? John Calvin said:

> It is plain that no man can arrive at the true knowledge of himself, without having first contemplated the divine character, and then descended to the consideration of his own. For, such is the native pride of us all, we invariably

esteem ourselves righteous, innocent, wise and holy, till we are convinced by clear proofs, of our unrighteousness, turpitude, folly and impurity. But we are never thus convinced, while we confine our attention to ourselves, and regard not the Lord, who is the only standard by which this judgment ought to be formed.[2]

Among other important things to note is this: God reveals himself as the God who requires holiness of all who would be in loving relationship with him. As the Bible says, "Without holiness, no one will see the Lord" (Heb. 12:14). It is only in the context of understanding something of God's character, of his righteousness and perfection, that we begin to understand the tremendous nature of saying that God truly is love, and his love has a depth, texture, fullness, and beauty to it that we, in our present state, can only begin to wonder at.

The Good News Is Not Simply That Jesus Wants to Be Our Friend

Other times the gospel message is represented to us rather simply as "Jesus wants to be our friend" or, as a variation of that, "Jesus wants to be our example." But the Christian gospel is not a matter of mere self-help or even of a great example or a relationship to be cultivated. There is a real past to be dealt with. Real sins have been committed. Real guilt has been incurred. And so what is to be done? What will our holy God do? Even if he, in his love, wants a people for his own, how will he have them without sacrificing his own holiness?

Did he simply come in the flesh to teach us that our sins are no big deal, that he's just going to forgive and forget? What would that do to the morality of God? What would that do to the character of the One who is said to love us?

What does Jesus want? What did he come to do? What is

amazing, when we study the gospels, is that we find that Jesus chose to die. This is what Jesus presented as the center of his ministry. Not teaching or even being an example, but, as he said, "The Son of Man did not come to be served, but to serve, and to give his life as a ransom for many" (Mark 10:45). Jesus himself taught that this choice of his to glorify the Father by his death on the cross was central to his ministry. It's not surprising, then, that the center and focus of all four Gospel accounts is Christ's crucifixion.

But what does it mean? And why would something that seems such a horrifying event be the focus of anything called "good news"?

The New Testament began to explain this event even before it happened in the words of Jesus himself. Jesus wove together two strands of Old Testament prophecy (Mark 8:27–38), which, to the best of my knowledge, had not previously been united. Here Jesus presented himself as a combination of the Son of Man (Daniel 7) and the Suffering Servant (Isaiah 53).

The apostles clearly learned from Jesus how they were to understand his death on the cross; and to teach Christians about this, the Holy Spirit has inspired various images in the New Testament that convey the reality to us: Jesus as a sacrifice, a redemption, a reconciliation, a legal justification, a military victory, and a propitiation.

None of this language in the New Testament refers to something potential, a mere possibility, or an option; rather, each image refers to something that actually accomplishes its end or purpose. So, for example, how can we say that God and sinners are reconciled if these "reconciled sinners" were then cast into hell? Or what kind of propitiation would it be if God's wrath was not assuaged, or what kind of redemption if the hostages were not set free? The point with all these images is that the benefit envisioned has not merely been made available; it has been secured not by the mere teaching ministry of Christ but by his death and resurrection.

There's no getting around the fact that the center of Christ's ministry was his death on the cross, and the heart of that death was God's certainly and effectively dealing with the claims of both his own love and justice. So much of this—blood, purchase, victory—comes together in the magnificence of the final vision given by God to John:

> Then one of the elders said to me, "Do not weep! See, the Lion of the tribe of Judah, the Root of David, has triumphed. He is able to open the scroll and its seven seals." Then I saw a Lamb, looking as if it had been slain, standing in the center of the throne, encircled by the four living creatures and the elders. . . . He came and took the scroll from the right hand of him who sat on the throne. And when he had taken it, the four living creatures and the twenty-four elders fell down before the Lamb. Each one had a harp and they were holding golden bowls full of incense, which are the prayers of the saints. And they sang a new song:
>
> "You are worthy to take the scroll
>   and to open its seals,
> because you were slain,
>   and with your blood you purchased men for God
>   from every tribe and language and people and
>   nation." (Rev. 5:5–9)

Christ isn't just our friend. To call him supremely that is to damn him with faint praise. He is our friend, but he is so much more! By his death on the cross Christ has become the lamb that was slain for us, our redeemer, the one who has made peace between us and God, who has taken our guilt on himself, who has conquered our most deadly enemies and has assuaged the personal, just wrath of God.

The Good News Is Not That We Should Live Rightly

Mistaking the gospel for "right living" is one more common error. Sometimes people think that the news, the message of the Bible, is simply that we should live moral lives. Christianity is sometimes presented as nothing more than virtues—public and private. Christians are thought to be simply about *doing* religious things, such as baptism, and communion, and going to church. The Christian life is nothing more than obeying the Ten Commandments and the Golden Rule, reading our Bibles, and praying. Being Christian means building up the community, giving to others, contributing to soup kitchens, and preserving historical buildings rather than making parking lots.

But as startling as it may be to those who think this way, the biblical gospel is not fundamentally about our love or our power. To be a Christian is not merely to live in love, or to live by the power of positive thinking, or to do anything that we can do ourselves. The gospel calls for a more radical response than any of these things allow for. The gospel, you see, is not simply an additive that comes to make our already good lives better. No! The gospel is a message of wonderful good news that comes to those who realize their just desperation before God.

So what response is called for? What is it you should do when your own sense of need, your understanding of God and of Jesus Christ, all begin to come together like this? God calls us to repent of our sins and to rely on Christ alone.

We find both repentance and faith in the New Testament, and often they occur together. As Paul met with the leaders of the church in Ephesus, a meeting which is recounted in Acts 20, he summarized his message this way: "I have declared to both Jews and Greeks that they must turn to God in repentance and have faith in our Lord Jesus" (Acts 20:21). This is the message that Paul and other Christians preached throughout the New Testament.

Once people have heard the truth about their sin and God's holiness, God's love in Christ, and Christ's death and resurrection for our justification, the message calls out for response. And what is that response? Is it to walk down an aisle? Is it to fill out a card or to lift up a hand? Is it to make an appointment to see the preacher or to decide to be baptized and join the church? While any of those things may be involved, none is absolutely necessary. The response to this good news is, as Paul preached, to repent and believe.

Where did Paul and the other authors of the New Testament get this message? If you turn to the first chapter of Mark's Gospel, you'll find out. They got it from Jesus, who called out, "Repent and believe the good news!" (Mark 1:15). The response to this news is believing and repenting.

We must honestly think the gospel is true. But there is more to saving belief than that. You can believe, for example, that the Angel Falls in Venezuela are nearly twenty times higher than Niagara Falls, that a spider's web applied to a bleeding wound helps the blood to clot, that the inhabitants of Iceland read more books per person per year than the inhabitants of any other country, or that Sir Christopher Wren had only six months' training as an architect. But none of these "believings" are what Jesus meant in Mark 1 when he called out for people to believe.

Saving belief is not mere mental assent, but a believing in—a living in—the knowledge of that news. It is a leaning on, a relying on. We must come to grips with the fact that we are unable to satisfy God's demands on us, no matter how morally we try to live. We don't want to end up trusting a little in ourselves and a little in God; we want to realize that we are to rely on God fully, to trust in Christ alone for our salvation.

And such a true believing and relying makes a difference and so demands not only faith but also repentance.

Repentance and this kind of belief, or faith, or reliance, are really two sides of the same coin. It's not like you can go for the basic model (belief) and add repentance at a later point when you want to get really holy. No! Repent is what you do if you really start thinking this way and believing Jesus with your life. Any purported belief without change is nothing but a base counterfeit. As J. C. Ryle said, "There is a common, worldly kind of Christianity in this day, which many have, and think they have enough—a cheap Christianity which offends nobody, and requires no sacrifice—which costs nothing, and is worth nothing."[3]

The repentance that Jesus demands is connected with believing this news, because if it's really "news," it's no surprise that you change your mind when you hear it. The word for "repent" is *metanoia* and means literally "to change your mind."

Real Christianity is never simply an addition to, or merely a cultivation of, something that has always been there. Instead, it is, in some radical sense, an about-face. And it's an about-face all Christians make, but only as a part of their relying on Christ's finished work on the cross. To say you trust without *living* as though you do is not to trust in any biblical sense. And you can see the truth of that from Abraham—the great example of faith—all the way through to Jesus Christ himself.

We change the way we act; we do. But we only change the way we act because we change what we believe. The good news of Christianity has a cognitive content; it's not simply a religious enthusiasm or a deep personal intuition. It is new; it is tidings, the latest. It says something. The gospel is news!

In our church in Washington, I always ask our prospective members to tell me the gospel in one minute or less. How would you do that? What would you say the message is? Here's what I understand the good news to be: the good news is that the one and only God, who is holy, made us in his image to know him. But we sinned and cut ourselves off from him. In his great love, God became a man in Jesus, lived a perfect life, and died on the cross, thus fulfilling the law himself and taking on himself the punishment for the sins of all those who would ever turn and trust in him. He rose again from the dead, showing that God accepted Christ's sacrifice and that God's wrath against us had been exhausted. He now calls us to repent of our sins and to trust in Christ alone for our forgiveness. If we repent of our sins and trust in Christ, we are born again into a new life, an eternal life with God.

Now that's good news.

But is this news too complicated for the average Christian to tell others? We'll think more about that in the next chapter.

Who Should Evangelize?

"**I couldn't do what** you just did."

"What?" I said, honestly clueless.

"Engage that person in conversation like that."

My friend was a strong Christian. He was growing spiritually like a weed. But he was a much younger Christian than I. Plus, he has, I would say, a normally balanced personality, whereas I am an off-the-charts extrovert, which brings blessings and challenges. But the extrovert's ability to talk to a lot of people is one of the pluses.

What isn't one of the pluses is what happened to my friend—he was left feeling that he couldn't evangelize. We went on to have a good conversation about evangelism and about his recent opportunities, but this experience did make me consider the fact that "clergy persons" such as I, whether intentionally or unintentionally, often give off the vibe that evangelism should be left to the professionals. After all, you wouldn't want just anybody to perform surgery on you, would you? You wouldn't want your bank account to be looked after at a gas station, would you? You wouldn't want to assign the keeping of the family checkbook to your second-grade son, would you? "All right then," you feel, "I'm not as eloquent as the man up front. I can't preach like that. I can't answer questions like that."

And then comes the killer conclusion: "I shouldn't share the gospel with others—at least, not much. And when I do, it will be only with close friends . . . and maybe only after a long time . . . and only if they ask me first . . . and only if I've had my quiet time that day. And only if . . ."

Whose job is it to evangelize? There are people in the New Testament who are said to have the gift of evangelism (see Eph. 4:11; Acts 21:8). We know that there are people today who are called evangelists. Sometimes they even set up companies with names like the So-and-So Evangelistic Association. Are they the ones called to spread the good news?

In Acts 4:29 Peter prays, "Now, Lord, consider their threats and enable your servants to speak your word with great boldness." Does that prayer apply only to preachers? Is evangelism really the work of pastors? Paul writes to Timothy, a pastor, to "do the work of an evangelist" (2 Tim. 4:5). Should the called and the equipped become professional evangelists? Are the rest of us to leave it alone for the most part? Are regular church members to be still and remain passive, inviting others to hear only pastors, preachers, speakers, and other trained evangelists? Is our evangelism to be merely inviting people to meetings rather than inviting them directly to Christ?

Is the ordinary Christian doing evangelism like the ordinary employee trying to do the company's accounting? Are we average Christians all to be evangelists, or should we leave that to Bible colleges and seminary graduates?[1]

However difficult this topic of evangelism may be for many of us, it is hard to avoid it without avoiding the Bible. Verses about spreading the good news are all through it. Paul wrote to the Romans, "I am obligated both to Greeks and non-Greeks, both to the wise and the foolish. That is why I am so eager to preach the gospel also to you who are at Rome" (Rom. 1:14–15). But are such statements simply statements of Paul's own calling rather than something that applies to us as well?

Of course, those statements *were* true of Paul. But when we read the New Testament, we don't read of the call to evangelism being limited to Paul, or even to the apostles. It was Jesus himself, in his final commission to his disciples, who taught, "All authority in heaven and on earth has been given to me. Therefore go and make disciples of all nations, baptizing them in the name of the Father and of the Son and of the Holy Spirit, and teaching them to obey everything I have commanded you. And surely I am with you always, to the very end of the age" (Matt. 28:18–20). This is commonly called the Great Commission, which Jesus gave to his disciples, and it would be difficult to overestimate its importance. John Stott concludes from Jesus' words:

> [This] commission . . . is binding upon every member of the whole Church. . . . Every Christian is called to be a witness to Christ in the particular environment in which God has placed him. Further, although the public ministry of the Word is a high office, private witness or personal evangelism has a value which in some respects surpasses even that of preaching, since the message can then be adapted more personally.[2]

These early disciples, having become apostles, took Jesus' Great Commission to heart. They evangelized constantly (see Acts 5:42; 8:25; 13:32; 14:7, 15, 21; 15:35; 16:10; 17:18). But, again, the question some are now asking is, who is supposed to do this today? Is it only preachers or professional religious types?

According to the Bible, all believers have received this commission. In the book of Acts we see glimpses of this universal obedience to the call to evangelize. In Acts 2 we see that all the Christians had God's Spirit poured out upon them. In the Old Testament, such an outpouring was preparation for the work of prophetically giving out God's Word. And so we are not surprised to find, as we continue through the book of Acts, that many people evangelized. We read in Acts 8:1–4:

> On that day a great persecution broke out against the church at Jerusalem, and all except the apostles were scattered throughout Judea and Samaria. Godly men buried Stephen and mourned deeply for him. But Saul began to destroy the church. Going from house to house, he dragged off men and women and put them in prison. Those who had been scattered preached the word wherever they went.

In the same chapter we read the story of Philip, a deacon, doing evangelism (Acts 8:5–12, 26–40); and later we read:

> Now those who had been scattered by the persecution in connection with Stephen traveled as far as Phoenicia, Cyprus and Antioch, telling the message only to Jews. Some of them, however, men from Cyprus and Cyrene, went to Antioch and began to speak to Greeks also, telling them the good news about the Lord Jesus. The Lord's hand was with them, and a great number of people believed and turned to the Lord. (Acts 11:19–21)

It's clear, too, from all the talk of persecution in the New Testament that the earliest Christians didn't try to keep their religion a secret, even though sharing it brought consequences. Paul wrote to the young Thessalonian Christians about their "severe suffering" (1 Thess. 1:6), and he refers to those who were troubling them (2 Thess. 2:5–7). We see this elsewhere in the New Testament also. Even though Christians were suffering because their lives had changed, they continued to speak in order to share the gospel and to explain their new faith.

And then there are Peter's instructions to Christians in 1 Peter 3:15–16:

But in your hearts set apart Christ as Lord. Always be prepared to give an answer to everyone who asks you to give the reason for the hope that you have. But do this with gentleness and respect, keeping a clear conscience, so that those who speak maliciously against your good behavior in Christ may be ashamed of their slander.

We know that Christ himself came to seek and to save what was lost (Luke 15; 19:10). In atoning for sinners Christ is uniquely our savior. In seeking sinners as he did, however, he is our example. So how can we follow Jesus Christ without inviting people to come to Christ? Can we be his disciples and not seek the lost coin, the lost sheep, the lost son? There is a lot of witnessing in the book of Acts. The lost were prayed for and sought after even by those who are not named as apostles, evangelists, or elders.

When Jesus is asked by a lawyer what the most important commandment is, he responds by quoting Deuteronomy 6, an exhortation to love God, and Leviticus 19, an exhortation to "Love your neighbor as yourself" (Mark 12:31). James calls this love the "royal law" (James 2:8). What does such love require of us? It seems to require that what we want for ourselves, we want for those we love, too. If you desire to love God with perfect affection, you will desire that for your neighbor, too. But you are not loving your neighbor as yourself if you're not trying to persuade him toward the greatest and best aspect of your own life—your reconciled relationship with God. If you are a Christian, you are pursuing Christ. You are following him, and you desire him. And you must therefore also desire this highest good for everyone whom you love. It is love itself that requires us to pursue the best for those we love, and that must include sharing the good news of Jesus Christ with them.

Furthermore, every Christian is to live a life that commends the gospel. The love that the New Testament community of believers shared is presented as an integral part of their witness to the world, as we see in John 13:34–35. This love was not shared only among the leaders; it was shared between all Christians. In fact, the outworking of faith through the community of a local church seems to be Jesus' most basic evangelism plan. And it involves all of us.[3] Paul wrote to the Philippian church commanding them to continue holding out the word of life (Phil. 2:16). They would do that by both their lives and their words.

We know that God's intent in establishing the church was to bear witness to himself and to his character. As Paul wrote, "His intent was that now, through the church, the manifold wisdom of God should be made known" (Eph. 3:10). And though Paul says that it was to be made known to the rulers and authorities in heavenly realms, we know from elsewhere in the New Testament that it was also God's plan to make known his character to other people.

Every Christian has a role in making visible the gospel of the invisible God. God's love, supremely, is to be revealed in the church. John Stott commented on this challenge and opportunity:

> The invisibility of God is a great problem. It was already a problem to God's people in Old Testament days. Their pagan neighbors would taunt them, saying, "Where is now your God?" Their gods were visible and tangible, but Israel's God was neither. Today in our scientific culture young people are taught not to believe in anything which is not open to empirical investigation. How then has God solved the problem of his own invisibility? The first answer is of course "in Christ." Jesus Christ is the visible image of the invisible God. John 1:18: "No one has ever seen God, but God the only Son has made him known." "That's wonderful," people say, "but it was 2,000 years ago. Is there no way by

50

which the invisible God makes himself visible today?" There is. We return to 1 John 4:12: "No one has ever seen God." It is precisely the same introductory statement. But instead of continuing with reference to the Son of God, it continues: "If we love one another, God dwells in us." In other words, the invisible God, who once made himself visible in Christ, now makes himself visible in Christians, *if* we love one another. It is a breathtaking claim. The local church cannot evangelize, proclaiming the gospel of love, if it is not itself a community of love.[4] (Emphasis in original)

One of the main reasons that the local church is to be a community of love is so that others will know the God of love. God made people in his image to know him. The life of the local congregation makes the audible gospel visible. And we must all have a part in that evangelism.

We can all contribute to evangelism simply by building up the local church—helping to organize it or lead it. We may teach and equip. We may provide hospitality and encouragement. We may pray and serve and show mercy and give. But we also all have a responsibility to speak of God and the good news both inside and outside of the church.

Martyn Lloyd-Jones taught, "Evangelism is pre-eminently dependent upon the quality of the Christian life which is known and enjoyed in the church."[5] A striking example of this truth is found in John Bunyan's experience. He recounted it himself in his autobiography, *Grace Abounding to the Chief of Sinners* (by which title he meant himself). Bunyan tells this story:

> One day, the good providence of God did cast me to Bedford, to work on my own calling; and in one of the streets of that town, I came where there were three or four poor women sitting at a door in the sun, and talking about the things of God; and being now willing to hear them discourse, I drew near to hear what they said, for I was now a brisk talker also myself

in the matters of religion, but now I may say, I heard, but I understood not; for they were far above, out of my reach, for their talk was about a new birth, the work of God on their hearts, also how they were convinced of their miserable state by nature; they talked how God had visited their souls with His love in the Lord Jesus, and with what words and promises they had been refreshed, comforted, and supported against the temptations of the devil. Moreover, they reasoned of the suggestions and temptations of Satan in particular; and told to each other by which they had been afflicted, and how they were borne up under his assaults. They also discoursed of their own wretchedness of heart, of their unbelief; and did contemn, slight and abhor their own righteousness, as filthy and insufficient to do them any good.

And methought they spake as if joy did make them speak; they spake with such pleasantness of Scripture language, and with such appearance of grace in all they said, that they were to me as if they had found a new world, as if they were people that dwelt alone, and were not to be reckoned among their neighbours (Num. 23:9).

At this I felt my own heart began to shake, as mistrusting my condition to be naught; for I saw that in all my thoughts about religion and salvation, the new birth did never enter into my mind, neither knew I the comfort of the Word and promise, nor the deceitfulness and treachery of my own wicked heart. As for secret thoughts, I took no notice of them; neither did I understand what Satan's temptations were, nor how they were to be withstood and resisted, etc.

Thus, therefore, when I had heard and considered what they said, I left them, and went about my employment again, but their talk and discourse went with me, also my heart would tarry with them, for I was greatly affected with their words, both because by them I was convinced that I wanted the true tokens of a truly godly man, and also because by them I was convinced of the happy and blessed condition of him that was such a one.[6]

"Sharing our stories" is no recent discovery by Christians. Bunyan—and these women before him—had been doing that as a part of their evangelism for centuries. These women, living their normal Christian lives, talking with each other, were part of God's evangelistic plan. It wasn't only sermons that God used to convert John Bunyan; he used normal Christians.

Let me share one more story of God using ordinary Christians to spread the good news: the story of James Smith. Smith was a slave near Richmond, Virginia. He was also a Christian. The inhuman cruelty of his "masters" separated him from his family—his wife, Fanny, and their children—for decades. But Smith's Christian faith sustained him. Each night after his day's work, Smith preached the gospel of Jesus Christ to fellow slaves, even after his master whipped him for it. But it wasn't in Smith's capacity as a preacher that God gave him one of his most amazing opportunities to evangelize. Smith was sold to a plantation in Georgia. His new "owner," concerned about a lack of obedience in Smith, ordered his overseer to give Smith a beating to get Smith to obey instructions, particularly those designed to limit his praying and meeting with others to worship. The overseer lashed Smith's back one hundred times. One hundred times! Later, that same overseer overheard Smith praying for his—the overseer's—soul, and when he heard that, he was cut to the quick and begged Smith's forgiveness. He also encouraged him to escape.[7]

God calls all Christians to share the good news. Our churches need to make sure that we know the good news and to make sure that we can all express it clearly. And we should work to train each other in having the kind of Christian lives and clear understanding that will help us to share the gospel. If we are honest, the main reason that we often want to shift the responsibility for evangelism to others is that we are not exactly sure how to do it. That's the question we want to consider in our next chapter.

4

How Should We Evangelize?

How should we evangelize?

We evangelize by preaching the Word and spreading the message (see Rom. 10:17). Okay, but how particularly should we spread the Word? This is a more important question than some people have realized. Whatever the specific means may be, publicly through various media, privately by personal conversation, through print and sermons, or through conversation and group study—*how* should we spread the gospel?

I want us to consider this in a couple of ways. First, and most basically, there is a certain balance that we want to strive for in our evangelism, a balance of honesty and urgency and joy. Too often we have only one, or at best, two, of these aspects rather than all three. The balance is important. These three together most appropriately represent the gospel. And then secondly, in the second half of the chapter, I have some suggestions for specifically how we can spread the gospel.

The Balance

Honesty. First, we tell people with honesty that if they repent and believe, they will be saved. But they will need to repent, and it will be costly. We must be accurate in what we say, not holding any important parts back that seem to us awkward or off-putting.

When considering how to evangelize, many people don't like to include anything negative in their presentation. There are thought to be negative and positive approaches to sharing the gospel, and talking about sin and guilt and repentance and sacrifice is thought to be a negative one, which is why it is currently out of favor. Here's what one leading television preacher said: "I don't think that anything has been done in the name of Christ and under the banner of Christianity that has proven more destructive to human personality, and hence counterproductive to the evangelistic enterprise, than the unchristian, uncouth strategy of attempting to make people aware of their lost and sinful condition."[1] Others more theologically orthodox suggest that while judgment and guilt were culturally relevant to a previous generation, they are alien today. They suggest that people today will respond better to a message of freedom.

But according to the Bible, although freedom is a wonderful aspect of our message (e.g., John 8:32–36), sin and guilt are at the very heart and core of the gospel. Making people aware of their lost and sinful condition is part and parcel of sharing the good news of Christ. If you read the summaries of Peter's sermons in the early chapters of the book of Acts, you will see that Peter is breathtakingly honest about the sin of those to whom he's speaking. His remarks were not calibrated to be flattering. By being frank, Peter was faithfully following the method Jesus had used with Peter and the others just a few months before, saying, "Anyone who does not carry his cross and follow me cannot be my disciple" (Luke 14:27).

Think about it. Let's not believe that we are simply all engaged in some search for truth. The fall did not leave people neutral toward God but at enmity with him. Therefore we must not pretend that non-Christians are seekers by the simple virtue of their having been made in the image of God. The

Bible teaches that people are by nature estranged from God, and we must be honest about that.

What is repentance? It is turning from the sins you love to the holy God you're called to love. It is admitting that you're not God. It is beginning to value Jesus more than your immediate pleasure. It is giving up those things the Bible calls sin and leaving them to follow Jesus.

When we tell the gospel to people, we need to do it with honesty. To hold back important and unpalatable parts of the truth is to begin to manipulate and to try to sell a false bill of goods to the person with whom we are sharing. So however we evangelize, we aren't to hide problems, to ignore our own shortcomings, or to deny difficulties. And we are not to put forward only positives that we imagine our non-Christian friends presently value and present God as simply the means by which they can meet or achieve their own ends. We must be honest.

Urgency. Also, though, if we are to follow a biblical model of evangelism, we must emphasize the urgency with which people ought to repent and believe if they will be saved. They must decide now. They certainly shouldn't wait until a "better deal" comes along. People might be careful enough with their money to wait to sign up for a cell phone plan or to renew their current plan until they've looked around on the Internet, maybe phoning and getting two or three offers and then comparing them all. But there's no point here in waiting for a better offer for forgiveness. According to the New Testament (John 14:6; Acts 4:12; Romans 10; all of Hebrews), Christ is the only way. How else would we suggest that sinners and the holy God be reconciled? And if Christ is the only way, then what are we waiting for? We don't know that tomorrow is ours, and we shouldn't act as if it is (James 4:13). "Today, if you hear his voice, do not harden your hearts" (Ps. 95:7–8; Heb. 4:7).

Jesus once told this story:

> A man had a fig tree, planted in his vineyard, and he went to look for fruit on it, but didn't find any. So, he said to the man who took care of the vineyard for him, "For three years now I've been coming to look for fruit on this fig tree and haven't found any. Cut it down! Why should it use up the soil?"
>
> "Sir," the man replied, "leave it alone for one more year, and I'll dig around it and fertilize it. If it bears fruit next year, fine! If not, then cut it down." (Luke 13:6–9)

It's not manipulative or insensitive to bring up the urgent nature of salvation. It's simply the truth. The time of opportunity will end.

As Christians, we've come alive to the truth that history isn't cyclical, always repeating in an endless rotation of events, spinning till any given part of it becomes meaningless. No! We know that God has created this world, and that he will bring it to a close at the judgment. We know that he gives us life, and he takes it away. The time that we have is limited; the amount is uncertain, but the use of it is up to us. So Paul tells us in Ephesians to "make the most of every opportunity (5:16)."

Like a collector buying up a collection, we should desire to capture each fleeting hour and to turn it into a trophy for God and his grace. As Paul said, "The time is short. From now on . . . those who use the things of the world [should use them] as if not engrossed in them. For this world in its present form is passing away" (1 Cor. 7:29, 31).

What are your circumstances right now? Trust the Lord to use you in them instead of seeking for new ones. Don't let the passing permanence of your world or the lulling tedium of certain long hours and minutes make a fool of you. The days are "evil" (Eph. 5:16) in the sense that they are dangerous and fleeting, and we must redeem the time and make the most of every hour. So we say with Paul that, in view of a certain judgment, Christ's love compels us to tell the good news to others (see 2 Cor. 5:10–15). We must be honest not only about the cost of repentance, but also about the expiration date of the offer. Such honesty compels us to urgency.

Joy. Now, if I stopped here, we might wind up with some rather grim evangelists. Driven by a careful conscience to be clear about what is condemned and forbidden, and driven by a sense of the brevity of time, we could end up with an intense, forceful practice of evangelism. But this wouldn't seem so much like *good* news. It would be imbalanced and inaccurate, because Scripture uses so much love language in relation to the gospel. We are built to love love. God loves us. We love God. Christ has loved us, and we love him even though we have not seen him. This news is good exactly because we want to spend an eternity with him. An eternity in relative prosperity without him would actually be hell to us.

The truth of this news of a restored relationship with God brings us great joy. So we should joyfully tell people that if they repent and believe they will be saved. It is all worth it, despite the cost. Which one of the people recounted in Hebrews 11 would not say that it was worth it? The Lord Jesus himself endured the cross, we read, "for the joy set before him" (Heb. 12:2).

At our church in Washington we have a bronze plaque on the pillar at the entrance to the church parking lot with this saying of Jim Elliot's: "He is no fool who gives what he cannot keep to gain what he cannot lose." What do we gain in coming to Christ? We gain a relationship with God himself, which includes forgiveness, meaning, purpose, freedom, community, certainty, and hope. All these and so much more are found in Christ. Just because we are honest about the difficulties, we don't have to mask the blessings or deny God's specific goodnesses to us through the gospel. We don't have to make the demands of the gospel sound worse than they are simply to make it all sound credible. We should tell others the good news with joy.

So that's the balance that we want to see—honesty, urgency, and joy. Honesty and urgency with no joy gives us a grim determination (read Philippians). Honesty and joy with no urgency gives us a carelessness about time (read 2 Peter). And urgency and joy with no honesty leads us into distorted claims about immediate benefits of the gospel (read 1 Peter).

Having gotten that balance in mind, though, here are some more specific ideas of how we want to share the gospel.

Specific Suggestions

1) **Pray.** Remember the importance of prayer in your evangelism. When Jonah was saved from the fish, he said, "Salvation comes from the LORD" (Jonah 2:9). If the Bible teaches us that salvation is the work of God, then surely we should ask him to work among those we evangelize. Jesus did. His prayer in John 17 was for those who would believe in him through the disciples' preaching and witnessing. And God answered that prayer. Jesus said, "No one can come to me unless the Father who sent me draws him" (John 6:44). If this is God's work, we should ask him to do it.

Paul also prayed for the salvation of those he was witnessing to. He wrote to the Roman Christians, "Brothers, my heart's desire and prayer to God for the Israelites is that they may be saved" (Rom. 10:1). We can work and witness for the salvation of someone, but only God can finally bring it about. It is his work.[2] So we must pray.

I remember once sitting in the library at seminary in the midst of my studies when suddenly I was struck with the fact that several people I loved had not been converted, even though I had been praying for them regularly for years. For a few moments, I wondered what use all these studies were if God wasn't listening and answering prayers that would obviously glorify him. I struggled with discouragement about this. Nevertheless, I knew it was my duty to keep on praying.

Some of those people I was praying for have never, to my knowledge, been saved. But others have been saved. By God's grace, slowly but surely over the years, I have seen many people for whom I was praying more than twenty years ago come to know Christ. Humanly speaking, some of these conversions were unlikely and surprising, which shows that ultimately it is God who is at work in evangelism, not you or me alone. And that brings about some wonderful fruit.

We pray about much less significant matters every day. Why wouldn't we pray about this? When you evangelize, remember to pray.

2) Use the Bible. The Bible is not only for public preaching and private devotionals. It can also be used in evangelizing. An interesting example of this, one we noted earlier, is found in Acts 8, when Philip came to the Ethiopian official. The official was reading Isaiah 53, a famous prophecy about the Messiah. Philip, as it says in Acts 8:35, "began with that very passage of Scripture and told him the good news about Jesus." The Bible is God's Word and is inspired by God's Spirit. God's message can go out not just through your words and mine, but through his own inspired words. And we can know that he will take a special delight in showing the power of his Word as he uses it in conversions.

This is one reason that I so enjoy doing a study of Mark's Gospel as a tool of evangelism. I am confident that God will use his Word in ways that I wouldn't have known to plan. I remember my own conversion and how crucial in that was my reading through the Gospels. Introduce a non-Christian (or a whole group of them in a Bible study) to the person of Jesus Christ as he is revealed on the pages of Scripture. Let them interact with the primary sources. Watch the power and majesty and love and penetrating conviction of Christ come through the stories, the works, the teaching.

Referring to the clear teaching of the Bible also shows our friends that we are not simply giving them our own private ideas; rather, we are presenting Jesus Christ in his own life and teaching. Just as we want the preaching in our churches to be expositional—preaching in which the point of the message is the point of the Bible passage being preached—we want to see people exposed to God's Word because we believe that God desires to use his Word to bring about conversions. It is God's Word coming to us that his Spirit uses to reshape our lives.

In your evangelism, use the Bible.

3) **Be clear.** When you share the gospel, think carefully about the language you use. One of the best conversations I can remember having about evangelism was with a secular Jewish friend of mine. I was to give talks soon on a college campus about evangelism, and I decided to ask my friend about evangelism. We'll call him Michael. (In fact, that was his name.) "So, Michael," I said, "have you ever been evangelized?"

"What's that?" he asked.

"You know," I said, "when someone who is a Christian starts talking to you about God and Jesus and asking if you're saved."

"Oh, that!" he said. "Yeah, I guess I have been."

Anyway, Michael and I got into a long and good conversation. Now, the truth is that I had evangelized Michael a number of times before, but he hadn't realized that's what I was doing. As we talked about it now, it became clear that he thought evangelism was something that someone did *to* him rather than a conversation in which he could engage.

I also realized that in my previous conversations with him I had taken the meaning of words for granted. "God," "prayer," "heaven," "good," "moral," "judge," and "sin" are all words that I realized I had not done a good job defining. If I had simply gone through a quick, persuasive sales presentation and gotten him to say "yes!" he would have been saying yes to much that he didn't understand. We need to be both engaging and clear when we present the gospel.

None of us ever has a complete understanding of the gospel, but we must have a clear idea of the basics of our message, and we must be clear in our expression of them. If there is a likely misunderstanding, we should address it. We should speak in such a way as to be understood. *Contextualization* is the big theological word for this.

So, for example, when we talk about justification (and we should), we should make sure to define it. Justification is being declared right with God. But because we sin, we are not right with God. So how can we be declared right? We can't, if God is truly good—unless, that is, we have someone act as a substitute for us. *Justification*, then, gets us talking about all kinds of issues right at the heart of the gospel.

So, when we are talking to non-Christian friends about the gospel, we want to make sure they understand what we mean. Christians in the Bible had a great concern about this. So it's often been noted that Paul began with the Old Testament when he was speaking to Jews, but when he spoke to a group of Greeks in Athens (Acts 17) he began by quoting their own sayings. As he wrote to the Corinthians, "To the Jews I became like a Jew, to win the Jews. . . . To those not having the law I became like one not having the law . . . so as to win those not having the law" (1 Cor. 9:20–21).

One part of providing clarity when we share the gospel, sometimes missed by earnest evangelists, is the willingness to offend. Clarity with the claims of Christ certainly will include the translation of the gospel into words that our hearer *understands*, but it doesn't necessarily mean translating it into words that our hearer will *like*. Too often, advocates of relevant evangelism verge over into being advocates of irrelevant non-evangelism. A gospel that in no way offends the sinner has not been understood.

Look at Peter at Pentecost in Acts 2. Peter wanted to be relevant, but that relevance gave his words more bite, not less. How did Peter witness to those he wished to see saved? He said to them, among other things, "Let all Israel be assured of this: God has made this Jesus, whom you crucified, both Lord and Christ" (Acts 2:36).

Relevant? Yes. Pleasing? No. Clear? Undoubtedly.

We must be clear about the fact of sin (Isa. 59:1–2; Hab. 1:13; Rom. 3:22–23; 6:23; Eph. 2:8–9; Titus 3:5; 1 John 1:5–6). We must be clear about the meaning of the cross (Matt. 26:28; Gal. 3:10–13; 1 Tim. 1:15; 1 Pet. 2:24; 3:18). We must be clear about our need to repent of our sins and to trust in Christ (Matt. 11:28–30; Mark 1:15; 8:34; John 1:12; 3:16; 6:37; Acts 20:21). How can we really evangelize without being clear about what the Bible says about these issues?

4) **Provoke self-reflection.** Something typical of our age is a heightened defensiveness that leads people to discover things for themselves rather than hearing things from other people. The desire for original discovery is what's behind the "journey" language that some use today. "Let people find the truth themselves. The days of simple tracts and surefire, sales-presentation evangelism is over. Don't tell people something; talk with them. Have a conversation." That's what we are hearing we have to do today, and to that I have a couple of replies.

First, it's true. Second (and surprising to some) it's always been true. It's nothing new. Our parents and grandparents were not the naïve, unquestioning followers that so much of current literature makes them out to be. Skepticism about particular facts can be borne out of a general cynicism about truth or out of a deep certainty about human character. Sherlock Holmes asked questions not because he wanted to know someone else's perspective, *their* truth; he wanted to know *the* truth. Detective stories always presuppose a right and wrong with certain actions and motives that explain them. Otherwise, there's no puzzle to be solved.

We Christians know that there is a right and wrong, but we also know our own hearts. We know that we don't like to be shown up easily and clearly when we are in the wrong. I'm a pastor. I write books telling you what to do, and yet the other day my wife most lovingly and respectfully corrected me on something that I had said in the presence of our son. She was right. I was wrong. I believe in absolute truth. I know she loves me. I know the theological truth that I am sinful. And yet she had to labor with me with patience, determination, perseverance, and love to get me to even be in the position to consider that I was perhaps wrong in that situation. And I've been a Christian for over twenty years.

Defensiveness is natural to the fallen human heart, so we want to do our best to help people hear the good news. We want to live and talk in such a way that we provoke people to reflect on themselves, on their own desires and actions. We can do this by asking good questions—questions about the origin of life or about how they understand bad things in this world. We can ask about what they're struggling with in their lives, and what they think the answer might be. We can even ask them what they think about death, and Jesus, and God, and judgment, and the Bible, and Christianity. But afterward we'll have to do what some witnessing Christians find very hard to do, something that surprises some of our non-Christian friends—listen to their answers![3]

Ask good questions and listen to their answers. Explore them. You may be helping them to enunciate and articulate their own thinking for the first time ever. And you don't even need to try to pretend that this is easy for you.

This is what you do for someone you love, and you surely love the person you're witnessing to. Insofar as you have opportunity, befriend people. Lower their defensiveness toward you (but not toward your message). Make suggestions of what you think is the case. Be clear in your presentation of the gospel. Pray that you will be able to put things in such a way as to undermine their disbelief and cause them to doubt their denials of the truth of the gospel. Be provocative in your conversation.

In fact, try to live in a distinctly Christian "salty" way around them—in your words and actions. Make them thirsty. Make your whole life before them provocative. I sometimes introduce myself to people as being a fundamentalist, because I'm hoping there will be an intriguing disconnect between their assumptions of what a fundamentalist is and what kind of person I seem to be. Live a Christian life before them. And that brings me to my final suggestion for you.

5) **Use the church.** By "use the church," I mean invite the person to whom you're witnessing to the church at which you're a member or to some other gospel-preaching church. But by saying "use the church," I also mean so much more than that. Realize that how the Christian life is lived out in the Christian community is a central part of our evangelism. Like those washer-women that Bunyan overheard, our lives are to give our words credibility. Not that any of us can live perfectly, but we can live lives that commend the gospel. Remember

Jesus' words in the Sermon on the Mount: "Let your light shine before men, that they may see your good deeds and praise your Father in heaven" (Matt. 5:16; cf. 1 Pet. 2:12).

Remember Jesus' statement in John 13:34–35: "A new command I give you: Love one another. As I have loved you, so you must love one another. By this all men will know that you are my disciples, if you love one another." Our words alone are not a sufficient witness—we must speak; we have *news*. Our lives are the confirming echo of our witness. Evangelism should include our way of living and our way of living together in the new society that is the local church.

The temple in Jerusalem was destroyed in A.D. 70, and there is nothing about a great Christian temple in the New Testament—a place of grandeur and majesty to which we can point our non-Christian friends and say, "Look! Aren't you impressed? Doesn't this show how wonderful and mysterious and beautiful and true and good our God is?" What happened to the temple in the New Testament era? There is nothing like it, because the temple has become us. We Christians have together become the temple of the Holy Spirit. When you read the New Testament, you find that it's not our church buildings but us, Christians. We Christians have together become the temple of the Holy Spirit.

So the community we live in will be given hope by those of us who live distinctive Christian lives, not by your church or mine, not by how similar we are to those around us (a common mistake Christians can make), but by how attractively different we are. That's why we are to live the distinctive lives that we do—because we are God's picture, God's billboard, in our city. Thus Paul wrote to the Philippians, "Do everything without complaining or arguing, so that you may become blameless and pure, children of God, without fault in a crooked and depraved generation, in which you shine like stars in the universe as you hold out the word of life" (Phil. 2:14–16).

The people around us are lost in darkness; we have the wonderful and attractive call to live out a new life in our congregations—a good life that reflects the good news. Think about the role of your church in your evangelism. Yes, you can invite people to services and special evangelistic events, but also consider bringing them into your own life, into the network of relationships that is your congregation. That may be to them as a shining star in the dark night of their lives. That may provoke them to do some honest soul searching. They may ask, as a friend once asked me, "So, you're a Christian? Then tell me the gospel! Witness to me, or somethin'!"

Those are just some suggestions, but suggestions that I hope encourage you in evangelizing. Of course, sometimes we share the gospel wrongly because we misunderstand what evangelism actually is. And that brings us to our next question.

5

What *Isn't* Evangelism?

I remember as a little child hugging my father's leg at a gas station only to realize it wasn't his leg I was hugging. I was embarrassed! It was a case of mistaken identity.

Other times mistaken identity has more serious consequences. I'm amazed at the number of predatory animals that can camouflage their bodies so perfectly that their prey doesn't ever suspect that a branch or rock is actually another creature preparing to eat and run!

In the matter of evangelism, I'm concerned about a number of things that people take to be evangelism that aren't. And this case of mistaken identity can have consequences more serious than mere embarrassment. Let me mention five things mistaken for evangelism.

1) Imposition

Probably the most common objection to evangelism today is, "Isn't it wrong to impose our beliefs on others?"

Some people don't practice evangelism because they feel they are imposing on others. And the way evangelism is often done, I can understand the confusion! But when you understand what the Bible presents as evangelism, it's really not a matter of imposing your beliefs.

It's important to understand that the message you are sharing is not merely an opinion but a fact. That's why sharing the gospel can't be called an imposition, any more than a pilot can impose his belief on all his passengers that the runway is here and not there.

Additionally, the truths of the gospel are not yours, in the sense that they uniquely pertain to *you* or *your* perspective or experience, or in the sense that you came up with them. When you evangelize, you are not merely saying, "This is how I like to think of God," or "This is how I see it." You're presenting the *Christian* gospel. You didn't invent it, and you have no authority to alter it.

In biblical evangelism, we don't impose anything. In fact, we really can't. According to the Bible, evangelism is simply telling the good news. It's not making sure that the other person responds to it correctly. I wish we could, but according to the Bible, this is not something we can do. According to the Bible, the fruit from evangelism comes from God. As Paul wrote to the Corinthians:

> What, after all, is Apollos? And what is Paul? Only servants, through whom you came to believe—as the Lord has assigned to each his task. I planted the seed, Apollos watered it, but God made it grow. So neither he who plants nor he who waters is anything, but only God, who makes things grow. (1 Cor. 3:5–7; cf. 2 Cor. 3:5–6)

I remember one time in Cambridge talking with Bilal, a Lebanese Muslim friend of mine. We were talking about a mutual friend of ours who was a fairly secular Muslim. Bilal wanted our friend to embrace a more faithful Muslim lifestyle, and I wanted him to become a Christian. We commiserated together on the difficulty of living in the midst of a secular British culture. Bilal then commented on how corrupt the Christian country of Great Britain is. I responded that Britain is not a Christian country, that in fact there is no such thing as a Christian country. That, he said, quickly seizing the opportunity, is the problem with Christianity compared to Islam. Christianity, he said, does not provide answers and guidelines for all of the complexities of real life. It has no overarching social-political pattern to give to society. I responded that this is because of Christianity's realistic portrayal of the human condition, of the problem of the human situation. He asked me what I meant.

I said that Islam has a shallow understanding of man's problems because it teaches that our problems are basically a matter of behavior. The solution to our problem is merely a question of the will. However, Christianity, I said, has a much deeper, more accurate understanding of the human situation, which includes a frank admission of human sinfulness as not merely an aggregate of bad actions but as an expression of a bad heart in rebellion against God. It's a matter of human nature. I said that Christianity has nothing that Bilal would recognize as a comprehensive political program because we don't think that our real problem can be dealt with by political power. I could put a sword to a person's throat and make him a sufficiently good Muslim, but, I said, I can't make anyone a Christian that way.

The Bible presents the human problem as one that can never be solved by coercive force or imposition. Therefore, all I can do is present the good news accurately, live a life of love toward unbelievers, and pray for God to convict them of their sins and give them the gifts of repentance and faith.

True biblical, Christian evangelism by its very nature involves no coercion but only proclamation and love. We are to present the free gospel to all; we cannot manipulate anyone to accept it. Biblical Christians know that we can't coerce anyone into life.

2) Personal Testimony

Some think of personal testimony as evangelism. Surely personal testimony is a wonderful thing. The psalmist is a model of it: "Come and listen, all you who fear God; let me tell you what he has done for me" (Ps. 66:16). So, too, we see in the New Testament that the lives of Christians test, prove, and confirm the claims of Christ. Paul wrote to the Corinthians, "In him you have been enriched in every way—in all your speaking and in all your knowledge—because our testimony about Christ was confirmed in you" (1 Cor. 1:5–6). The truth of the gospel, which someone once shared with us, is proved in our lives daily. We should testify to this wonderful experience. We should delight in God and share our delight verbally with others. Such testimony can certainly *contribute* to evangelism.

Michael Green tells the story of being at an outreach event. It was a time that was full of Christians giving testimonies about their Christian life. At one point, Green recounted, a non-Christian professor leaned over to him and whispered: "You know, I don't believe any of this." Green responded, "Yeah, I know, but wouldn't you like to?" As recounted, "with that remark, tears welled up in the woman's eyes. Her head told her 'no,' but her heart yearned to hear."[1] Testimonies are powerful.

One of the classic testimonies was given by a blind man Jesus healed. When he was questioned after Jesus healed him, he responded, "Whether he [Jesus] is a sinner or not, I don't know. One thing I do know. I was blind but now I see!" (John 9:25). The man disregarded the menacing threats of those more honored and respected than he in order to give this verbal witness to the power of God. It's a wonderful, powerful testimony, but it's not evangelism. There is no gospel in it. The man didn't even know who Jesus was.

In our own congregation in Washington, one of the highlights of our morning service comes after the sermon on Sundays when we have baptisms. After a hymn is sung, the congregation is seated, and those who are to be baptized come forward. We ask them one by one to introduce themselves and to share their testimonies. We noticed, however, the first few times we did this, that people could recount their own conversions—and quite movingly—but without ever clearly sharing the gospel. While it was encouraging for the congregation gathered there, the non-Christians present (including friends and families of those to be baptized) weren't hearing the gospel in the testimonies.

So we began asking those coming forward for baptism to write out their testimony the week before and to go over it with a staff member. One of the main things such a check does is to make sure that the gospel isn't merely implicit in the testimony but is, rather, explicit and clear, so that non-Christians present will be evangelized even as they're listening to the testimony of their friend. An account of a changed life is wonderful and inspiring thing, but it's the gospel of Jesus Christ that explains what it's all about and how it happened. And it's the gospel that turns sharing a testimony into evangelism.

Certainly a testimony of what we know God to have done in our lives may include the good news, but it also may not. In telling people how we have seen God help us, we may not actually make clear his claim on our lives or explain what Christ did on the cross. It's good to share a testimony of what God has done in our lives, but in sharing our testimonies we may not actually make clear what Christ's claims are on other people. In order to evangelize, we must be clear about that.

Let me share with you one word of special caution. Testimony is, of course, popular in our postmodern, that's-good-for-you age. Who would object to your thinking you've gotten something good from Christ? But wait and see what happens when you try to move the conversation from what Jesus has done for you to the facts of the life, death, and resurrection of Christ, and how that all applies to your nonbelieving friend. That's when you discover that testimony is not necessarily evangelism.

3) Social Action and Public Involvement

Some people mistake social action and public involvement for evangelism.

As this book is being written, a new biography of William Jennings Bryan has just been released. Bryan was the Democratic candidate for president of the United States three times. He was a fervent evangelical Christian, an evangelist in his own right, and a tireless worker for social reforms. He went all over the country giving speeches on factory conditions, working for a shorter workweek, promoting the idea of minimum wages, and championing graduated taxation. While Bryan was so laboring, was he evangelizing? Certainly he was involved with the best of motivations for the good of the most vulnerable members of society. His desire to change societal wrongs was excellent; his desires commend the character of the God Bryan claimed to represent. But was he evangelizing?

If someone had agreed that Bryan was pointing out real problems but disagreed with the solution he offered, would that have indicated he was also opposed to evangelism, the gospel, and the kingdom of God? I remember one prominent evangelical leader in the 1980s who was a proponent of unilateral nuclear disarmament. He upheld the idea that regardless of what "the other side" did, the United States government should simply eliminate their nuclear weapons. He justified this in the name of advocating peace. But what if such action, ironically, despite all the best intentions, actually encouraged war? Or what if peace was actually best achieved by "peace through nuclear superiority," as one t-shirt said?

Of the many actions designed to improve society, some are wonderful (e.g., the abolition of slavery), and some are terrible (e.g., legalizing the killing of unborn children). But none of them, not even the best, are the gospel of Jesus Christ.

Being involved in mercy ministries may help to *commend* the gospel, which is why Jesus taught, "Let your light shine before men, that they may see your good deeds and praise your Father in heaven" (Matt. 5:16). Peter echoed this when he wrote that we should "live such good lives among the pagans that, though they accuse you of doing wrong, they may see your good deeds and glorify God on the day he visits us" (1 Pet. 2:12). Displaying God's compassion and kindness by our actions is a good and appropriate thing for Christians to do. Jesus commended it when he told the story of the sheep and the goats (Matthew 25). Matthew concluded that story by quoting the Lord: "Whatever you did not do for one of the least of these, you did not do for me" (Matt. 25:45). But such actions are not evangelism. They commend the gospel, but they share it with no one. To be *evangelism*, the gospel must be clearly communicated, whether in written or oral form.

When our eyes fall from God to humanity, social ills replace sin, horizontal problems replace the fundamental vertical problem between us and God, winning elections eclipses winning souls. But Proverbs 11:30 says, "The fruit of the righteous is a tree of life, and he who wins souls is wise." Our practice of evangelism might be crusades for public virtues, or for programs of compassion, or for other social changes. But, as Donald McGavran, the well-known missionary from the middle of the last century, said, "Evangelism is not proclaiming the desirability of a liquorless world and persuading people to vote for prohibition. Evangelism is not proclaiming the desirability of sharing the wealth and persuading people to take political action to achieve it."[2]

Evangelism is not declaring God's political plan for nations nor recruiting for the church—it is a declaration of the gospel to individual men and women. Societies are challenged and changed when, through this gospel, the Lord brings individual men and women together in churches to display his character and to pursue their own callings in the world. As we learn from King David, it is a good thing to govern well (see 2 Sam. 23:3–4), but it is not evangelism. It's also a good thing to be a husband, wife, father, mother, employer, or employee—the list could go on. These are parts of what Christians are called to do, but fulfilling them is not the same thing as obeying the command to share the gospel of Jesus Christ.

4) Apologetics

Other people mistake apologetics for evangelism. Like the activities we've considered above, apologetics itself is a good thing. We are instructed by Peter to be ready to give a reason for the hope that we have (1 Pet. 3:15). And apologetics is doing exactly that. Apologetics is answering questions and objections people may have about God or Christ, or about the Bible or the message of the gospel.

Apologists for Christianity argue for its truth. They maintain that Christianity better explains that sense of longing that all people seem to have. Christianity better explains human rationality. It fits better with order. They may argue (as C. S. Lewis does in *Mere Christianity*) that it better fits with the moral sense that people innately have. It copes better with problems of alienation and anxiety. Christians may—and should—argue that Christianity's frankness about death and mortality commends it. These can be good arguments to have.

Other times they're not. Once, when I was giving a series of evangelistic talks at a university in England, I was so taken up in one talk with trying to anticipate objections to the Christian gospel—and answer them!—that I fear I suggested new ways to doubt the gospel far more effectively than I presented it to anyone that night. Since I used to be an agnostic, apologetics have been very important to me. God used things such as reasoning about the resurrection of Christ to help bring me to faith in Christ. But not all people have the same questions. We are not all built the same. And I shouldn't evangelize in such a way that I'm assuming that every non-Christian is just like I was with all my issues, questions, objections, and arguments.

However, just as we've observed with giving a testimony or working for social justice, practicing apologetics is a good thing, but it's not evangelism. Answering questions and defending parts of the good news may often be a part of conversations Christians have with non-Christians, and while that may have been a part of our own reading or thinking or talking as we came to Christ, such activity is not evangelism.

Apologetics can present wonderful opportunities for evangelism. Being willing to engage in conversations about where we came from or what's wrong with this world can be a significant way to introduce honest discussions about the gospel. For that matter, Christians can raise questions with their non-Christian friends about the purpose of life, what will happen after death, or the identity of Jesus Christ. Any of these topics will take work and careful thought, but they can easily lead into evangelism.

In college I led a discussion group for many of my college friends who were atheists. We met in a dorm room, just a number of atheists and me and occasionally another Christian. The atheists set the agenda. They posed questions, and we discussed them. I would try to answer their questions, and I'd also ask them some of my own. At the end of the day, for all the time it took, I can't really say how helpful that meeting was.

It should also be said that apologetics has its own set of dangers. You might unwittingly confirm someone in their unbelief by your inability to answer questions that are impossible to answer anyway. You can easily leave the impression that if you don't know how to answer your friends' questions, then you don't really know enough to believe that the Christian gospel is true either. But just because we don't know everything doesn't mean we don't know anything. All knowledge in this world is limited. We proceed from what we know, and we work that out. Everyone, from the youngest child to the most celebrated research scientist, does this. Apologetics can be very important work, but it should be undertaken with care.

By far the greatest danger in apologetics is being distracted from the main message. Evangelism is not defending the virgin birth or defending the historicity of the resurrection. Apologetics is defending the faith, answering the questions others have about Christianity. It is responding to the agenda that others set. Evangelism, however, is following Christ's agenda, the news about him. Evangelism is the positive act of telling the good news about Jesus Christ and the way of salvation through him.

5) The Results of Evangelism

Finally, one of the most common and dangerous mistakes in evangelism is to misinterpret the *results* of evangelism—the conversion of unbelievers—for evangelism itself, which is the simple telling of the gospel message. This may be the most subtle misunderstanding, yet it is a misunderstanding still. Evangelism must not be confused with its fruit. Now, if you combine this misunderstanding with a misunderstanding of the gospel itself, and of what the Bible teaches about conversion, then it is very possible to end up thinking not only that evangelism is seeing others converted, but thinking that it is within our power to do it!

According to the Bible, converting people is not in our power. And evangelism may not be defined in terms of results but only in terms of faithfulness to the message preached. John Stott has said, "To 'evangelize' . . . does not mean to win converts . . . but simply to announce the good news, irrespective of the results."[3] At the Lausanne gathering in 1974, evangelism was defined as follows:

> To evangelize is to spread the good news that Jesus Christ died for our sins and was raised from the dead according to the Scriptures, and that as the reigning Lord he now offers the forgiveness of sins and the liberating gift of the Spirit to all who repent and believe.[4]

Paul wrote, "We are to God the aroma of Christ among those who are being saved and those who are perishing. To the one we are the smell of death; to the other, the fragrance of life. And who is equal to such a task?" (2 Cor. 2:15–16). Note that the same ministry has two different effects. As with the parable of the soils, it's not that certain evangelistic techniques always lead to conversions. The same seed was planted in various places. The response varied not according to how the seed was planted but according to the nature of the soil. Just as Paul could not judge whether he was preaching correctly based upon how people responded to his message, so we cannot finally judge the correctness of what we do by the immediate response that we see.

Making this error distorts well-meaning churches into pragmatic, results-oriented businesses. It also cripples individual Christians with a sense of failure, aversion, and guilt. As one book puts it:

Evangelism is not persuading people to make a decision; it is not proving that God exists, or making out a good case for the truth of Christianity; it is not inviting someone to a meeting; it is not exposing the contemporary dilemma, or arousing interest in Christianity; it is not wearing a badge saying 'Jesus Saves'! Some of these things may be right and good in their place, but none of them should be confused with evangelism. To evangelize is to declare on the authority of God what he has done to save sinners, to warn men of their lost condition, to direct them to repent, and to believe in the Lord Jesus Christ.[5]

Who can deny that much modern evangelism has become emotionally manipulative, seeking simply to cause a momentary decision of the sinner's will, yet neglecting the biblical idea that conversion is the result of the supernatural, gracious act of God toward the sinner?

D. Martyn Lloyd-Jones recalls the story of a man who was disappointed that Lloyd-Jones hadn't given a public altar call after the previous night's sermon. "'You know, doctor, if you had asked me to stay behind last night I would have done so.'

"'Well,' I said, 'I am asking you now, come with me now.'

"'Oh no,' he replied, 'but if you had asked me last night I would have done so.'

"'My dear friend,' I said, 'if what happened to you last night does not last for twenty-four hours I am not interested in it. If you are not as ready to come with me now as you were last night you have not got the right, the true thing. Whatever affected you last night was only temporary and passing, you still do not see your real need of Christ.'" [6]

And such problems sometimes go further by becoming established in a church culture. One minister recounted:

I sat across the table from a 'big' preacher. His church had five thousand on a Sunday morning. I asked him about his evangelism strategy. He said his church employed two seminary students, each of whom was required to have two people come forward for baptism each Sunday. Therefore, a minimum of four people would 'profess faith' each Sunday—208 a year. He added, 'You can't get invitations to evangelism conferences unless you baptize 200 a year.' I was dumbfounded! I probed a bit. 'What if Sunday comes and the seminarian doesn't have two who will profess faith?' He responded, 'I will get students who can get the job done.' I questioned, 'What if these fellows are forced to cut some theological corners to meet their quota?' He was unconcerned and thought my question trivial, pesky, and the child of a too lively conscience.[7]

When we are involved in a program in which converts are quickly counted, decisions are more likely pressed, and evangelism is gauged by its immediately obvious effect, we are involved in undermining real evangelism and real churches. History is full of people coming to Christ months and years after the gospel is presented to them. That may be the case with you. I know it was with me, and it is with many other Christians. Most of us don't respond the first time we hear the gospel. Do you know the story of Luke Short?

It took a long time for the conversion of Mr. Short. He was a New England farmer who lived to be one hundred years old. Sometime in the middle of the 1700s he was sitting in his fields reflecting on his long life. As he did, "he recalled a sermon he had heard in Dartmouth [England] as a boy before he sailed to America. The horror of dying under the curse of God was impressed upon him as he meditated on the words he had heard so long ago and he was converted to Christ—eighty-five years after hearing John Flavel preach."[8] The preacher, John Flavel, had been a faithful evangelist eighty-five years earlier. And he was wiser than to have thought that the day he preached the sermon, he would quickly see all its fruit.

The Christian call to evangelism is a call not simply to

persuade people to make decisions but rather to proclaim to them the good news of salvation in Christ, to call them to repentance, and to give God the glory for regeneration and conversion. We don't fail in our evangelism if we faithfully tell the gospel to someone who is not converted; we fail only if we don't faithfully tell the gospel at all. Evangelism itself isn't converting people; it's telling them that they need to be converted and telling them how they can be.

Evangelism is not an imposition of our ideas upon others. It is not merely personal testimony. It is not merely social action. It may not involve apologetics, and it is not the same thing as the results of evangelism. Evangelism is telling people the wonderful truth about God, the great news about Jesus Christ. When we understand this, then obedience to the call to evangelize can become certain and joyful. Understanding this increases evangelism as it moves from being a guilt-driven burden to a joyful privilege.

But what happens once we've understood correctly what evangelism is, and we've done it? What happens then? That's what we'll take up in our next chapter.

6

What Should We Do *After* We Evangelize?

I had assured my young Christian friend that I would do all of the talking. "Besides," I said, "people are often interested in having a conversation. And even if they're not, most people are very polite."

I don't think my friend was buying it, but he followed along with me. When we came up to the first guy, reading a book, leaning with his back against a large, old tree, I began to engage him in conversation.

He just looked up at me, seeming mildly irritated, and said, "Go to hell!" While we didn't follow his instructions, we did move on at that point.

As my friend and I continued initiating conversations, we found different responses. And that's the way it is with all our evangelism. We get various responses to the gospel. This is true in contact evangelism. And this is true in the more long-term-relationship evangelism that we are doing all the time with our non-Christian friends.

When people are confronted with Jesus' command to repent and believe, many people do, and many people don't. And with those who do, their responses don't all look alike. Even those who reject the gospel don't all do it in the same way.

Negative Responses

"I'm undecided." Most of us have trouble making up our minds from time to time. We might be very decisive about some matters but not at all about others. We want to delay many decisions as long as possible in order to leave our options open.

I was an "undecided" for years. I spent probably two to four years (depending on how I count) considering the claims of Christ. I understand now from John 3:36 that as long as I was unbelieving, God's wrath remained on me. But at the same time, I was reading the Bible and thinking about following Christ. From a theological standpoint, I would now say that God was drawing me. But at the time, the Christians around me could see only that I was an "undecided." And that's all I could see of myself.

Considered at one level, people are undecided for various reasons. Maybe they aren't sure of their need and, therefore, of the importance of the message we are sharing with them. They might be undecided on something as basic as the existence of God or whether we, the ones sharing the message, are confident about the truth of the Bible. A lot of people are undecided simply because they are apathetic and indifferent. They're not convinced that they're in any danger. They can't conceive of anything they might have done that would be bad enough to merit any kind of terrible consequences from which they need to be saved. But whatever the reason, they're not sure. They're not aware of the danger of indifference to God, let alone their rebellion against him personally. Being undecided, they might reason, is not the same as being against something or someone.

Of course, "undecideds" don't count—at least, not as disciples. Silence may be construed as consent in legal reasoning, but it isn't in following Jesus. Jesus said, "He who is not with me is against me" (Matt. 12:30; Luke 11:23).[1] If people tell us that they can't make up their mind, we can't force them to, but at the same time we must not comfort them in their indecision, as if God recognizes the validity of a kind of spiritual in-between state. In humanity's rebellion against God, there is no neutrality.

In the book of Acts, Luke records Paul's preaching to all kinds of people. Among them were people Paul evangelized who did not respond by repenting and believing, but who wanted to hear him again.

We know that Felix, the Roman governor of Caesarea, told Paul after Paul had witnessed to him, "That's enough for now! You may leave. When I find it convenient, I will send for you" (Acts 24:25). But when we continue to read, we find that Felix's motivation was greed. Felix "was hoping that Paul would offer him a bribe, so he sent for him frequently and talked with him" (Acts 24:26).

A little different was Paul's witnessing to King Agrippa. After Paul had shared the gospel with him, Agrippa responded, "Do you think that in such a short time you can persuade me to be a Christian?" (Acts 26:28). That was essentially a negative response. Agrippa was rebuffing Paul's evangelistic witness and even seeming to reprove him for his forwardness. It's interesting that Agrippa didn't simply deny the gospel, but rather he implied that, were he to become convinced of it, he would need more time to do so.

We can't know what Agrippa was thinking. And we may not know what those we've witnessed to are thinking. But they should know that, even if they don't think that they are making up their minds about Christ, they are still making up their lives. They can't help it. They will either live as if Christ is Lord or as if he's not. We can hold our conclusions in suspense; we can't hold our living in suspense. No one will ever experience a truce in the conflict of lordship. There are only two options. And each of us in the world lives as if only one of these is Lord—God or self.[2]

Another negative response is "*I want to wait.*" Not only was I an "undecided"; I was also a "wait." A "wait" is a lot like an "undecided." A "wait" may or may not be an "undecided"; both waiting and not deciding have some similarities. Those who are undecided do wait. But they may wait simply because they don't want the consequences of a decision. A "wait" could be a person who doesn't want to close the door on Christian faith by rejecting it, at least not yet. Or he could be a person who doesn't want to repent of his sins, at least not yet. Such people may not be self-consciously undecided, but they want freedom from having to make a decision. For whatever reason, they want more time.

As with the "undecided," we should respect the "wait." We can't force someone to make a decision. We can't force her to make up her mind. But we can be clear about the danger of waiting.

Waiting is a negative response, even if couched in the most polite, ambivalent hesitation. "Wait" is another form of "no." That doesn't mean that it can never become a yes, but it isn't one yet. Both "no" and "wait" can, by God's grace, be turned into a "yes" to the gospel but until that time, both are "no" answers.

A famous story about the danger of a delayed response involves the famous nineteenth-century evangelist D. L. Moody. As an evangelistic meeting he was holding came to a close, Moody said, "Now, I want you to take that question with you and think it over, and next Sunday I want you to come back and tell me what you are going to do with it." His song leader, Ira Sankey, sang a hymn, "Today the Savior Calls." Sometime after the meeting that night, a fire began.

And before noon the next day, much of Chicago had been destroyed by fire, including Moody's own church building. Perhaps as many as three hundred people were killed, and thousands were made homeless. Moody vowed, as a response to this, that he would never again give a congregation a week to think over their need for salvation.

If, after you have evangelized people, they give you a "I want to wait" response, they may be expressing fear of the demands that would come on them if they were to commit themselves. "Wait" means I want something to stay like it is right now.

If you sense that they are not really attracted to the gospel, be clear and then drop it. Continue to pray for them. Make sure they understand what you are saying, but realize that you have indeed evangelized. You have witnessed. You have shared the gospel. You have been faithful. We share, but, as Paul told the Corinthians, "I planted the seed, Apollos watered it, but God made it grow" (1 Cor. 3:6). Clearly, more has to happen inside these people, and we should aid by praying for the Spirit's work and by trying to live a salty, provocative, attractive, joyful, authentic life around our friends.

Perhaps they want to wait, because, although they have basically decided to continue as they are—apart from Christ—they want to preserve their relationship with you. They know you are a Christian. They want your approval, or at least your friendship. And so, rather than cutting you off, they simply avoid, procrastinate, and delay. They wait.

On the other hand, perhaps they recognize that they are becoming convinced, that they are deciding to follow Christ. But they are reluctant to repent of certain sins. Perhaps it's a relationship with a girlfriend, a love of getting drunk, or a desire to continue in a sinful avoidance of responsibility. Whatever it is, they find within themselves, as they're coming to recognize the truth of the gospel and to take seriously God's claim on their lives, a desire to pause. "Hold on!" they say. "Am I really sure I want to give up this much?" I can understand that reaction. While sin's ugliness is often apparent once we have given up a particular sin, it was once attractive, even beguiling, to us.

So, if you sense that someone is becoming attracted to the gospel, be patient. I've read books on personal evangelism that talk about the need to protect a person's privacy while they are deciding. I remember one book that even suggested we should lock the door so that we and the one we are leading to Christ won't be interrupted. I wonder about that . . .

I don't know what you think, but I agree with D. Martyn Lloyd-Jones's statement in the previous chapter to the man who wanted to make a decision one evening but did not because Lloyd-Jones hadn't given a public invitation. The man told him the next day that he wouldn't be making a decision at all, though he would have the previous night. Lloyd-Jones responded, "If what happened to you last night does not last for twenty-four hours I am not interested in it. If you are not as ready to come with me now as you were last night you have not got the right, the true thing. Whatever affected you last night was only temporary and passing, you still do not see your real need of Christ."[3]

Interrupting someone in the process of deciding to follow Christ can actually help him. After all, his life as a Christian will be full of interruptions, of people who will distract, disturb, discourage, and even mock him for following Christ. Having a little of that right at the beginning is no bad thing.

As I'm writing this section, I've been watching a squirrel in our backyard. At first he was perched on the fence and about to leap to a tree branch. But he waited. He stood there for several seconds, eyeing the branch, poised to spring, but not yet springing. He was waiting. I don't know why. I guess it was to make sure the moment was right, that the wind wasn't too high, or that our dogs weren't around, or that there was no other predator awaiting him in the tree. Who knows what all was involved in that situation? But the squirrel waited.

People can be like that too. Even if they've decided that they want to become a Christian, they realize that what we've described to them will mean a tremendous change. A new turn in their lives—a new life, really—is about to begin. I can understand the natural tendency to pause and take stock. To wait—even if for the squirrel's few moments—before they take the plunge. Pray for wisdom to know how to respond, even as you pray for God's Spirit to continue his work in their hearts.

Another negative answer is "*Not now.*" I won't say much about a "not now." Most of it has been covered in our consideration of an "undecided" and a "wait." A "not now" says, "I might think about it more later, but I'm not persuaded. I don't like the cost. I'm not just a 'wait.' I'm being a little more definitive. I'm saying, 'No—at least, for right now.' I'm not an 'undecided.' I understand that you want me to follow Christ now, and to that I'm saying no. Perhaps at some point in the future I might think differently about this, but for this year, this month, for today, as I see things, I'm saying, 'No. Not now.'"

I was a "not now." I wasn't sure that Christianity was wrong; I was an agnostic. And even when I began moving toward Christianity, as I read the Gospels, I pondered for quite a while, turning over the question of becoming a Christian and concluding, "Not now." I thought it was too much to take in all at once and commit to. But I continued to read, attend church, and think. I didn't really pray, at least, not much.

Of course, there are less hopeful "not now's." A "not

now" can be a decided "no" expressed with some humility. Or he might be expressing a realization that he's open to his mind being changed, even though it hasn't happened yet. It can also be a polite way of saying the next response we want to consider.

"*No, never.*" I don't think I was ever a "no, never." This is the most severely negative response. Paul implicitly said "no, never" in Acts 7 and 8 as he went around persecuting Christians, even approving of Stephen's martyrdom. A "no, never" is saying "I've looked at Christianity all it needs to be looked at, and I've considered it all it needs to be considered. The passage of time will not change anything about this. The message is simply not true. It's certainly not true for me!"

The certainty of the "no, never" obviously informs us of how strongly the person feels. However, it doesn't tell us with unfailing accuracy what will end up happening. I'm sure that many Christians—you may be one of them—were at one time "no, nevers."

According to the Bible, non-Christians are spiritually blind. Their eyes are not open to spiritual truths. They are dead to the things of God. Their own statements on spiritual things may be sincere, but they're not necessarily accurate.

Of course, those who adamantly reject the gospel must still be treated with respect. We don't need to make an appeal to them every time we see them. Such appeals may simply drive them away. To friends like this we should continue to be faithful, knowing that the very strength of their response may indicate a strength God will someday convert and use for his own ends. Paul was a mighty opponent of the gospel, and yet he became a mighty evangelist. As with other negative responses, this one, too, is best met with continued prayer, and we can continue to live around the "no, nevers" in such a way as to demonstrate the great truths of the Christian gospel. Let them see your life and character. We can let them see our church family, a community of Christians following Christ together, helping and caring for each other.

Positive Responses

Now let's think about those who accept the gospel.

What do you do with those people who accept the news you've given and profess repentance and faith? No one book can fully answer this question. Certainly not this one. The Bible, however, gives us all the instructions that we need. And we find there that these new Christians are to be brought into the fellowship of the local church. They're to be given all the family privileges and all the family responsibilities. They're to be baptized and admitted to the Lord's Table. They are to be provided with guidance and counsel, love and support, care and teaching. Their relationship with the local church will mature and change just like their relationships with their spouse or friends. Sometimes one thing is needed; at another stage of life other kinds of support, correction, or instruction will be needed.

Throughout it all, the new Christian should continue to be taught what it means to follow Jesus. From sitting under the preaching of the Word, to being baptized and taking the Lord's Supper, to praying and studying the Word, to repenting and believing, evangelism should find its fulfillment in discipleship. The good news is not merely about the commuting of an eternal sentence but about the commencing of an eternal relationship. Truly trusting Christ will always show itself by following him.

However, some "yeses" are false ones. Sometimes people say that they have become a Christian when they haven't. Some of these will no doubt be revealed to us only in the next world. Sometimes this becomes obvious after years of apparent discipleship. Other times it happens more quickly, after only a few weeks, months, or years of Christian profession. Their zeal seems to lag. Their church attendance becomes spotty. They would continue to say they are Christians, but following Christ is of little practical concern to them. Little of their energy goes into it, little of their attention.

And then one day the flickering flame just seems to go out. It is extinguished by the cares of this world, the lust of the flesh, the pride of life. Jesus told a parable about the plants that sprang up quickly but then quickly died (Mark 4:5–7). It's exactly because of such supposedly sincere but actually false conversions that Christians have often been exhorted to be patient in their offering of assurance and in their counting of converts. George Whitefield said, "There are so many stony ground hearers, who receive the Word with joy, that I have determined to suspend my judgment till I know the tree by its fruits. I cannot believe they are converts until I see fruit brought back; it will never do a sincere soul any harm."[4]

I remember talking to a friend with whom I'd been studying Mark's Gospel. He told me one morning—after months of meeting—that he'd become a Christian. I asked him some questions, rejoiced with him, took him over to meet with the church staff to share his great news with them. Afterward we all prayed with him, and then the staff members filed out of the room until my friend and I were left alone again. I closed the door, sat down, and said, "I'm not sure exactly what's really happened to you, but it sounds like God is doing great things in your life. Time will tell." (I said more, but that's all that I need to recount for the point I'm making!) And time did tell. As we approached his baptism, he was confronted with further sins. At each one of those points, he had the choice to continue to follow God and trust Christ or, as he came to understand more clearly what repentance meant for his life, of turning back and deciding to live for himself and for his immediate pleasure as his god.

Praise God, he chose to follow Christ! My friend and those like him are the true "yeses," which are the evangelist's hope. These are the true Christians. At one time, we were not Christians. Perhaps you were converted when you were a small child. You may not remember a time when you didn't follow Christ. But the Bible tells us that we are all by nature at enmity with God. And at some point, our hearts came alive to God and our wills bent to his. We were converted. That's what we want to see as a result of our evangelism.

But is getting this result what motivates us to evangelize? If a yes answer seems obvious to you, don't skip the next chapter. We'll see why we should really go to so much trouble to share the good news.

7

Why Should We Evangelize?

So, we've seen that God calls us to evangelize, and he tells us how to do it. The message is about him. But we have one final question to consider: Why should we evangelize? In other words, what's the ultimate goal?

The French philosopher and mathematician Blaise Pascal once said, "Happiness is the motive of every man, even those who hang themselves." Really? Is our own happiness the reason that we do everything that we do? Or are there other motives as well?

But why even ask the question? Is there such a thing as having the wrong motivation for evangelism? Now, maybe this seems to be a silly question. After all, how bad can it be to share the gospel? Won't any reason do? What's the point of looking for a motive for something that is, in and of itself, evidently good? Isn't that like looking for a motive to love your spouse or to care for your kids? What can be gained from such assessment?

But there are problems when the motive is wrong. For example, you could have a *selfish* motive for evangelism. As grotesque as it may seem, you could evangelize out of wanting to be right, or wanting to win an argument with a friend, or wanting some kind of psychological reenforcement for your own beliefs, or wanting to look spiritual in front of your friends—or even in front of God—or to have a reputation as a successful evangelist. I know that sometimes I've shared the gospel, at least in part, so that I could tell others that I had witnessed to someone. I'm not particularly proud of that fact, but it's true.

So what is the right reason to tell the good news?

According to the Bible, good motives for evangelism are a desire to be obedient, a love for the lost, and a love for God. Let's consider each one of these. And then I'll close this chapter with a few encouragements.

A Desire to Be Obedient

When we read the Bible, we see that evangelism isn't an idea thought up by traveling revivalists or marketing specialists. It was the risen Lord Jesus Christ who commanded his disciples to "go and make disciples of all nations, baptizing them in the name of the Father and of the Son and of the Holy Spirit" (Matt. 28:19). We know from the book of Acts that the early disciples did this. And Paul refers to his own compulsion to preach the gospel (1 Cor. 9:16–17). Preaching the gospel was an obligation he had been given (Rom. 1:14). To evangelize was to obey.

And the command wasn't only given to these original disciples. We considered this back in chapter 3, but here's a brief refresher. We read in Acts 8:4: "Those who had been scattered preached the word wherever they went," and those scattered ones weren't just apostles or elders. Later on in Acts 8 we find the story of Philip the deacon evangelizing the Ethiopian official.

One of the clearest places in the New Testament where we find the command to evangelize is 1 Peter. In chapter 3, Peter commands young Christians: "Be prepared to give an answer to everyone who asks you to give the reason for the hope that you have" (1 Pet. 3:15). Doing so is said to be a part of setting apart Christ as Lord, that is, of obeying him.

We know that God is good. And we know that if we fear him uniquely (as Peter urged Christians to do), it's as if we are tied to him, and we must go where he leads. Have you ever been (or even watched) waterskiing? Following Christ is a bit like that. The person on the skis has special regard and respect for one particular boat, because it is that boat which determines where the one on the skis will go. Sometimes the lake may be placid and the water calm. At such times the skier may have no particular problem following the boat. But sometimes the boat goes through some rougher water. Then, as long as the skier is holding on to the tow rope, the skier, too, will go through rough water.

God is much better than any boat driver at knowing where we need to go, but it is the universal experience of all of us who are Christians that God will take us through some difficult waters. However, if we are truly going to fear him alone, then we will continue following him, doing good, and evangelizing, even when doing so entails suffering.

"But," some of you may be thinking, "today differs so much from the days in which Peter wrote. Where then there was tormenting persecution, today there is only tolerant pluralism, at least for us in the West. What does such talk of being willing to suffer mean for us in our prosperity and spiritual indifference? This stuff about suffering doesn't really apply to us, does it?"

I think it does. Robert Jenson, in one essay, gave an example of what it could mean. He noted:

> One of [the] chief and excruciatingly ironic effects [of the ideology of pluralism]: it silences a lot of people. . . . So far as my observation reaches, the silenced are almost always those who if they spoke would say something character-

istically Jewish or Christian or Islamic. Try, for example, arguing that unrestricted permission to abort the unborn is a social and political evil at a party in Manhattan or a college town in Minnesota. Your arguments will not be rebutted; heads will merely be turned as from one who has audibly broken wind. If, on the other hand, you argue what is in fact the *conventional* opinion, you will be praised for courage and compassion. Or relate two conversions, one to Christianity and the other away from it; one will be received as a tale of horrid narrow-mindedness and the other as an example of an open society's marvelous possibilities.[1]

Have you ever tried to be open about your Christian discipleship? If so, you know that sometimes it's a wonderful experience, but other times you're simply made to feel strange or stupid.

We typically want to process our experiences immediately, and if they are unpleasant, we are inclined to change course in order to some way avoid the discomfort of the difficult comment or the pain that comes to us by a long obedience. But Peter says (1 Peter 3) that navigating our lives that way won't do; at least, not for those who really want to serve God more than themselves. Because this world is in rebellion against God and good, and if we would fear him and follow him, then our former false peace will leave, and we will become the focus of a pitched battle, sometimes around us, sometimes inside us. Following a good God in an evil world will sometimes involve suffering—even as we evangelize. But we do it, because we are believers in Jesus Christ.

If you are a believer, you have been commanded to share the good news of Jesus Christ with others.

Love for the Lost

Another reason to share the gospel is out of love for those who are lost. It is a godly, Christlike thing to have compassion and mercy on those in need. God himself, we read, "so loved the world that he gave his one and only Son, that whoever believes in him shall not perish but have eternal life" (John 3:16). If God has loved in this way, we, too, should love those who are lost. We ourselves have been the objects of his saving love, so how very appropriate it is for us to show such love to others. The Lord Jesus, whom we follow, "when he saw the crowds . . . had compassion on them, because they were harassed and helpless, like sheep without a shepherd" (Matt. 9:36). Such compassion should mark us and motivate our evangelism.

Compassionate love marked the evangelism of Paul. We read in Romans these words: "Brothers, my heart's desire and prayer to God for the Israelites is that they may be saved" (Rom. 10:1; cf. 9:1–5). Paul loved the lost, and so he shared the gospel with them. He wrote, "I am talking to you Gentiles. Inasmuch as I am the apostle to the Gentiles, I make much of my ministry in the hope that I may somehow arouse my own people to envy and save some of them" (Rom. 11:13–14). Paul loved them and, therefore, wanted to see them saved. So he was motivated, he told the Corinthians, to become "weak" if he needed to, in order to "save some" (1 Cor. 9:22).

Augustine talked about this over 1500 years ago. Speaking of Jesus' great command, he wrote:

> "Thou shalt love thy neighbor as thyself." Now you love yourself suitably when you love God better than yourself. What, then, you aim at in yourself you must aim at in your neighbor, namely, that he may love God with a perfect affection. For you do not love him as yourself, unless you try to draw him to that good which you are yourself pursuing. For this is the one good which has room for all to pursue it along with thee. From this precept proceed the duties of human society.[2]

The gospel helps us to love the lost. We are instructed by

God's own love. We are moved by the needs of the lost. We are compelled by Christ's sacrifice. And we feel, ourselves, the benefit of betraying our sins and turning to Christ in full trust. As we so experience the gospel, we find ourselves loving others more, and we want to share this good news with them.

Sometimes at our meetings of church elders or staff, we'll have to decide who gets to tell someone a piece of good news. Maybe it's a seminarian we've decided to support or a missionary. Maybe it's someone we want to ask to preach, or someone we've decided to approach about serving the church in a certain position, or a prospective intern whose application has been accepted. It's good news, and we know the recipients will like it, so we all want to be the one to tell them.

Can you imagine being less excited about telling someone the infinitely better news of the gospel of Jesus Christ? And, yet, too often we are. I am!

Evangelism is a duty of the Christian, and it is a duty born of love for others. And it's a privilege.

Love for God

Finally, though, our love for people can prove inadequate. The motivating force of our whole life, including our evangelism, must be our love for God.

> Love for God is the only sufficient motive for evangelism. Self-love will give way to self-centeredness; love for the lost will fail with those whom we cannot love, and when diffi-culties seem unsurmountable [sic], only a deep love for God will keep us following his way, declaring his Gospel, when human resources fail. Only our love for God—and, more important, his love for us—will keep us from the dangers which beset us. When the desire for popularity with men, or for success in human terms, tempts us to water down the

Gospel, to make it palatable, then only if we love God will
we stand fast by his truth and his ways.[3]

Ultimately, our motive in evangelism must be a desire to
see God glorified. This was the end of all of the Lord Jesus'
actions (see John 17). Again and again throughout Ezekiel we
read the phrase "then they will know that I am the LORD" as
God's explanation for his actions with his disobedient people
(e.g., Ezek. 12:16; 20:20; cf. verses about intra-Trinitarian love:
John 3:35; 5:20; 14:31). Jesus taught that the actions of those
who follow him would bring glory to his Father: "This is to my
Father's glory, that you bear much fruit, showing yourselves to
be my disciples" (John 15:8). So we share the gospel to glorify
God, which happens as we declare the truth about God to his
creation.

God is glorified in being known. To see others truly come
to know him glorifies God and honors him. To tell the truth
about one another does not necessarily convey honor. We
have all done things that bring us shame rather than glory. But
God is perfect. To tell the truth about God is to praise him, to
glorify him. When others come to know him, it tells the truth
about his *desirability*. This is why Christians like John Harper,
whom I mentioned in the introduction, are so zealous to share
the truth, the good news, about Jesus Christ.

The call to evangelism is a call to turn our lives outward
from focusing on ourselves and our needs to focusing on God
and on others made in his image who are still at enmity with
him, alienated from him, and in need of salvation from sin
and guilt. We bring God glory as we speak the truth about
him to his creation. This is not the only way that we can bring
glory to God, but it is one of the chief ways that he has given
us as Christians, as those who know him through his grace in
Christ. It is not a way that we will bring him glory eternally in

heaven; it is one of the special privileges of living now, in this fallen world.

Peter exhorted Christians in the first century toward the glory of God: "Live such good lives among the pagans that, though they accuse you of doing wrong, they may see your good deeds and glorify God on the day he visits us" (1 Pet. 2:12). Peter knew that the Christian life that bears witness to God and the gospel will be a ground for God to be glorified in the last day. This is a never-ending motive to evangelize.

Sometimes we ignore even the most important things in our lives. There have been times when I've run out of gas while driving my car. I actually remember doing it twice in one summer! Just as with my disregard for a low gas tank, evangelism is one of those most important things that we can forget or ignore or neglect. We should commit ourselves to combat this neglect. So in order to help you do that, let me finish off this chapter with some encouragements to evangelize.

Encouragements to Evangelize

Following are five simple practices to encourage you in evangelism.

1) Ask for testimonies. As I mentioned in chapter 5, I love hearing people share how they came to Christ. I am encouraged to share the gospel with others as I hear such stories. I am reminded of the change Christ has made in my own life and in the lives of so many others I know and love.

In order to join our church, you must meet with me (or with one of the other elders), and part of what we ask you to do is to share your testimony with us. That is one of my favorite parts of being a pastor. I've gotten to sit and listen to literally hundreds of people share how they've come to Christ. And they've come in all kinds of ways, but it's always Christ they've come to by repenting of their sins and trusting in him.

And, inevitably, how did they get to that point? They came to Christ because someone shared the gospel with them.

2) **Consider the reality of hell.** I do think about the shortness of this life, and I think about the life to come. I think about people meeting God in his wrath. As one Puritan said, "Outside of Christ, God is terrible." Do you understand what he meant? He meant that God is good, and because he is unswervingly, uncompromisingly, unerringly good, he will not accept any kind of evil. As the prophet Habakkuk said to God, "Your eyes are too pure to look on evil; you cannot tolerate wrong" (Hab. 1:13).

Since that's the case, it's no surprise that God is committed to punish those who are in rebellion against him, those who are in sins that they will not repent of. And the penalty is not merely an annihilation or an absence but the active punishment of the sinner for their sins. And that state of being punished forever for those sins you will not repent of is called hell.

Thinking of such things sobers me. It clarifies what the big issues are in my day and my week. Remembering this truth helps me in conversations with people that I meet. Not that I immediately or always think, "This person is going to hell." But I do think, "This is a person who is liable to fall under God's wrath. I want to share with them the wonderful work that Christ has performed for all who will turn from their sins and trust in him!"

Apart from such turning and trusting, however, there is only God's deserved wrath. We read in John 3:36: "Whoever believes in the Son has eternal life, but whoever rejects the Son will not see life, for God's wrath remains on him." How will someone ever escape this wrath? They never will, unless they come to believe in the Son. But how will they come to believe? It will happen only by someone sharing the gospel with them.

3) **Consider God's sovereignty.** This one may surprise you, but I'm actually just following God's lead in pointing out the doctrine of his sovereignty. Paul was becoming a reluctant evangelist—or at least a tired and discouraged one—in Corinth. We read in Acts 18:9–11: "One night the Lord spoke to Paul in a vision: 'Do not be afraid; keep on speaking, do not be silent. For I am with you, and no one is going to attack and harm you, because I have many people in this city.'" When the Lord said that he "had many people in this city," he wasn't referring to Corinth's population; Paul was surely aware already of the size of the city. So then what was the Lord saying to Paul?

God was telling Paul that the fact that God had elected some (in this case, many, in Corinth) for salvation meant that Paul should continue preaching so that the elect would be saved. Paul knew that God had willed Paul's evangelism to bear such good fruit.

Have you heard it said that the doctrine of God's choosing some for salvation (the doctrine of election) undercuts evangelism? It didn't in Paul's life. As he later wrote to Timothy, "I endure everything for the sake of the elect, that they too may obtain the salvation that is in Christ Jesus, with eternal glory" (2 Tim. 2:10). Romans 10 contains Paul's clearest and most impassioned plea for Christians to send out people to preach the gospel because it is the only way people are saved; but this impassioned plea comes after what many consider Paul's plainest teaching about the doctrine of election in Romans 9. He didn't see any inconsistency that a sovereign God is also a saving God.

Somehow, Paul found the doctrine of God's sovereignty an encouragement in his evangelism. Do we need to recover this confidence in a day of increasing opposition to the public preaching of the gospel? I think that we do. I fear that much of today's evangelism will soon end. As evangelism becomes more and more unpopular, I fear that some Christians will simply dilute it, water it down, alter it, or even stop sharing the good news altogether. I think a better understanding of the Bible's teaching on God's election would help them. I think it would give them confidence and joy in their evangelism.

But isn't the doctrine of election not only narrow-minded but also narrow-hearted? I know some people think so. I like the prayer I've heard attributed to C. H. Spurgeon: "Lord, save the elect, and elect some more." I don't mean that disrespectfully. I'm sure I could never be more generous than God. But I'm also sure that God is not disappointed by our aspirations that more and more people should come to know him in his wonderful, majestic, saving love. But how will they come to know God's love? They will only do so by someone sharing the gospel with them.

4) **Meditate on the gospel.** I find the gospel message itself compelling. To think about who God is (for the Christian) is to be attracted to him. It is to be enthused. It is to be drawn to him and his heart, to his holiness and his just claims on our allegiance.

Meditating on man's need is also an encouragement to evangelize. Man's need concerns more than just his eternal state; it also involves his current enslavement by and to sin. Such a creature, made in the image of God, should not be spending his life in rebellion, as if there were a better government for his soul than God's. He should, rather, be in fellowship with God, submitted to him, and adopted as God's own child. How can someone so repent of their sins and believe in Christ? It is only by someone sharing the gospel with him.

5) **Consider the cross.** Meditating, too, on what God has provided in Christ is a special encouragement to share the gospel. To think that God has loved us at all is amazing, con-

sidering how we have treated him. But to think of him loving us to the extent that he has in Christ—this is *truly* amazing. He bought the church with his blood (Acts 20:28). On the cross, Christ showed us the extent of God's love; would you know its height and breadth and depth and length? Then look at Christ's arms outstretched on the cross.

Perhaps you have sometime in your life received a gift that absolutely embarrassed you. The expense of the gift, its rarity, or even the sheer thoughtfulness so overwhelmed you that you almost wanted to shrink back from it. That's the way it is with the cross of Christ. We almost can't believe that Someone so good could love people like us, and love us so thoroughly and to that extent!

How can someone come to know the beauty of God's love in the cross of Christ? Only by someone sharing the gospel with them. In light of all this, evangelism should be both a discipline and a worshipful act of devotion.

I thought that this was going to be a small book on evangelism, but it's getting to be a big one! I'd better bring this thing to a conclusion. Before you go, I want us to think together about "closing the sale."

Conclusion
Closing the Sale

So this is the end. Almost.

This is to be our evangelism: a God-given commission and method, a God-centered message, and a God-centered motive. We should all evangelize. Evangelism isn't all those other things we considered; it is telling the good news about Jesus, and doing it with honesty, urgency, and joy, using the Bible, living a life that backs it up, and praying, and doing it all for the glory of God.

I remember reading a little book by C. S. Lovett, *Soul-winning Made Easy*, in which Lovett lays out a "Soul-Winning Plan," as he calls it, which is based on sales techniques of the time. "You are in command," he says, talking about Christians as salesmen.

> In much the same way the trained soul-winner can bring his prospect to a decision for Christ. There is no middle ground as he moves with surety and deftness right up to the point of salvation. It is his conversation control that makes this possible. He knows exactly what he is going to say each step of the way and can even anticipate his prospect's responses. He is able to keep the conversation focused on the main issue and prevent unrelated materials from being introduced. The controlled conversation technique is something new in evangelism and represents a real break-through in soul-winning.[1]

Lovett then instructs the earnest Christian about various tools needed and gives some helpful hints such as, "Get your prospect alone."[2] At one point, he teaches how to press for the decision. He writes, "Lay your hand firmly on the subject's shoulder (or arm) with a semi-commanding tone of voice, and say to him: 'Bow your head with me.' Note: Do not look at him when you say this, but bow your head first. Out of the corner of your eye you will see him hesitate at first. Then, as his resistance crumbles, his head will come down. Your hand on his shoulder will feel the relaxation and you will know when his heart yields. Bowing your head first causes terrific psychological pressure."[3] It causes terrific psychological pressure.

Terrific psychological pressure. Psychological pressure. Pressure. How many churches today are full of people who have been psychologically pressured but never truly converted?

At my church in Washington, we had a visitor one Sunday who came up to me at the door after the service. He had appreciated the message and wanted to tell me so. I steeled myself for the encouragement. After he told me that the sermon was good in various ways, he characterized it as "perhaps the best sales pitch I have ever heard. And," he added, "that should mean something, because that's what I do for a living. I'm a salesman."

At this point I was trying to accept the remark kindly, feigning slight but godly humility, all the time beginning to chew on the compliment like a dog on a bone.

"But" he added, "I have one criticism."

"What's that?" I asked, honestly curious.

"You didn't close the sale!" And with that statement, it was like an adult had just entered a room of childish daydreams. My attention snapped to. I saw a different view on the gospel and evangelism, one that pivoted on that one statement.

We need to know what kind of sales we can close and what

kind we can't. The redemption of an eternal soul is one sale that we, in our own strength, cannot accomplish. And we need to know it, not so that we won't preach the gospel, but so that we won't allow the gospel that is preached to be molded by what finally gets a response!

That last sentence was important, so I'm going to repeat it. We need to know what "sales" we can "close" and what "sales" we *can't*—not so that we won't preach the gospel, but so that we won't allow the gospel that is preached to be molded by what finally gets a response.

As I was falling asleep last night, I read an essay by the late liberal theologian Paul Tillich.[4] In this essay, Tillich suggested that Christianity has powerful symbols (creation, fall, incarnation, salvation, heaven), which lose their connection with modern life when they are taken literally. My salesman friend sounded like a modern disciple of Tillich. You can close the sale. If you don't get a response, change the way you present the message until you do get a response—until you can close the sale. That can get perilously close to changing the message.[5]

You and I aren't called to use our extensive powers to convict and change the sinner while God stands back as a gentleman, quietly waiting for the spiritual corpse, his declared spiritual enemy, to invite God into his heart. Rather, we should resolve to preach the gospel like gentlemen, persuading while knowing we can't regenerate anyone, and then stand back while God uses all his extensive powers to convict and change the sinner. Then we'll see clearly who it is that can really call the dead to life, and although he'll use us in the doing of it, it's not you and I who are actually doing it.

God can use anybody, and he likes to do just that for his own glory. He used Moses the stutterer to confront the world's mightiest king and to bring God's law to his people. God used Paul the Jewish nationalist to reach the Gentiles.

George Whitefield, the great eighteenth-century evangelist, was hounded by a group of detractors who called themselves the Hell-fire Club. They derided his work and mocked him. On one occasion, one of them, a man named Thorpe, preached a sermon in which he mimicked Whitefield to his cronies with brilliant accuracy, perfectly imitating Whitefield's tone and facial expressions. When Thorpe himself was so pierced that he sat down and was converted on the spot.[6]

The gospel is powerful, and God is committed to using this good news through our spreading of it to every tribe and tongue and people and nation on earth.

Sometimes the charge is leveled, "If you're a believer in election, you won't evangelize." But haven't many of the greatest evangelists in the history of the Christian church believed that salvation is by God's election? Has that dulled the evangelistic zeal of a Whitefield or an Edwards, of a Carey or a Judson, of a Spurgeon or a Lloyd-Jones, of a D. James Kennedy or an R. C. Sproul.

My concern is the opposite: if you *don't* believe that the gospel is the good news of God's action—the Father electing, the Son dying, the Spirit drawing—that conversion is only our response to God's giving us the grace-gifts of repentance and faith, and that evangelism is our simple, faithful, prayerful telling of this good news, then you will actually damage the evangelistic mission of the church by making false converts. If you think that the gospel is all about what we can do, that the practice of it is optional, and that conversion is simply something that anyone can choose at any time, then I'm concerned that you'll think of evangelism as nothing more than a sales job where the prospect is to be won over to sign on the dotted line by praying a prayer, followed by an assurance that he is the proud owner of salvation.

But evangelism isn't all about our ability to hawk our

religious wares. Discouragement can be painfully sharp sometimes as we share this best of news only to have it received as unimportant or unbelievable. But that's where we must remember that it is our part simply to give out the message; God will bring the increase.

I pray that we see an end to a wrong, shallow view of evangelism that simply tries to get people to say yes to a question or to make a one-time decision. As David Wells recently said, "We live in a day when it is very easy to make converts, very hard to make disciples." Of course, such non-disciple converts are no true converts, so we want to see an end to the bad fruit of false evangelism:

- worldly people feeling assurance because they made a decision one time;
- real revival being lost amid our own manufactured and scheduled meetings that we euphemistically call "revivals" (as if we could determine where and when the wind of God's Spirit will move);
- church memberships markedly larger than the number of those involved with the church;
- inaction in our own lives, as we ignore the evangelistic mandate—the call to share the good news. We want to see the end of this debilitating, deadly coldness to the glorious call to tell the good news.

We want to see a renewed commitment to and joy in the great privilege we have of sharing the good news of Christ with the lost and dying world around us. Only because Someone Else was so faithful can anyone be saved.

Pray that God will use you as a faithful messenger of the good news. Pray that you will see others saved from God's good punishment for their sins because they accept the good news of Christ's substitutionary death. And if God, in his mysterious sovereignty, ordains it not to be so with those to whom we witness, may it not be because we have failed in our commission to make him and his grace in Christ known to every creature made in his image.

This good news of Jesus Christ is crucial. Until you recognize that, I can say nothing helpful to you about evangelism. It will be no more for you than an unpleasant duty or an occasional impulse. When the message of the cross captures your heart, then your tongue—stammering, halting, insulting, awkward, sarcastic, and imperfect as it may be—won't be far behind. As Jesus said, "Out of the overflow of the heart the mouth speaks" (Matt. 12:34).

What is your heart full of?

What do you spend your words on?

The Christian call to evangelism is not simply a call to persuade people to make decisions, but rather to proclaim to them the good news of salvation in Christ, to call them to repentance, and to give God the glory for regeneration and conversion.

We do not fail in our evangelism if we faithfully tell the gospel to someone who is not subsequently converted; we fail only if we do not faithfully tell the gospel at all.

Recommended Reading

A few suggestions for further reading in evangelism are these:

- Will Metzger's *Tell the Truth*, rev. ed. (InterVarsity Press, 2002) may be the single best book on evangelism that I've read. Metzger makes it clear both theologically and practically that our evangelism should not be "man-centered" but "God-centered." The book contains old illustrations and good charts.
- Mack Stiles's *Speaking of Jesus* (InterVarsity Press, 1995) provides masterful examples of naturally speaking about Jesus Christ to friends and family. Mack is one of the best personal evangelists I have ever met and never ceases to exhibit a personal and spiritual empathy for those around him. His ability to relate and remember spills over into his book in the entertaining and instructive stories he recounts.
- Iain Murray's *Revival and Revivalism* (Banner of Truth, 1994) recounts some crucial changes in the history and practice of evangelism that still affect us negatively today.
- J. I. Packer's *Evangelism & the Sovereignty of God* (InterVarsity Press, 1991) is a modern classic in explaining the theology of Christian activity in evangelism and how that fits with the Bible's teaching on God's election. This is a great introduction to a doctrine (election) that God used to encourage Paul in his evangelism (see Acts 18).
- Among resources pertaining specifically to the actual gospel, I know of nothing better (outside of the Bible) to sug-

gest to you than the canons of the synod of Dort. Look them up, then read them and meditate on them slowly, carefully, paragraph by paragraph. Be amazed at God's love for us in Christ. Also, Robert Letham's book *The Work of Christ* (InterVarsity, 1993) is a great meditation on the center of the gospel.

- Tools to consider using for doing evangelism are *Christianity Explained* (Scripture Union) and *Two Ways to Live* (Matthias Media).
- More tools and articles on evangelism can be found at www.9marks.org.

Appendix
A Word to Pastors

Many people feel that evangelism should be left up to pastors. (We thought about that back in chapter 3.) The truth is that pastors often have an especially hard time finding ways to do personal evangelism.

Think about it. We pastors spend our workdays with Christians. We spend our evenings with our families, or church officers, and maybe the occasional neighbor or other friend. How can we pastors evangelize? We need to for all the reasons other Christians need to and also to serve as models.

First, we must remember that our preaching is the primary way that God has uniquely called us to evangelize.[1] We want to preach the gospel to non-Christians, and we desire to see the fruit of conversions.

To this end, we should be careful to include a summary of the gospel in every sermon. I remember my friend Bill coming up to me after I had preached a sermon on Lamentations. He told me that it was a good sermon, and then, after a pause, he asked me something like, "But did you have the gospel in the sermon?"

I was surprised by the question, but as I later went back and examined the sermon, I found that I had nowhere clearly explained what Christ had done, and how he calls us to repent and believe. I resolved from that point on to try always to clearly present the gospel in each sermon.

Other truths, too, in our sermons can help in our evangelism, and we can help Christians listening to us preach by modeling how to speak the truth. Plough up the ground often by speaking of God's holiness and our sin. Be clear about the problem of our sin in relation to a God who is all good. Try to expose Satan's lie that sin is petty. Try to help people see sin's weightiness and the depth of its opposition to God.

Make sure that your sermons both instruct people about the gospel and appeal to people to respond to it. If you make an appeal without the instruction, you are making an assumption that your listeners understand the gospel, when they may not really know what it is. On the other hand, if you only tell gospel truths in the third person, in other words, if you tell only your experience of it, then people may not understand that the Bible teaches clearly that they themselves are to repent and believe.

Be available after preaching also. Stand at the door, go to the reception, somehow make yourself available to folks who have just heard you deliver God's Word, and who, therefore, may have special questions about how the message relates to them or about particular issues that they want to understand more fully.

My pastor friend, even beyond your preaching, be sure to pray regularly for non-Christian neighbors, friends, and family. Pray publicly for conversions in your pastoral prayers before the sermon. Encourage and model praying for God to save non-Christians. And spend time thanking God for your own salvation; keep your gratitude fresh.

Pray to be a faithful evangelist as well. I have in the past gone regularly to certain restaurants, shopped at certain stores, and frequented certain places of business in order to build relationships in those places as opportunities for sharing the gospel. Undertaking personal evangelism of this nature requires being a patient customer, a good tipper, and a conversationalist—even when you may not have budgeted the time for it.

Realize, too, that you are called to equip the saints to evangelize. C. H. Spurgeon said:

> With all that you can do your desires will not be fulfilled, for soul-winning is a pursuit which grows upon a man; the more he is rewarded with Conversions the more eager he becomes to see greater numbers born unto God. Hence you will soon discover that *you need help if many are to be brought in.* The net soon becomes too heavy for one pair of hands to drag to shore when it is filled with fishes; and your fellow-helpers must be beckoned to your assistance. Great things are done by the Holy Spirit when a whole church is aroused to sacred energy. . . . Contemplate at the outset the possibility of having a church of soul-winners. Do not succumb to the usual idea that we can only gather a few useful workers, and that the rest of the community must inevitably be a dead weight: it may possibly so happen, but do not set out with that notion or it will be verified. The usual need not be the universal; better things are possible than anything yet attained; set your aim high and spare no effort to reach it. Labor to gather a church alive for Jesus, every member energetic to the full, and the whole in incessant activity for the salvation of men. To this end there must be the best of preaching to feed the host into strength, continual prayer to bring down the power from on high, and the most heroic example on your own part to fire their zeal.

The pastor should make sure that others in the congregation are equipped in evangelism. We can equip not only through our preaching, but by our conversations, the books we give out, the way we admit new members (we always ask them to recount the gospel and their testimony with us). We can provide the congregation with training in specific evangelistic tools (such as *Christianity Explained* or *Two Ways to Live*[2]). We can model a concern for evangelism and conversions in our prayers. We can sponsor special evangelistic events. We can encourage the members by having times for sharing and praying in which we specifically pray for evangelistic initiatives and for particular conversions.

Through all this, we must lead by example. As pastors, we are called to lead by our teaching but also by our actions. So we must heed Paul's charge to Timothy: "But you, keep your head in all situations, endure hardship, do the work of an evangelist, discharge all the duties of your ministry" (2 Tim. 4:5). In everything, from our personal prayer life to conversations with family and neighbors, we should work to present Christ well.

We pastors should accept the role of leadership that God has given us. Certainly, we pastors sacrifice personal opportunities to do evangelism when we work full-time in ministry. We are, in a sense, willing to be pulled behind the front lines in order to equip others. We realize the front line of the contest, the "skin" of the church, if you will, is represented by the members of the local congregation after they leave church on Sunday. It is then, throughout the week, that the church presses in on the kingdom of darkness as believers live out their callings around hundreds or even thousands of non-Christians each week. It is our task as pastors to lead all believers in accepting, embracing, and using the opportunities that God richly gives them. In all of this, we should work not so much merely to implement programs as to create a culture in our church. We want our congregations to be marked by a culture of evangelism. In order to do that, we are going to have to watch how many nights we encourage our members to be doing some program at church. We must give our members time to develop friendships with non-Christians.

So, my pastor friend, be encouraged in evangelism. Share stories about evangelism with your friends. Ask them to recount recent evangelistic experiences. Read books that remind you of the priority of evangelism in your own ministry. Let me suggest a few that kindle my own soul: Richard Baxter, *The Reformed Pastor*; Charles Bridges, *The Christian Ministry*; Horatius Bonar, *Words to the Winners of Souls*; C. H. Spurgeon, *Lectures to My Students* (or, really, anything by Spurgeon).

Notes

Introduction

1. Moody Adams, *The Titanic's Last Hero: Story About John Harper* (Columbia, SC: Olive Press, 1997), 24–25.

Chapter One

1. Everett Gill, *A Biography of A. T. Robertson* (New York: Macmillan, 1943), 187.

Chapter Two

1. Thomas A. Harris, *I'm Okay, You're Okay: A Practical Guide to Transitional Analysis* (New York: Avon, 1969).

2. John Calvin, *Institutes of the Christian Religion,* 2 Vols., in The Library of Christian Classics, Vol. 20, ed. John T. McNeil (Philadelphia: Westminster Press, 1960), 1.1.35.

3. J. C. Ryle, *Holiness* (1883; repr., Grand Rapids, MI: Baker, 1979), 204.

Chapter Three

1. For more on this question, see Robert Plummer, "Paul's Understanding of the Church's Mission: Did the Apostle Paul Expect the Early Christian Communities to Evangelize?" (Carlisle, UK: Paternoster Biblical Monographs, 2006).

2. John Stott, *Personal Evangelism* (Downers Grove, IL: InterVarsity; 1949), 3–4.

3. This is Rob Plummer's conclusion in his excellent study cited above. "The apostolic mission devolves upon each church as a whole—not upon any particular member or group. Each individual member within the church, then, will manifest missionary

activity according to his or her particular gifting and life situation. All but the unrepeatable aspects of the apostles' mission (e.g., eyewitness testimony and initial promulgation of authoritative revelation) devolve upon the church as a whole." Plummer, "Paul's Understanding of the Church's Mission," 144.

4. John Stott, "Why Don't They Listen?" *Christianity Today* (September 2003): 52.

5. Iain H. Murray, *D. Martyn Lloyd-Jones: The First Forty Years 1899–1939* (Edinburgh: Banner of Truth, 1983), 246.

6. John Bunyan, *Grace Abounding to the Chief of Sinners* (1875; repr., Grand Rapids, MI: Baker, 1986), 29–30, 37–40.

7. Donna Britt, "Love Stories That Transcend Bonds of Slavery, Time," *Washington Post* (February 11, 2005), in Betty DeRamus, *Forbidden Fruit: Love Stories from the Underground Railroad* (New York: Atria, 2005), 15–27.

Chapter Four

1. Robert Schuller, *Milk & Honey* (December 1997): 4.

2. For more on this topic, see J. I. Packer, *Evangelism and the Sovereignty of God* (Downers Grove, IL: InterVarsity, 1991).

3. Two books that have excellent examples of conversations are Mack Stiles, *Speaking of Jesus* (Downers Grove, IL: InterVarsity, 1995), and Randy Newman, *Corner Conversations* (Grand Rapids, MI: Kregel, 2006).

Chapter Five

1. Graham Johnston, *Preaching to a Postmodern World* (Grand Rapids, MI: Baker, 2001), 136.

2. Donald McGavran, "The Dimensions of World Evangelization," in *Let the Earth Hear His Voice,* ed. J. D. Douglas (Worldwide Publications, 1975), 109.

3. John Stott, "The Biblical Basis of Evangelism," in *Let the Earth Hear His Voice,* ed. J. D. Douglas, 69.

4. "The Lausanne Covenant," in *Let the Earth Hear His Voice,* ed. J. D. Douglas, 4.

5. John Cheeseman, *Saving Grace* (Edinburgh: Banner of Truth, 1999), 113.

6. D. Martyn Lloyd-Jones, *Preaching & Preachers* (Grand Rapids, MI: Zondervan, 1971), 276.

7. Cecil Sherman, "Hard Times Make for Hard Thinking," in *Why I Am a Baptist: Reflections on Being Baptist in the 21st Cen-*

tury, ed. Cecil P. Staton (Macon, GA: Smyth & Helwys, 1999), 136–37.

8. John Flavel, *Mystery of Providence* (1678; repr., Edinburgh: Banner of Truth, 1963), 11.

Chapter Six

1. In Mark 9:40 Jesus says, "Whoever is not against us if for us" (see also Luke 9:50). Here, however, he seems to be speaking to the disciples regarding good work done in Christ's name by someone who wasn't one of their number. In the statements in Mark 12:30 and Luke 11:23, Jesus seems to be warning unbelieving religious leaders about the danger of indifference to him.

2. A great evangelistic presentation that majors on this dichotomy is *Two Ways to Live* (Kingsford, Australia: Matthias Media, 1989). Or see an online presentation at http://www.matthiasmedia.com.au/2wtl/.

3. D. Martyn Lloyd-Jones, *Preaching & Preachers* (Grand Rapids, MI: Zondervan, 1972), 276.

4. Carey Hardy, "Just as I Am," in *Fool's Gold,* ed. John MacArthur (Wheaton, IL: Crossway, 2005), 136–37.

Chapter Seven

1. Robert Jenson, "The God-Wars," in *Either/Or: The Gospel or Neopaganism,* ed. Carl E. Braaten and Robert W. Jenson (Grand Rapids, MI: Eerdmans, 1995), 25.

2. Augustine, "Morals of the Catholic Church," in *The Nicene and Post-Nicene Fathers,* Vol. 4, ed. Philip Schaff (Peabody, MA: Hendrickson, 1994), 55.

3. John Cheeseman et al., *The Grace of God in the Gospel* (Edinburgh: Banner of Truth, 1972), 122. For some reason, this paragraph was not retained in John Cheeseman's revision of this book, *Saving Grace* (Edinburgh: Banner of Truth, 1999).

Conclusion

1. C. S. Lovett, *Soul-winning Made Easy* (Lockman Foundation, 1959), 17–18.

2. Lovett, *Soul-winning Made Easy,* 23.

3. Lovett, *Soul-winning Made Easy,* 50.

4. Paul Tillich, "The Lost Dimension in Religion," in *Adventures of the Mind,* ed. Richard Thruelson and John Kobler (New York: Vintage, 1958) 52–62.

5. A concern for evangelistic outreach has often been the path to liberalism. This is in no way to suggest that a concern for evangelism is bad—it's essential!—It's just more dangerous than is often recognized. For more on this, see the writings of Iain Murray, especially *Revival and Revivalism* (Edinburgh: Banner of Truth, 1994), and *Evangelicalism Divided: A Record of Crucial Change in the Years 1950–2000* (Edinburgh: Banner of Truth, 2000).

6. Spurgeon recounts this in *Metropolitan Tabernacle Pulpit,* 34: 115.

Appendix

1. See my chapter, "Evangelistic Expository Preaching," in Philip Graham Ryken et al., *Give Praise to God* (Phillipsburg, NJ: P&R 2003), 122–39.

2. *Christianity Explained* (Kingsford NSW, Australia: Matthias Media, 2003); *Two Ways to Live* (Valley Forge, PA: Scripture Union, 1975).

THE KING

of Main Street

business • mentorship • succession • legacy

Harry

long and good life

chai

To 120!!!

THE KING

of Main Street

business • mentorship • succession • legacy

By **Peter J. Merrick**

This work is dedicated to my children. I wish to give to you what I believe is infinitely more important and personally meaningful than any material gift. These are some of the discoveries and insights I have stumbled upon in my lifetime that may be of value to you as you venture forth on your own journeys. Life might be short, but your opportunities are boundless.

IT COULDN'T BE DONE

BY EDGAR GUEST

Somebody said that it couldn't be done
But he with a chuckle replied
That "maybe it couldn't," but he would be one
Who wouldn't say so till he'd tried.
So he buckled right in with the trace of a grin
On his face. If he worried he hid it.
He started to sing as he tackled the thing
That couldn't be done, and he did it!
Somebody scoffed: "Oh, you'll never do that;
At least no one ever has done it;"
But he took off his coat and he took off his hat
And the first thing we knew he'd begun it.
With a lift of his chin and a bit of a grin,
Without any doubting or quiddit,
He started to sing as he tackled the thing
That couldn't be done, and he did it.
There are thousands to tell you it cannot be done,
There are thousands to prophesy failure,
There are thousands to point out to you one by one,
The dangers that wait to assail you.
But just buckle in with a bit of a grin,
Just take off your coat and go to it;
Just start to sing as you tackle the thing
That "cannot be done," and you'll do it.

PROLOGUE

THE RIDDLE

I HAD FORGOTTEN. AND then I met a man who would remind me of the dream I had once had when I had been a teenager. It was to observe, learn and then write—to share and pass on my knowledge. At age 16, I had felt a deep urge to one day write something bold, something of significance, something lasting, something that would help me and others understand and live our lives to our fullest potential.

At the time, I'd had no idea what that something would be. I had just had this burning desire of youth to discover a treasure map that would lead to a holy grail, whatever it was. I had been young, cocky and naive. Since then, I have learned through experience that sometimes life teaches best by kicking and punching our egos into submission. And the thing is, more often than not, that happens at the very moments we need timeless wisdom most. Those are the moments when we need to step back from our lives to take stock of the path we are on. Only then can we correct course.

I have discovered that life's lessons are sadly missing in our society today. Not only that, but they are missing at a time when they are absolutely necessary for finding greater self-awareness and our purpose in the cosmos. They help us break free of constraints in our lives.

At the time I met the man, I was going through one of the darkest moments of my life. My youthful hopes had become so distant. Distant, yes. Gone, no. I still had the desire to one day synthesize my discoveries and experiences so others could avoid my mistakes and benefit from my life's learnings.

I had a big pit in my stomach as I sipped my coffee. I was in a diner in La Jolla, San Diego. It was the spring of 2004. And in my hands I held an envelope from the taxman. I didn't need to open it to know what was inside this "THIRD NOTICE." It was the government saying, "Hey you! Pay up all your back taxes."

So there I was with my coffee, wondering how I was going to dig myself out from this big hole. The only thing I knew for sure was that the paperboy who had just dropped off the *San Diego Union Tribune* had more money in his pockets than me.

I felt I had to do something quick and bold, but what? I didn't want to mess with the taxman. I understood he meant business. Even if I tried to avoid the issue, the taxman was not about to ignore me. I knew that if needed, he would bring the full force of the government down on my head in order to get my undivided attention.

But still, my first instincts were to run and duck, rather than face up to my life. Two weeks earlier, I had taken my last few dollars, googled "sunny destinations" and purchased the cheapest ticket to the first warm destination that popped up on my internet search. And now, it was almost time to say goodbye to the West Coast. I had to be at the airport for an early evening flight back home.

How did I get to this point? How did my life come to this crossroad? Only two years earlier, I had felt a strong breeze of optimism flow over me. I had sold my practice after being in the financial services industry for more than a decade, to invest in a new emerging financial solution for business owners. Some might say that this was forward-looking, that I was on the leading edge. But for me, as I learned firsthand, it turned out to be the "bleeding edge."

I had been a little too early to market. At the end of my first year into this entrepreneurial venture, I found myself without a business, and I was finding myself increasingly in the throes of an early midlife crisis. Just shy of my 35th birthday, I didn't know if I had what it took to start all over again. Could I get myself up from ground zero?

I had always been told that when one door closes, another opens. But no one tells you about the bloody hallway in between opportunities! What was I going to do next? How would I do it? Most importantly, why would I be doing it—whatever that "it" was going to be?

And as I sat there drowning in self-pity, I heard a voice call to me.

"Oh, life can't be that bad," the man at the next table assured me.

I immediately looked up. What first caught my eye was the man's hard-covered copy of Herman Melville's novel *Moby Dick*.

"Would you like to see it?" he asked as he motioned it towards me.

"Yes, indeed," I replied. "I was supposed to read it for my senior year in high school. I regretted that I'd never got around to finishing it."

Leafing through the book's pages, I was taken aback to see that it was a signed first edition, from 1851.

"This is a true American classic," I said.

He smiled, saying, "I find it required reading at any age. It has some important life lessons that I still need to learn."

"What sort of lessons?" I asked.

As it turned out, this was no small question. He described Ahab, the captain of a whaling ship who was on the hunt for Moby Dick, the great white whale that had chewed off his leg on a previous voyage. But this was not just a tale of questionable revenge. It was the story of a once-good man, a great leader, who had become fanatically obsessed with hunting down Moby Dick. He put this obsession above profit, above his crew's livelihood and, in the end, above their lives. Ahab had failed to let go, and that had robbed him of all restraint, denying him of life's joys. Obsession eventually killed Ahab and most of his crew.

At that moment I thought, *I have allowed myself to feel as Ahab did. My obsession has led me to my own self-destruction.*

"What brings you out this morning?" the man asked.

"Failure," I blurted out.

He smiled kindly and said, "Sometimes it takes the eruption of the darker sides of life to jolt us into breaking free from the inner voices of self-doubt." Then he added, "They can restrain and prevent us from becoming who we truly are."

He continued, "I have found through my attendance at the University of Hard Knocks that there is no such thing as failure in life, only feedback. It's all about making sure to fall forward, picking oneself up afterward, learning the lesson being taught, correcting course and then moving onward and upward."

He said this confidently and clearly, making it sound so straightforward.

"Have you heard of the story about the French-Canadian lumberjacks?" he asked.

I told him I hadn't.

"This is your lucky day, kiddo; it's one of my favorites," he said, again smiling.

"Once there were two famous lumberjacks named Pierre and Nicolas. They were the two best lumberjacks in the world, but no one knew who the better of the two was. One day, a promoter decided to host a competition between Pierre and Nicolas to see who could cut down the most trees in seven hours. At the end, the judges would count the number of trees each had cut down. The winner would be crowned the world's greatest lumberjack.

"The conditions on the day of the competition were perfect—there was not a cloud in the sky. And with the shot of the starter pistol, the competition began. Pierre and Nicolas started cutting feverishly. One hour into the competition, Pierre didn't hear any sound at all coming from Nicolas' direction. He had stopped chopping.

We're just an hour in, and there's no way I'm about to stop, Pierre thought. So he kept on. But 10 minutes later, Pierre could hear that Nicolas had resumed chopping.

"It seemed strange to Pierre. Why did Nicolas take a break for 10 minutes? The next hour it happened again: another 10-minute break. The same thing occurred the next hour and the hour after that, until the finishing gun went off.

"Pierre couldn't believe his luck. Nicolas had stopped chopping for 10 minutes every hour of the competition. Pierre was sure that he would be declared the winner at the end of the count. After all, judging by the regular 10-minute silences during the event, he'd had a lot more chopping time—those 10-minute breaks added up to over an extra hour of chopping time for him. So, he was positive that the additional time would give him the crown of the greatest lumberjack of all.

"The judges counted the trees that had been cut down, and then they recounted and recounted again. When they were sure, they announced the winner—Nicolas!

"Nicolas was crowned the greatest lumberjack of all. Pierre was dumbfounded. *How could this be possible?* He couldn't believe it, so he walked over to Nicolas and said in disbelief, 'It's impossible that you won. It just couldn't be—it couldn't be done! When we were chopping those trees, I could tell from the silence in the distance when you put your ax down. It was always for 10 minutes, on the hour, every hour during the competition. So that means I cut at least one more hour than you!'

"Nicolas simply replied: 'I did not stop once during the entire competition. I was simply sharpening my blade.'"

What a pertinent story, I thought as I took another sip of coffee. But I guess the worry on my face was still there, because the man said, "You look like you need to take a load off your shoulders. You have my ear."

What prompted me to continue our conversation? That he was

reading *Moby Dick*—and something else, a feeling that I couldn't put into words at the time. I thought, *Here is a man who seems comfortable in his own skin*. I could sense it. I wanted nothing more than to hold that feeling, even if only for a fleeting moment. Perhaps he could distill some of it for me, share his hard-won wisdom before I had to catch my flight home. At the very least, I would kill some time.

He looked to be in his early 70s. He took his coffee straight up: black, no sugar. From what I could observe, there was nothing pretentious about him—not in the way he dressed, not his shoes, not his watch. They were all simple, practical and reliable.

Something in my being told me to trust this man. I felt compelled to accept his invitation to talk. I wanted to listen, and on the other hand, I also wanted to really hear myself, perhaps for the very first time. That morning I was open to listening, sharing and learning. I was his student, and the diner had become our sacred space.

It would be a life-altering conversation. He would become my sacred elder, someone who would initiate me into the next stage of my journey. I looked him in the eye and began to tell the story of my personal misadventures and business mishaps. It was time to stop feeling sorry for myself. I needed some sobering introspection. Through our conversation, I realized that I had been asking all the wrong questions.

I told the man what I had been doing for the past two years, that I had focused on creating a revolutionary manager/owner business solution. But I had failed to successfully bring it to market. It would have allowed business owners to personally take out corporate monies in the most tax-effective way during and especially at the end of their careers, when it was perhaps most needed.

This stranger made me realize that I had failed to ask myself the most important questions:

Why would a mature, successful business owner want—for perhaps the first time—to pull out large sums of money from his company? Why wouldn't he reinvest it back into his business? Why would he instead want to take it out for personal use at that particular stage in his career?

Through his probing questions, the answer slowly emerged. I had missed it entirely. The business owners who would adopt my solution were actually saying, even if they didn't know it at the time, that they had had *enough*.

They wanted out of their businesses so that they could enjoy the fruits of their labor while they were still healthy and capable of enjoying their lives. They wanted to have the satisfaction of knowing that if they died too soon, got sick, became disabled or lived too long, their financial situations and that of their families would be secure—that they would be able to continue to live their lives on their own terms, without compromise.

In my botched business venture, I had failed to address the human need that the fully mature business owner longs to create, that of a positive and lasting legacy. It's a legacy that enriches his community, family and children, with the gift of both his time and money. The business owner who would have been attracted to my solution wanted to exit his business on his own terms. At some level, he did not want to be at the mercy of someone or something else. He wanted to be in charge; he wanted to be the captain of his fate.

The man kept probing: Why does this discussion in society need to happen right now? Why not tomorrow or next week?

I heard myself saying, "The statistics speak for themselves."

By 2020, up to 70 percent of the workforce will have passed or be approaching the traditional age of retirement. Also, half of all privately held businesses will be going through transition. Privately held companies, collectively worth tens of trillions of dollars, will go through an ownership or control change—transitioning to family members, employees or third-party buyers.

If these business owners don't receive the proper counsel from the right professionals, and if they don't have the proper supporting resources, their businesses will be driven into the ground. There are predictions that, if that happens, our economy could shrink by as much as 30 percent.

That morning turned out to be a satisfying and productive surprise. I gained incredible new insights. And this man who had been a stranger just a short while before had one more lesson to teach me. As our conversation drew to a close, he left me with a riddle to contemplate. He told me to take my time and made me this promise that *how* I chose to answer it would act as the guiding principle for *how* I would approach my business and life from then on.

Here's the riddle: If you are alone in an ancient redwood forest and the largest tree cracks and falls right in front of you, taking down with it several large neighboring trees, does it make a noise?

It was already 10:30 a.m. The time had just flown by, and I was running late. I needed to do some errands and get back to the hotel to pick up my bags before my flight home. As I was getting up to leave, saying goodbye and thanking him for gifting me his time, insight and wisdom, I realized I had forgotten to ask him his name.

"Harold," he said.

Who was this Harold? I asked myself. I felt that I had just had one of those rare life-changing conversations. I'd heard about such experiences, but now I understood what having one of them meant. Even though I would meet this man, this Harold, only once, he continues to have a profound influence on the path I have chosen to take in my life.

Up until this chance encounter, I was chronically fixated on seeking out an elusive prize. But I hadn't yet earned it. I had much more experience to gain. I left Harold with a reawakened sense of the excitement. I felt as I had when I was 16 and thinking about writing my opus. What's more, new possibilities for the direction my life could take were emerging. I knew I couldn't just ignore my inner calling. That would only lead to a slow spiritual death and to my physical and mental decay.

I left that day preoccupied with the riddle. I needed to discover the answer to it. It would take another decade for me to answer it to my satisfaction. Once I did, I had another epiphany. Harold's riddle had shown me how someone's life's work can create their true legacy. I became even more determined to share the knowledge I had acquired from my venture in business, mentorship, succession and legacy. But I did not want to do this through a dry textbook. Instead, I wanted to write a timeless story that brings these lessons and morals to life.

This is the story you now hold in your hands.

CHAPTER 1

————⟫⟨————

DON'T JUDGE A MAN BY WHAT HE WEARS OR WHAT HE DOES

"I READ AN INTERESTING study last night," said Mitch. "Did you know that 80 percent of American families either did not buy or did not read one book in the past year? It also said that, on average, businesspeople who read at least seven business books a year earn at least 2.3 times more than those who read only one book. Have you ever wondered why?"

"It's obvious," replied Michael. "One percent of society creates, and the remaining 99 percent are sheep who just eat what they are fed. Readers earn more than nonreaders because they get a constant stream of new ideas and strategies. They can then apply them to their lives, careers and companies."

Michael wasn't finished. He thought about how that would shape the future, how it had shaped him personally.

"We are moving into a thought-based economy, where good ideas matter. And to make it in this new economy, you need to have access to the best ideas. I know this firsthand," he said. "When I was growing up, my surroundings did not match the picture I had in my head of the life I desired, the one I intended to live when I grew up.

"Only through reading was I able to inoculate my mind against the negative forces that were saying, 'Why bother trying in the first place; it's foolish to think that there could be a better life for a kid like me.' Through reading I was given a lifeline to other worlds. I was introduced to the likes of Mark Twain, Alexis de *Tocqueville,* Ralph Waldo Emerson, Henry David *Thoreau*, Buckminster Fuller, Thomas Jefferson and Eric Hoffer. There are too many to count or for me to thank. Through their writings they became my mentors, my peers and my constant companions. These great men gave me a lifeline to the life I intend to create for my family and myself."

Mitch was impressed with his friend. "No one can accuse you of being illiterate," he said. "But your thirst for knowledge may get you killed! I watched you cross the street just now to meet me, lost in your damn book again. No worries in the world—not even all those cars rushing towards you. Did you know you were almost flattened by a truck? We can't make you an all-star businessman if you become a hood ornament first."

Mitch had been teasing Michael like this since their freshman year in college. They had been a bit of an odd couple when they were first placed as roommates back in the fall of 1976. They had grown up on opposite sides of the tracks.

Mitchell Meadows was raised in Evanston, Illinois, a wealthy Chicago suburb. After high school, he set into motion a plan based on what he had intuitively felt since he was a child. From the earliest age, he had known what he was going to do with his life and why. He was going to do what his father did—and his great-grandfather before him. He was going to distinguish himself through a legal career.

And now at age 34, Mitch was doing it. He was one of the best mergers and acquisitions (M&A) lawyers around. In the office, he was known as the M&A go-to guy. It was the reason he had just been named partner at his law firm, and this was no small accomplishment, considering its reputation as one of the country's top M&A firms. It was something he had always wanted, having come from a long line of accomplished lawyers and judges.

His maternal great-grandfather had received nationwide prominence during the prohibition era. Justice James Wilkerson hadn't been soft on crime. And he sure hadn't let anyone who had been caught on the wrong side of the 18th Amendment—which made alcohol illegal for 13 years—just slide by. He had also been the judge who had slammed the gavel on Al "Scarface" Capone.

It would be a big task for Mitch to measure up to a man still remembered in the US District Court for the Northern District of Illinois as the one who sent Capone to prison. The beauty of the conviction was its simplicity. The most feared gangster in the nation was taken down by the most mundane of nonviolent crimes: tax evasion.

If his great-grandfather's accomplishments weren't enough, there was Marv Meadows, Mitch's father. Marv completed his law degree after serving as an officer in the US Navy during the Second World War. He put his education on hold upon hearing of the attack on Pearl Harbor. He just couldn't believe the news on the radio. On December 7, 1941, Imperial Japan had hit the heart of America's sea power.

Marv was a patriot; his country was at war and it needed him. He had to act. And so he volunteered for active duty and was deployed to the South Pacific. His first assignment was to the aircraft carrier USS *Yorktown*. He was one of its few survivors when it sank during the Battle of Midway in June 1942. He saved three of his crewmates that day and was awarded the Navy Cross for valor.

After finishing law school, Marv clerked for the US District Court for the Northern District of Illinois. Marv met Rose Wilkerson at the court's annual Christmas party. It was love at first sight, and it wasn't long before they were married. Soon Mitch's older brother was born. Ten years later, Mitch arrived.

After his clerkship ended, Marv went into private practice as a trial lawyer. He successfully mounted class-action protection lawsuits for abuses of consumer trust against many of the top Fortune 50 companies. During his stellar 35-year law career, Marv was considered among the top hundred trial lawyers who had ever practiced in the United States. Many of the cases he won now constituted required reading in law schools.

From the time Mitch was able to understand his legal lineage, he had dreamed of making his own mark on the law. After law school, he was laser-focused on his goal: to rise to the top of the emerging M&A field.

Michael Stevens' upbringing could not have been more different from Mitch's. Michael had been brought up in a working poor family and raised since early adolescence by his widowed mother. What he remembered most about his childhood was that his mother had worked three jobs just to pay the bills, and that she had worked tirelessly to keep food on the table and a roof over his and his siblings' heads.

What Michael lacked in pedigree he sure made up with internal drive—he worked harder than a combustible engine in a Ford Mustang. Like Mitch, Michael was determined to create meaning in his life. He had bet the farm on his dream, which he had always known was his ticket out of the life of his childhood. He believed that if he built a great business, it would be his ticket to independence and to financial security, something his family had lacked during his youth.

Michael's childhood was shaped significantly when he was 11, when, one afternoon, he was called out of his grade six class and asked to go see the principal. His father, Leslie Stevens, had died. He was one of the last fatalities at *Chicago's* Union Stock Yards, known to everyone as "The Yards." A heavy piece of machinery had fallen on Leslie, killing him instantly.

Leslie had come to the United States from Northern Ireland as a baby in the 1920s. His parents had packed him up, along with his two brothers and three sisters, in search of the American Dream. Unfortunately, Michael's father never found it in his lifetime. He grew up on *Chicago's* South Side. It was a rough working-class neighborhood, and no one there got anything without working for it.

At age 15, Leslie dropped out of school to join his father and brothers in working at The Yards. He was there until Japan and Germany declared war on the United States. The attack on Pearl Harbor, and the war against Germany, ignited something in the young Leslie. It was a patriotism he had never felt before. He had also never been much beyond Illinois. So, with a patriot's heart and a youthful sense of adventure, Leslie Stevens joined the US Army as a foot soldier. His regiment was one of the first to land on Omaha Beach on D-Day, during the Allied invasion of German-occupied France on Tuesday, June 6, 1944.

Leslie returned stateside after the war and went back to work at The Yards. It wasn't long before he married Connie, his childhood sweetheart. And before they knew it, they had started a family. Leslie Stevens was a union man to his core, and he was a proud shop steward at the United Packinghouse Workers of America. The war was over, but Michael's father was always fighting the good fight for the underdogs, his fellow employees. But it wasn't a two-way street between him and the company and union he worked for. After Michael's father was killed on the job, his mother didn't get much. She was given the proceeds from a small life-insurance policy and a meager pension. It sure wasn't enough to support a young family. Michael, his siblings and his mother had to fend for themselves.

Leslie's death was also a hard emotional blow for the young Michael. He often recalled the weekend adventures his dad had taken him on over the years. The last trip had been to the *Museum of Science and Industry, where father and son had both marveled at the tremendous accomplishments and inventions of the great men of industry and business. They had turned their visions into reality through hard work. Michael remembered how his father had turned to him and said: "I don't have much in the way of money to give you. Whatever you accomplish, you are going to have to earn it yourself, son. But what I have given you is something much more valuable. It's a good name and a strong work ethic."*

A little less than a week later, Michael's father was dead.

When Michael became old enough to work, he started contributing to the family's household income. And when he was not working, he was either studying or nose-deep in some book. He was young, but he didn't have time for a social life. He knew what he wanted to do, even if all the details were still not worked out.

When he turned 17, he applied for a university scholarship. As part of the application, he was required to write an essay explaining to the selection committee why he was worthy of the scholarship. Michael was wise beyond his years, and his essay reflected this. He wrote about the importance of responsibility, being a good citizen and achieving financial success. But he also noted that he wanted to live a complete and honorable life. He told the committee about his desire to give back to society. He pledged that if he was awarded the scholarship, he would commit his life to achieving success with the aim of contributing back by creating a worthwhile lasting legacy for those less fortunate than him.

The selection committee was impressed with the essay, and it was even more impressed by Michael in person when he came for the interview. His hard work and focus earned him the scholarship. Michael Stevens would be the first in his family to attend college. Michael's perseverance had paid off. He was on the first leg of his journey to achieving his dream. And thinking about the opportunity ahead of him at university made him think back to his last conversation with his father, at the *museum.* His father's words echoed in Michael's mind: *"Whatever you accomplish, you are going to have to earn it yourself, son."*

When he first met Michael, Mitch wondered why they had been paired off as dorm roommates. They had so little in common. Mitch came from a prominent family, and his career path was set. Anyone who was anyone on campus knew his family lineage. All he had to worry about was squeezing in the odd frosh event, attending home-coming parties, and maybe pledging a fraternity. In college, he was also laser-focused on his goal: to earn high enough marks for the dean's list.

Michael, on the other hand, was just another kid on a scholarship. He kept mostly to himself and, unlike with Mitch, life wasn't laid out in front of him. He had no clue about his future. He was just worried about getting through his freshman year. He split his time by either studying at the library or working at his part-time job as a janitor at the university. Cleaning up after your classmates wasn't exactly a path to social acceptance. Mitch noticed that when Michael wasn't working or studying, he regularly slipped off—to where, Mitch had no idea. This happened every week. He would stay out into the late hours of the night, returning to their dorm room exhausted and ready to crash.

At first, the two roommates didn't have much to do with each other. The divide was so bad that Mitch even approached his resident advisor to see about moving in with a different roommate. He was told that it would be a long process and that it would be best to just try to get along. But everything changed when Mitch came down with a bad case of mononucleosis. It couldn't have happened at a worse time. He was laid up in the hospital, with an important pre-law paper due in just two weeks. The illness was jeopardizing his carefully made plans. His future depended on getting nearly perfect grades, so his future depended on that paper. Lying there in the hospital bed, Mitch realized there was no way he would ever get it done in time.

Rarely did his fraternity friends come to visit while he was in the hospital. But every night, no matter how late, there was Michael. He would somehow make time to try to cheer up his roommate. Michael could tell Mitch was worried about more than his illness. Mitch finally confided in him why he was feeling so anxious. Time was slipping away to write the paper that his future depended on. It turned out that he didn't need to be so worried. When Mitch returned to his dorm room from the hospital a week later, he discovered 50 pages of notes, with full citations, neatly placed on his bed.

Knowing how important the paper was to Mitch, Michael had taken it upon himself to spend two days straight in the library to scan articles on microfilm and pull as much research material from the stacks of books as he could. He didn't want his roommate to fall behind. Mitch was taken aback. No one had shown him that level of loyalty and friendship before. Sure, his other friends showered him with get-well cards, but no one else had ever taken the time to visit, never mind do what Michael had done for him. And Mitch couldn't believe Michael's modesty when he thanked his true friend.

"Don't worry about it," Michael replied quietly.

Mitch had once thought Michael a sort of odd bird, but he realized there was much more to this guy than met the eye. So Mitch decided to play detective and get to know his roommate much better. One night, Mitch followed Michael when he slipped out of their dorm room. *Where does he go?* wondered Mitch. He trailed Michael to a building not far from campus, which Michael entered through the backdoor. Mitch waited outside for 45 minutes, but when Michael didn't come back out, Mitch decided to go in to check the place out for himself.

As he entered the building, he realized that it was a seniors' residence. He could hear Michael in one of the common rooms, chatting away and joking around with some of the residents. Later, Mitch learned that Michael had been going to the residence for several years. He had been taking what little extra personal time he had to assist seniors who had little or no family. Mitch realized that Michael could relate to the residents' sense of loneliness and isolation.

Did I ever get this guy so wrong, he thought. Michael really had a soft heart under what appeared to be a cold veneer. That night, Mitch experienced a real paradigm shift when it came to how he viewed his friend. He believed he could learn a lot from Michael and pledged to put in a committed effort to do this. He wouldn't let Michael close himself off; Mitch was determined to get to know this roommate of his, who seemed to be a truly genuine person.

But getting to know Michael wasn't easy. It took time to get Michael out of his shell. But Mitch wasn't going to waiver from his commitment. And he was determined to get his buddy a social life. Whenever there was a party on campus, Mitch would drag his reluctant roommate to it with him.

Good thing that he did; Michael would never have met the future Mrs. Stevens if Mitch hadn't been so pushy. They were at a frat party where they saw Dawn Martin, a girl in one of Michael's classes. Years later, Mitch would deliver Michael's best man speech, telling the guests how Michael almost messed up his big opportunity.

"I knew he liked her, and I knew she was going to be at the party," he said, laughing at the memory. "But he wouldn't get his head out of the books. I finally dragged him out. But my work was far from done. Michael wasn't exactly a smooth operator with the ladies back then—or ever. At the party, I kept telling him to talk to her, but he was so scared, he wouldn't move."

The guests laughed. They could all picture a petrified Michael.

"And then Dawn was about to leave with her girlfriend," Mitch continued. "Jeez, I'd had enough. Here she was about to leave, and he just stood there like a bump on a log. So as Dawn walked by I blurted out to Michael, 'Stupid! Aren't you going to say one word to this beautiful girl?'"

The crowd laughed again. They knew how the story ended. An embarrassed Michael ended up asking Dawn out that night, and before long, the two were inseparable. As it turned out, Dawn was quite a matchmaker herself. As Mitch was delivering his speech at their wedding, she smiled at her best friend, Wendy Smith, seated strategically near her new husband's best friend.

As Dawn predicted, Mitch and Wendy hit it off immediately. The four of them went on a couple of double dates, but it wasn't long before Michael and Dawn's friends were off doing their own thing. Almost two years to the date of Michael and Dawn's wedding, Wendy and Mitch walked down the aisle themselves. Dawn served as the matron of honor, and Michael got back at Mitch with a few jabs and jokes during *his* best man speech. The marriage helped forge an even stronger bond between the two couples. Over the next few decades, they would share in the births of their children and grandchildren, attend countless weddings together, vacation together and mourn together when friends and family passed away.

After Michael and Mitch finished their undergraduate degrees, Mitch went off to law school. Michael's career path was a little less straightforward. He had dreams of taking his business degree and getting a position in hospitality with one of the international luxury hotel chains. He wanted to get out of Chicago, to work and experience life in exotic locations around the world. And he also wanted to find out more about his own country and fellow Americans.

But in 1980, there was a deep recession. The luxury hotel market was hurting, and no one was hiring, especially for junior management positions. So Michael found himself taking a managing job at the seniors' residence where he had volunteered.

Michael did not lose hope that one day he would enter the hospitality industry. He subscribed to many of the industry publications in order to keep up to date. By the end of Ronald Reagan's first term as president, the economy was in full recovery. And when Michael read an article about how many of the large national hotel chains were looking to unload properties at deep discounts, the timing could not have been better. Many of these hotels were located just off the exits of the highways that crossed the country. Now the chains were selling off these properties in an effort to write down the huge losses on their balance sheets.

It was at that moment that Michael had his billion-dollar idea. What if he could raise the money to buy one of these hotels off an interstate? The hotels were in great shape. They had indoor pools, workout rooms and large restaurants and banquet rooms. Any one of the properties could be easily converted into a seniors' residence. Michael thought long and hard about bringing together the two worlds he knew best. He was graduating with a first-class education in hospitality, and he never felt more at home than when he was at the seniors' facility, managing it.

As Michael researched the demographic opportunity for his idea he understood what he had to do. The linchpin in his business plan was finding the right investors and lenders, those who also saw this untapped potential. Over the past few decades, the United States had become less rural and more urban. Young adults were moving in large numbers away from the small towns and into metropolitan areas, sometimes thousands of miles from where they had grown up.

That typically meant they had to leave their parents behind, and as they aged, those parents would need living facilities designed to accommodate the elderly. Michael saw that there was already a real shortage of seniors' residences in rural America, and he knew he could find a way to meet the demand. And Michael also knew that, over the next 25 years, the shortage of these residences would only worsen, as baby boomers would be turning 65 at an astounding rate—some ten thousand per day.

With help from Mitch, Michael was able to raise seed money from an anonymous source. That helped him purchase his first seniors' residence. It wasn't long before he was finding success. Twelve years after graduating, Michael had successfully implemented his formula. He was buying properties from large hotel chains and converting them into profitable seniors' residences. And the best part of all was that he was getting a phenomenal three-year return on investment.

By the early 1990s, Michael wanted to take his winning business formula and go national. The country was just pulling itself out of yet another recession, and there was some hope for optimism. Bill Clinton had just been elected as the 42nd president of the United States. So Mitch talked to Michael about possible funding options. Mitch set up an appointment for Michael to meet his mentor, Richard Saunders. Richard was the founding and managing law partner of Mitch's firm. Michael was hoping he would be able to provide some good investor ideas so that he could take his business to the next level and achieve its full potential.

Michael felt a bit nervous as he walked with Mitch to the law firm for his first meeting with Richard. He noticed just how huge downtown Chicago's skyscrapers around him were, and how out of place he felt. He also noticed something he would normally have ignored. It was a man in his early 60s, dressed in a plaid shirt, khaki pants and work boots, and sweeping up trash outside one of the towers.

For some reason, Michael had a visceral negative reaction upon seeing this man doing such menial work. He lost his focus on the conversation he was having with Mitch.

"Do you know why I work so hard and am willing to sacrifice so much at this point in my life?" asked Michael, almost in anger.

"No. I've often wondered where your drive comes from," answered Mitch.

"I watched my father doing manual labor, and it literally killed him—he died in a workplace accident," Michael continued. "And for what? My father was a committed employee and union man, but his company and union were not that committed to him or his family. All that my mother, my sisters and I got after his death was a little money from an inadequate life-insurance policy and a small pension from the company. It was a trivial amount for my father's life. I saw my mother having to take whatever jobs she could find to raise me and my sisters.

"It's all for my kids. I don't want my children to ever have to go without—like I had to when I was growing up. I never want to be that poor again. When I'm in my 60s, I want to have created a company so sturdy that I will not have to collect trash or do anything I don't want to do. I don't want to just survive, like that man over there. I intend to thrive."

As Michael was speaking he remembered his university essay, the one that had won him his scholarship. He knew why financial success was important, and how it could transform lives. It's what he had outlined in his letter to the scholarship committee; he wasn't just being mean when he referred to the man who was picking up garbage.

Michael wanted to create a very successful business so that he would have the financial resources to provide opportunities to men and women so they could reach their full potential. He wanted everyone to have the same opportunities he had. He also wanted to provide assistance and dignity to the elderly. Many had not been as fortunate as him.

Michael's mind snapped back to his conversation with Mitch. Mitch was looking intently at the man who had set off such a powerful reaction in Michael. He then did a double take.

"That is not just *any* man," said Mitch.

"What do you mean, that isn't just any man?" Michael asked.

"You really don't know who that is?" asked Mitch in disbelief.

"Of course I don't. What's your point?"

"That's Harold Bloom, the King of Main Street. Only the senior partners at my firm deal with him. He most likely owns that tower—and everything else that surrounds it for blocks. He's probably one of the wealthiest men in America. No one knows for sure how rich he is because his companies are all private."

"I guess I shouldn't have been so judgmental," Michael muttered.

"We have to move along quickly if we are going to make it to our meeting," Mitch said, before giving Michael some advice.

"If you get it right today with Richard, you'll be on the way to becoming like Harold—so successful you won't have a care in the world if some cocky young kid mistakes you for the trashman."

CHAPTER 2

---><<---

RAISING MONEY

A T 8 A.M. sharp, Mitch walked Michael into the boardroom on the 54th floor of Chicago's Sears Tower. Michael was awe-struck by the expansive mahogany walls. And he was about to meet Richard Saunders, the founder and managing law partner of Mitch's firm, and his mentor.

"Mitch must love you, Michael," Richard said as he gave Michael a firm handshake. "A few months ago, he looked me right in the eye and told me I'd be a fool. Can you believe that? He actually said I would be a fool not to invest in your retirement homes. I couldn't believe it. No junior partner had ever spoken to me that way."

Michael looked over at his friend, and Mitch smiled at him.

Richard continued. "So let me get this straight, Michael. You want me to consider investing my time and money in your project. And you want me to convince some of the firm's clients to do the same."

"Yes," Michael said, without hesitating a beat.

It was Richard's business to read people, to know what made them tick. He already liked Michael, and he could see his hunger. "You have my full attention," he said. "The floor is yours."

Michael had prepared for this moment. "Demographics are destiny," he began.

"Yes," he continued, "it's a bold statement and a big topic. But I am telling you, the country cannot afford to ignore this fact any longer. We are an aging nation that needs to face this reality. We, as businessmen, need to see and seize this opportunity."

Michael studied Richard carefully as he spoke, noticing as he underlined the word "destiny," written in his notepad.

"We don't know what new technologies and industries there will be in the future," said Michael. "What we do know is that people age, and at different stages in their lives they have different wants and needs. What someone wants or needs when he is young is vastly different from what he will want and need in the future. And that's what I want to focus on. Demography, the future and how we can serve a growing need in our communities."

Richard liked this guy more and more with every sentence he spoke. He was confident, but he wasn't smug. What impressed Richard most was that Michael came prepared with more than just facts and figures.

"If we are lucky enough, we will have independent, successful and happy lives," Michael said. "But a fact of life none of us can escape is that as we age we lose independence. Many of us will need assistance when we are elderly. My business model is simple: to be the premier retirement living and assisted-care provider in the nation."

Richard didn't say anything, just listened.

"Let me give you some numbers that will illustrate to you just what I mean. They show just how we can use this opportunity to help an aging population that's about to explode. Did you know that demographers believe that 107 billion people have lived on this planet? And in all that time, only 500 million have lived past age 65?"

Michael could see that Mitch was watching him. Mitch was impressed with his friend: Michael was on top of his game. He was paying attention to every detail, the way he always did.

"Here's the interesting part," Michael said. "Right now, half of the seniors who have ever lived are alive today, and the total number is about to skyrocket even higher. In 2050, there will be 1.5 billion alive. That's equivalent to the entire population at the turn of the 20th century."

Richard looked over at Mitch, impressed. Michael had already convinced him. He was in. But he was fascinated by the details.

Michael went on to explain that by 2030, worldwide, there would be fewer children under the age of 15 than seniors, a first in human history. And he wasn't talking small numbers of seniors either. There were 77 million boomers in the United States alone, and they were heading into retirement fast. The first wave would hit age 65 in 2011.

"Think about it," Michael said to Richard. "That's just 19 years from now."

"It'll go by in the blink of an eye," Richard added with a smile. "You young guys don't know just how fast that time will fly. Take the word of a real old-timer—it'll be in the blink of an eye."

By now, Michael was feeling more relaxed. "And no one knows this generation better than people like me and Mitch," he said. "We were both born in 1958, the year with the largest bulge in boomer births. Our generation and the country as a whole are really going to feel the pressure. There's going to be an explosion of seniors, but not many people are preparing for it. Senior care is already underserved, and it's only going to get worse."

Michael explained that there are three plagues of old age: loneliness, helplessness and boredom. Traditional nursing and seniors' homes are sterile environments, breeding grounds for isolation and neglect. That was no environment for people who had spent their entire lives among family and friends to live in.

"The elderly at nursing homes need assistance, but they don't want to feel like they've been shuffled off into a corner to die," Michael said.

"For many people, the loss of a caring community is accompanied by a wrenching disconnection from a past that had purpose and dignity. And this is exactly what is happening at the vast majority of seniors' homes today."

"Michael," Richard interjected, already thinking of people who would jump at this opportunity, "give me a pitch I can present to potential partners."

"Richard, my company has four seniors' residences. All of them have one aim: to give people dignity and a good life in their golden years. We want to alleviate those three plagues I just mentioned. There's no reason people have to feel lonely, helpless or bored just because they're at a seniors' residence. It all goes back to the demographic tsunami I was talking about, and the impact it will have on our economy and business opportunities.

"You can bet there are a lot of people who don't see what's coming, or don't care. Some will continue to survive doing things that have worked for them in the past. There will be others who aren't as fortunate and won't be able to adapt to the new demographic realities.

"We plan to be the big winner in this marketspace because we embrace the new truths. You may find this outrageous, but not too long from now we are going to turn on our television sets and see commercials for medicines for erectile dysfunction."

Richard laughed. That wasn't something people talked about, at least not his generation. But he saw Mitch nodding when Michael brought up the commercials. *Maybe I'm out of touch*, he thought.

Michael continued. "Seniors' residences are going to be big winners in our economy. Right now, our government is not doing enough in the way of leadership in this area. And there's not much competition in the private sector. Very few businesses are preparing to serve; those that do rise to this opportunity will be profitable."

Michael went over some charts he had brought with him, along with his company's financials, showing how his team had successfully created its four profitable seniors' residences. The numbers spoke for themselves: the return on investment was expected in less than three years.

"What we offer is unique," Michael told Richard. "Our residences are basically all-inclusive. The residents can live the lifestyle they want. They'll never be bored if they don't want to be. And we are talking about residents who want to keep their active lifestyles. They want fine dining, outstanding amenities, fully equipped gyms, pools and great service. It's the quality of life they have earned and deserve."

Michael could see that Richard saw what he saw. He understood right there and then why Mitch had sought Richard out as his mentor. Richard instinctively understood how businesses worked; this knowledge was in his DNA. That's when Michael went all out.

"We have proven that we have a profitable formula," he said in a firm tone. "We're a company known for our commitment to our residents. You have to remember, these seniors' residences aren't just our business. This is our community too.

"We are in the process of building a reputable brand. What we need is a cash infusion for our company to go the distance and be the name in seniors' residences."

Richard leaned in. "How much are we talking about?"

"Thirty million—for now—to keep up and fund our rapid growth, with access to more," Michael said, ending his formal presentation.

He had done what he had set out to do: deliver the perfect presentation.

"I understand where Mitch gets his passion for your business," Richard said to Michael. "You've struck a chord with me. You have the mindset of the type of clients we want to work with. These are individuals who have always viewed themselves as entrepreneurs and want to improve the world.

"If you ask five people, you'll get five different definitions of what makes someone an entrepreneur. I've always believed it is someone who has an ability to identify the needs and wants of people and translate them into products and services. While many folks may be able to come up with these ideas, an entrepreneur uses a mix of knowledge, intuition, creative problem-solving, perseverance and drive to bring his idea to fruition in the only place that counts—the marketplace."

Yes, exactly, thought Michael.

"It's this ability to wear many hats and overcome whatever obstacle comes his way that distinguishes the entrepreneur from others," Richard continued. "You've shown that you have many of these traits. I would like to explore how we can get your company to the next level."

Richard explained why entrepreneurs are the ideal clients for his firm. Their success, for various reasons, frequently outpaces their cash needs for spurring on growth in their companies, and they find themselves in a situation similar to the one Michael was in. Oftentimes, they need to raise new funds, and weigh their options carefully. And they need to consider giving up ownership or share control in their business by inviting investors and lenders to help grow their enterprises.

If the owner of a business decides not to raise equity financing, Richard explained, one of two traditional forms of debt can be utilized: senior or subordinated.

Senior debt comes in three forms: an operating revolver (also known as a line of credit), a term loan or a capital lease. A senior debt means that the lender will have preference over all lenders on the asset that lender has security over.

An operating line of credit is set up on the basis of the amount of accounts receivable the business owns, which is reassessed monthly. Most commercial lenders will lend between 60 percent and 80 percent of the value of the accounts receivable. This form of debt is usually the cheapest, as interest rates are set at the bank's best rate—prime or prime plus 2 percent. Another attractive feature of this debt instrument is that there is no defined debt repayment schedule.

A term loan is similar to an operating line of credit but it takes into account the tangible assets of the business, such as buildings, land, inventory and so on (but excluding the business's accounts receivable). Most commercial lenders will lend between 40 percent and 60 percent of the value of the tangible assets, depending on the condition of the asset. With this form of debt, the interest is usually at a rate of prime to prime plus 4 percent. Unlike the operating line of credit, the term loan has defined repayment terms.

As for a capital lease, most business owners are familiar with the notion of taking a lease out with the manufacturer or a third-party leasing company to buy an asset such as a vehicle or piece of equipment. But what they often neglect to consider is the hidden value of the tangible asset once the lease is paid off and perhaps fully depreciated on the balance sheet. There are companies that lend money as capital leases against assets that have been fully written off but where the market value is greater than zero. The interest cost of an asset-based loan is similar to a term loan and will usually have a three- to five-year repayment schedule.

Subordinated debt, Richard then explained, is the second type of debt. Much like an equity investor, the subordinated debt lender typically looks at the business as a whole. The lender considers the value of the assets that are secured and those that are unsecured. The lender also considers the cash-flow the business has generated and should generate in the future. For those who have a business with an operating revolver in place, a subordinated debt lender may be the best option.

This lender will charge more for the loan than would a senior lender—in most cases, from prime plus 8 percent to prime plus 10 percent. However, the lender will postpone their security to other lenders. This type of debt has a fixed repayment plan.

Richard then turned to another option, one where an entrepreneur decides to raise equity financing by selling partial or all ownership in the business venture. He could not emphasize enough that entrepreneurs need to be aware of the three key questions seasoned private equity investors will ask before they part with their cash:

1. Is there a large definable market?

2. How big a share of that market can the company earn and then defend?

3. Is the management team capable of executing and managing growth?

Private equity investors invest in specific individuals and their ability to execute. The private equity investor merits more credit than he may garner, precisely because he is not an investment analyst skimming the cream from the top but is actually creating new real value, building the economy. Working together, the market-savvy entrepreneur and the experienced private equity investor can create something bigger than either could achieve on their own: a growth business.

"Our firm believes that private equity investors bring more than capital to the table," Richard said. "In reality, they become partners with the ownership/management group of a business. They work closely with management teams on issues related to acquisitions, financial structure and strategic planning.

"The relationship also goes well beyond these things. Private equity partners can help enhance many intangibles. Partnering with the largest private equity funds can bring relationships and credibility that are unique and helpful to many independent businesses such as yours."

Richard pointed out that although private equity investors are as diverse as the operating companies they seek to invest in, there are many characteristics common to the potential candidates that private equity investors find attractive. In general, these investors are looking for well-managed companies that generate annual operating income in the millions. Michael had already proven that his company had accomplished this for the past five consecutive years.

Richard then laid out the criteria that private equity investors consider when evaluating potential investment opportunities:

• Consistent and growing business.

• Stable revenue streams.

• Expansion opportunities.

• Predictable cash-flows.

- The current market position of a business within its industry.

- The presence of meaningful barriers to entering the company's market segment or geographic region.

In any case, a private equity partner will seek assurances that operating managers will stay on with the enterprise to increase sales and profits in order to achieve maximum value for all stakeholders.

"That fits your profile, Michael," Richard said. He looked over to Mitch. "You two still look like kids from where I'm sitting. It's important to recognize that a lender or private equity partner will want to be very comfortable with the business's ability to service the company and/or grow the business. Both lenders and private equity investors will want to see the company's historical performance, understand the business strategy going forward and assess the business plan."

Richard rose from the table to excuse himself—he had a full day of meetings ahead of him. As he was leaving, he said, "Michael, what you need to think about before going forward is the route you want to take. I am sure this was a lot to take in. So, what I suggest is that you spend some time thinking about what you plan to do next. When you're ready, I want my firm to be a part of the process, and Mitch to be our point man, working with you every step of the way."

CHAPTER 3

—>→>⊁≪<—

MENTORSHIP

MITCH AND MICHAEL stayed in the boardroom for a few minutes after Richard had left. They wanted to recap the options presented to Michael for injecting capital into his seniors' residence business to fund its expansion.

"As Richard said, it's a lot to take in all at once, selling ownership versus taking on additional debt," Mitch acknowledged.

Michael was still thinking about the meeting. "I'm going to take Richard up on his suggestion," he said, "but I need some time to think before I get back to you on what I believe will be best for the business and for me personally."

When Michael left Mitch's office that day, the streets of downtown Chicago were bustling. To Michael, they seemed to reflect the activity in his mind, which was buzzing with ideas and possibilities. He decided to take a walk along North Michigan Avenue, *Chicago's* Magnificent

Mile, to clear his head and gain some perspective on the morning meeting with Richard and Mitch.

"What's my next move?" he asked himself under his breath.

He was at a crossroad. He was hesitant. And he was scared. He knew that how he made his choices when it came to taking his business national was extremely important. It would show who he really was as a human being and determine who he would become. Taking on either debt or active investment partners would be a crossover into an area Michael had so far avoided. Either path would mean giving up some of his autonomy. But the opportunities and his business were demanding that he step over the threshold and into a new business universe.

No one else in his family had been an entrepreneur, at least not a successful one. He had lacked true mentorship in the art of business of any kind. Michael felt he had gotten by up to then with a lot of luck, and as he walked he wished he had a mentor.

Michael knew after his meeting with Richard that he had to stop being "unconsciously incompetent" in the art of running a large business. So far he had managed with luck and instincts—and his business was relatively small. He had mastered the skill set for that particular level. It had become second nature for him. But now he knew he couldn't continue to build his business with the ease and confidence he had had in the past. He needed guidance.

Michael knew that if he were to succeed, he would have to become "consciously competent" in order to perform the new tasks that would lie ahead of him. To grow his business and perform at a higher level, he would need to be extremely focused. If he committed to learn absolutely everything that is required for growing a successful business, eventually he would become unconsciously competent again. That would require pure devotion and determination, but ultimately he would no longer have to think when applying those skills—they would just be second nature. They would just be a part of who he was, so that he would be able to focus his attention on other things. He would be able to take on new tasks and acquire more knowledge, to spur on the rapid growth and expansion of his business.

Michael thought again about mentorship relationships, a subject that had occupied his mind for some time now. A few weeks earlier he had popped into his favorite bookstore, where he had found Robert Bly's *Iron John*. It was a masterpiece on mentorship. His copy was now well read: he had highlighted much of the text, and made countless notes in the margins.

Bly had articulated a lifetime of observations on what it took for an individual to graduate from being an immature youth to being a mature, responsible and productive adult and citizen, someone who would benefit all of society. He had taken a complex topic and made it tangible and simple to understand. In Bly's opinion, a mentorship relationship is one of the most complex, developmentally important and life-enhancing events that anyone could ever engage in.

Bly wholeheartedly believed that the tradition of mentoring relationships and its benefits were missing in our modern world, that we no longer teach and value responsibilities and obligations to those in our society—not to one another, and not to ourselves. He believed people give a lot of lip service to the concept of rights and privileges, but they don't give much thought to our responsibility to continuously earn our rights and reaffirm our obligations—certainly not in the same way preceding generations had.

Mentorship relationships have been an essential part of every ancient culture. Considering the relative difficulty of our ancestors' daily struggle for existence, Michael thought that it seemed illogical that they would have supported mentorship if there had been no big return on investment for their society. Why else would they have used their precious resources or invested their time creating mentorship relationships? Bly highlighted through his writing and in life that three criteria must be met for any one of us to reach our full potential in any worthy pursuit. Michael pondered Bly's criteria as he strolled over to the Wabash Avenue Bridge.

The first criterion: There must be a strong and well-rooted structure—how an individual unconsciously or consciously chooses to live his life—that the initiant engages in and becomes a full member of. Michael thought of his friend Mitch, the perfect example of someone who was actively applying this criterion to his life. Mitch had earned his Juris Doctor degree from one of the best law schools in the nation. He had then had to show a certain level of competency via standardized testing in order to be certified. He had also needed to meet a set amount of supervised and verifiable work experience. And he'd had to pledge to commit to a binding code of ethics by the state bar associations of Illinois, New York and California—the states in which he had planned to practice. Mitch had had to do all this before he could use his law degree to practice law.

It wasn't as straightforward for Michael. In the entrepreneurial world, there were no established routes set out for reaching goals. There was no formal process or roadmap for creating a revolutionary business from scratch. Michael smirked as he remembered Robert Frost's famous poem "The Road Not Taken."

Two roads diverged in a wood, and I—
I took the one less traveled by,
And that has made all the difference.

The words "the one less traveled by…that has made all the difference" echoed in his head.

The second criterion: Bly believed that for an individual to reach a level of proficiency and excellence, that individual needs to have a self-generated internal drive to excel far beyond just competency. His aim is to be excellent in any pursuit he intends to master. Bly says that the most important ingredient in accomplishing this is ownership of one's free will. Bly believed that, in the big scheme of things, our vocations choose us, rather than us choosing our vocations. He tells us that we must really listen to what our lives are saying we must do with ourselves. He defined free will as being given the choice to either accept one's destiny or fight it. If we choose to fight our destiny, we have to live with the consequences of not living up to our full potential.

Mitch met this second criterion in spades. He had been hearing stories about the importance of the law, and how it made people's lives and society better, since he was a child. He had always known he was going to be a lawyer. He had always had a burning desire to make his mark on the law. It was this internal drive that had propelled him to pursue—and complete—formal legal education. Mitch hadn't "predicted" his future; he had created it by implementing an internally driven vision, a vision that would match his external accomplishments. This had created many opportunities for unconventional experiences and for him to take an active part in writing his own destiny.

All of Mitch's education and career choices had been guided by this inner drive, desire and vision. Michael thought about Mitch's craving for the highest achievement in his chosen field. It reminded him of Victor Frankl, one of the great luminaries in psychology and the author of the groundbreaking book *Man's Search for Meaning*, which he wrote after surviving the Auschwitz concentration camp. Frankl made the point that it is absolutely essential for a man to find his own *logos*, Greek for "purpose." Once a man finds a meaningful reason for doing what he does, it is amazing how, as if by magic, many of the holes in his life become filled in.

The third criterion: Bly believed that intent and structure would take an individual only so far towards reaching his goals. To cross the final threshold of meaningful purpose and excellence, one needs to find mentors who have walked the desired path and found success. The luckiest of men are those who find the right mentor in their youth.

Michael had read that Merlin, the legendary wizard of the King Arthur stories, had been a warrior king long before he came to magic. In middle age, Merlin abdicated his throne and went into the forest alone. He wanted to learn how to regulate weather, which was a metaphor for controlling one's emotions. He did not become the beloved magician of Western lore until he had a great vision of what Camelot could become. It is with this vision that he found a boy whom he would mentor. That boy would later become King Arthur of the Round Table. Michael had this inner understanding that when the teacher is ready, the student will appear. The same is also true the other way around: when a student is seeking a mentor, the mentor will appear.

It wasn't by luck that Mitch had paired himself with Richard. Richard Saunders was a legend in the field of mergers and acquisitions. Mitch had followed Richard's career exploits via legal and business journals ever since he was in high school. He had negotiated some of this country's most difficult and comprehensive business transactions. Mitch had no doubt that Richard was the best M&A lawyer in the country, and he had long been determined that Richard would become his teacher.

Mitch had finished at the top of his law school graduating class. He'd had his pick of the litter when it came to where to practice. Richard had been the reason Mitch had declined all the offers that had come from more than a dozen of the top national firms. He hadn't solicited any of them. Mitch had wanted to stay in Chicago. He had known Richard would be the best mentor for him, and he had committed himself to earn Richard's respect and patronage.

As Michael contemplated and worked out his thoughts, he reflected on a more recent and powerful example that perfectly illustrated the importance and benefits of finding the right mentor—the Rubik's Cube. He had read that if you gave a Rubik's Cube to a blind man, statistically it would take him 126 billion years to solve the puzzle if he made random moves. But if this same blind man received information about the correctness of each twist of the cube from a Rubik's Cube master, the blind man would unscramble the cube in an average of 120 moves, within three minutes. That was the true power of finding the right mentor and earning the right to work with him.

As Michael continued his walk down State Street, Michael felt a burning need to seek out his own mentor. He wanted someone who would act as a teacher, to enhance his skills and development. The idea that his mentor could also serve as a sponsor began to cement in his mind. His mentor could use his influence to facilitate his entry and advancement into the world of business stardom. The mentor Michael needed was someone who showed who he was through his virtues, achievements and way of living. He would be Michael's example, the person that he, as the protégé, would admire and seek to emulate.

His mentor would provide wise counsel and moral support in times of stress and transition from one stage of life to the next. He needed this wise counsel right now as he decided how to make his seniors' residence business go national. Bly had found that the mentor's most crucial role is to support the protégé's dreams and facilitate the realization of them. A true mentor believes in his student's potential, sometimes well before the student believes in it himself.

Michael's mentor would be motivated by the immaterial rewards of knowing that he has aided the protégé in realizing his full potential. A true mentor is driven primarily by his wish to create a lasting legacy for the people his life has touched.

Michael thought of his father. He now understood that his father had played the essential role of parent but had never been Michael's mentor. He now understood that a true mentor has different experiences and knowledge, and a different role to play, than a parent. A mentor can also become a valued peer once his protégé has passed through the necessary trials and tribulations of the journey he faces. A successful mentoring relationship is one in which a mentor's guidance and experience helps the student become a full and equal peer, in every possible way, of his mentor. This was the type of relationship that was developing between Richard and Mitch. Michael's musing on why a father could not fulfill the role of mentor brought to mind the old adage, "When a father helps a son, both laugh, and when a son helps a father, both cry."

Michael's thoughts were starting to crystalize now. He understood that he must select his own mentor, as Mitch had done. For Michael this was absolutely essential, and he had to be selective in choosing the teacher. Thoughts were racing through his mind. He realized that until young men like him were willing to find wise men, they would remain boys. Without wise men to initiate them into the band of brothers, they would always remain boys—even though their bodies might grow and age; their inner beings would remain immature and childish.

Several hours had passed and it was now well past noon. Michael had spent a great deal of the day soul searching. He kept thinking about what was missing in his life, what he needed in order to continue his healthy development. Suddenly Michael awoke from his walking daydream and became aware of his surroundings. He had been so caught up in his thoughts that he had walked back to Daley Plaza without even realizing it.

He needed something to eat, so he walked to a nearby diner. It was nothing fancy, but the food must be good, he thought, because sitting there was Harold Bloom, the King of Main Street. Michael remembered how he had mistaken him for a trash collector just before his meeting with Richard that morning.

Michael knew that this was more than a meaningful coincidence. Harold had successfully walked the path Michael was now prepared—and determined—to walk down himself. Michael wondered if this man could help take him to the mental, emotional and spiritual levels necessary for him to move towards the next stages in his life's development. Michael understood that this answer would have to be earned. He knew he would have to work for it.

Michael paused, then made his approach.

CHAPTER 4

---><>⋘<---

HAROLD BLOOM

IT WAS THE beginning of the end for Germany's fledgling Weimar Republic. On March 13, 1932, the German people were going to the polls to vote in the presidential election. On the ballot was President Paul von Hindenburg. The 84-year-old hero of the First World War was facing off against Adolf Hitler and his National Socialist German Workers' Party of thugs, otherwise known as the Nazis.

That day, buried beneath headlines in *The Berliner Tageblatt*, Germany's largest circulated newspaper, was this:

Berlin: At 12:05 a.m., Dr. Mendel and Ester Bluhm became the proud parents of their third child, a healthy baby boy. Weighing 8 pounds 6 ounces and named Harold, after his late paternal grandfather, David and Rachelle are excited to welcome their baby brother to the family.

Harold's father, Mendel Bluhm, had been an army medic, stationed on the Western Front in France during the First World War. Mendel had had to put his medical studies—and his dream of becoming a doctor—on hold in the spring of 1916. The war was dragging on, and there were heavy losses on both sides, creating shortages of qualified medical personnel. Mendel was called up to serve at the front.

When hostilities ceased on November 11, 1918, Mendel felt the relief that all real men feel when they no longer have to witness the carnages of war. But it was not long afterward that he, like most Germans, felt a sense of betrayal as the new German government signed the Treaty of Versailles, officially ending the war. Germany had not lost on the battlefield but in a Paris conference room. The German government had been shut out of the negotiations on the terms of its final surrender. With the stroke of a pen, the German government had accepted total responsibility for starting the war. It had committed its people to pay war reparations to the Allied victors, which planted the seeds for the second world conflict.

After returning home to his young wife, Ester, Mendel completed his medical studies and together they started a family. Upon graduation, he took a prestigious medical research position at the Charité, one of Germany's top research and teaching hospitals. Here he would work under Dr. Otto Heinrich Warburg, who would win the 1931 Nobel Prize in Physiology or Medicine. Mendel was getting his own recognition for his contribution to the groundbreaking cancer research being done at the hospital. Mendel's future looked bright. Everyone believed Warburg was grooming him to take over the research department one day.

Things had seemed a lot less certain when Ester and Mendel had first met at a German war bond drive. The war had just started, and every day young men across Germany had been being called up to join the cause. Mendel or any young man could have been called into service at any time. Aware of their uncertain future, they had quickly married.

Mendel was much different from the other men Ester knew. He came from a long line of celebrated scholars, who could be traced to the Genius of Vilna, which dated back to the 18th century. Ester had fallen in love with Mendel for his kind heart, modesty, reserved nature, intelligence and commitment to humanity. Ester had grown up in the presence of business titans. She was the granddaughter of Georg Wertheim, the founder of Germany's largest department store chain and one of Germany's greatest philanthropists.

After election day—and their son's birth—things seemed to be even more uncertain than when Ester and Mendel had first met. As little Harold learned to walk, Germany was falling further into chaos. Hindenburg had won the presidential election but had lost the streets to Hitler's Brownshirts, who, with Hitler, essentially functioned as the Nazi Party's paramilitary wing. Hoping to curb the violence, Hindenburg appointed Hitler to head a Nazi-led coalition government, less than a year after Harold was born.

In February 1933, Hindenburg's appeasement failed when the Reichstag building, which held the German Parliament, went up in flames. The Communist Party was blamed. It was a convenient scapegoat, and the party was immediately banned. A few months later, Hitler and the Nazis achieved total supremacy over all areas of German life when President Hindenburg died. The Nazis' first totalitarian act was to eliminate all opposition to their rule.

Young Harold was shielded from much of this turmoil, at least until September 1935, when the Nuremberg Laws were passed. These laws robbed many Germans of their right of citizenship and other civil liberties. It wasn't long afterward that Dr. Warburg called Mendel into his office. With a heavy heart, he requested Mendel's resignation. He told Mendel that he was forced to by the Nuremberg Laws and that his hands were tied. The governing medical authorities had revoked Mendel's medical license.

Although Ester *Bluhm*'s family had once held considerable financial resources and clout, it was not able to provide much protection and financial assistance during those troubling days. The Nazis had confiscated many of the Wertheim family's financial assets, including the company her grandfather had built. The situation was bad, and it became even worse on *Kristallnacht*, the Night of Broken Glass. In November 1938, thousands of institutions classified as enemies of the Nazi state, along with homes, schools and businesses, were torched or otherwise vandalized. At least a hundred people were killed. More than thirty thousand men were arrested without cause. And by the end of the night, Mendel *Bluhm* was being held in a Gestapo detention center.

The Wertheim family used what little influence it could to secure Mendel's release, to no avail, so they bribed a Nazi official. That was the breaking point for the *Bluhms*. Within days they set in motion their escape from the Nazi terror—and the Germany they had once loved—by securing safe passage to Uruguay.

South America wasn't to be the *Bluhms'* final destination. Mendel's younger brother, Max, choosing adventure over academics, had seen the writing on the wall in Germany. He had fled Germany in 1923 after Hitler's failed treasonous takeover of Bavaria's government. Max had left Berlin behind to settle in the village of Skokie, Illinois, which was on the northern edge of Chicago. Max had started up a scrap-metal yard there, and in 1940, the *Bluhm* family crossed the US-Mexico border as legal refugees. The family reunited with Uncle Max, and their surname underwent a slight change. The US border officer who prepared and stamped their immigration documents changed its spelling from the German *Bluhm* to its American equivalent, *Bloom*.

With his new Americanized surname, Mendel Bloom immediately set his focus on studying for the grueling medical board exam in the state of Illinois. But the man who had once been on his way to being one of the top medical researchers in the world failed the exam several times. He lacked proficiency in English, and eventually he had to come to terms with the fact that he would never practice medicine again.

Ester soon found herself becoming the primary breadwinner for the Bloom family. She opened a dress shop in Skokie with seed money from Uncle Max. The Bloom children worked in the store when they could. In 1943, Harold's older brother, David, received his draft notice.

During the Second World War, he served in the Twenty-Fifth Air Force, also known as Air Force Intelligence, translating top secret German submarine transmissions coming in from the North Atlantic.

After the war, David accomplished what his father had failed to do. He attended Harvard Medical School on the GI Bill, with a partial scholarship. He went on to become a successful heart surgeon at Mount Sinai Hospital in New York City. Harold's older sister, Rachelle, met a brilliant lieutenant at a USO dance during the war. She and Richard Saunders got married and started a family, all while Richard completed law school. It wasn't long before Rachelle's husband made a name for himself. Richard would quickly become one of the country's top attorneys in the emerging fields of investment banking and mergers and acquisitions.

Harold had always been the black sheep of the family, the rebellious one. He didn't really care much for school. Being young, bored, daring and bold, Harold sought out adventure—deciding early on that he would have to chart his own destiny if he wanted true success. Harold didn't even graduate from high school. Instead, he dropped out, and on his 18th birthday he enlisted in the US Marine Corps. As fate would have it, three months after his enlistment, on June 25, 1950, the United States declared war on North Korea. Private Harold Bloom was put on a boat and shipped thousands of miles across the world to fight on the Korean Peninsula.

Harold's initiation into manhood was by mortal combat. He earned it through a Purple Heart after fighting in the Battle of Triangle Hill, and witnessing the horrors of war. The experience forced him to grow up fast. He became more serious about grabbing hold of his future and making something of himself. During the war, he had completed his high school equivalency certificate. When he returned stateside, he enrolled in business school at the University of Chicago.

Even before he turned towards a new seriousness about life, Harold had been certain about one thing: his love for Sara. Sara Landis was his high school sweetheart, the girl he called Chailee, which means "life for me." He had not lost contact with Sara, not even after he went off to war. In fact, their relationship grew stronger during this time, through heartfelt letters they wrote each other every week. In these letters, they expressed their innermost selves, their aspirations and their deep love for each other.

Harold wanted to lasso the moon for Sara and never disappoint her. The two of them got married in a civil ceremony soon after he returned from Korea, and they embarked on a life together. What they lacked in material wealth they more than made up for with their love for one another.

Sara often would smile and tell everyone how she truly fell in love with Harold through their wartime letters, how she knew he was the man she wanted to spend the rest of her life with. She saw him for the man he wanted to become, could become and one day would become. She always knew he would be a good, loving husband and father and grandfather, an inspiring businessman, a leader and a pillar of the community—even if he could not see it in himself.

They say that behind every successful man is a stronger, more loving and smarter woman. Sara was all this and more. She was a powerhouse in her own right. She was the eternal optimist, even more than Harold. Sara was always right there any time Harold was down and thought he was about to fail. She would have none of that type of thinking from him. Staying in the background, she was his counsel and the driving force that helped him overcome all obstacles. Sara wasn't shy, and she would proudly tell people that her job in life was to support Harold Bloom in whatever Harold Bloom deemed important. They always had a united front. Together they built a wonderful life, and had a loving family, with healthy children and grandchildren.

As a returning veteran, Harold received a monthly allowance of $110 for living and tuition expenses. It wasn't enough for a young married couple who were expecting their first child. It seemed they were always struggling to make ends meet. But one day, Harold happened to overhear a conversation while in the main cafeteria on campus. It would change the direction of his life.

A member of one of the college fraternities was complaining that he was trying to get sweaters made with his fraternity's crest but couldn't find anyone to do it. Harold's ears perked up at hearing this opportunity. He knew he could fill this need—and make some desperately needed cash. He interrupted the conversation.

"I can get those sweaters for you at a deep discount," he pledged.

And just how did Harold plan to get it done? When Harold was growing up in Skokie, his Uncle Max had stepped in as his surrogate father when his own father had checked out emotionally. Max had always seen much of himself in Harold. Often Harold would skip school to meet up with Uncle Max at Manny's Deli. There, Harold was schooled in the University of Life by Max and his buddies. They were all street-smart men who had built successful *garment factories or other manufacturing businesses, supplying the American war effort.*

Harold's new business opportunity brought him back to Manny's to talk to his Uncle Max. This was his chance to earn the right to sit at the big boy's table, and it would be the first of many opportunities he would successfully explore.

His trip to Manny's was well worth it: Max placed a call to the owner of a local sweater manufacturer. Harold was off to a great start! Before long, he had sold 120 sweaters at a deep discount while earning a 35 percent profit margin. Building on this success, Harold made many more connections—with the help of Uncle Max, who sponsored him with his buddies, as well as with other local factory owners.

Harold also made good money in other ways while he was at college. He became a door-to-door salesman in the university's rich fraternal system—peddling, among other things, discounted clothing, encyclopedias, radios, refrigerators, ovens, toasters and jewelry. He also began selling what was then the hottest new technology—television sets. He was so good at sales that on the college campus he picked up the nickname "Bargain Harold."

When Harold graduated in 1957, he was earning $2,000 a month from his entrepreneurial ventures. It was then that Harold made up his mind to go into wholesaling as a full-time vocation, a move strongly supported by Sara. He began by opening a deep-discount store, basing its name on his college nickname: Bargain Harold's. The whopping 6,000-square-foot outlet opened in July of 1957.

As usual, Harold did things his own way, trying things that had never been done before. The prevailing practice of American discount-store chains at the time was to locate their outlets in central business districts of large cities. Instead, Harold decided to leverage off the country's population shift to suburban areas.

He opened shops in small cities and towns in the bedroom communities of growing metropolitan centers, first in the Midwest, then expanding the model across the country. The first Bargain Harold's was located off Interstate 94 in Gurnee, Illinois, right between Chicago and Milwaukee. Harold stocked the store with all kinds of odd merchandise, purchased at bankruptcies and fire sales. He bought only from American manufacturers that could supply goods at low prices, and he quickly innovated the wholesale discount industry. He instituted a membership program, a technique that had never been applied to a department store before. Most discounting was outlawed at the time, but these membership cards legally allowed Harold to undercut suggested retail prices on all the items in his store. In doing so, Harold could accept large discounts from suppliers, something his competition could not.

Harold was also a master pitchman. He ran in-store promotions on everything in the store, including televisions, Christmas trees and even turkeys. He also came up with the idea of the loss-leader. Loss-leaders were selected items sold at below-cost discounts, designed to lure buyers into the store.

Soon Bargain Harold's success formula was propelling the business's rapid growth. Before long, the original Bargain Harold's store expanded to 12,000 square feet. Then Harold took a huge calculated risk. In 1962, he replaced his original store with a 120,000-square-foot super center. The new store was designed to offer the customer a unique shopping experience. Here he offered a revolutionary innovation just introduced into the retailing industry: this location accepted the Bank of America's licensed credit card, which became known as Visa. This gave his customers greater credit convenience, making shopping easier and a better experience.

Harold was a strong believer in taking care of his employees, because he knew they were the bedrock of his success. All full-time employees were invited to join a profit-sharing plan. They also received reimbursement for medical and dental expenses, along with a retirement benefit plan. His business model was ideal for meeting the demands of the growing suburbs, towns and cities that were rapidly being connected by the new Interstate Highway System, which spanned the country. But beyond his monetary success, Harold was learning important lessons. He realized that the real money in the postwar economic expansion was in owning the real estate that this growth was being built upon.

Harold had made the promise to himself that when he took a risk, he would get paid for it. He had split his business into two main entities, which fell under a third master corporate structure called the Menter Group of Companies, named in honor of his parents, Mendel and Ester. Harold liked this name because it sounded like "mentor." The Menter Group of Companies would be owned by a trust established in the state of Nevada. This allowed him to maintain complete privacy and anonymity, which was his highest priority—followed closely by tax efficiency of all his financial affairs. One of the beneficiaries of the trust was a dormant charitable foundation.

The first entity would hold the Bargain Harold's Super Store Center portfolio; the other would own and lease out plots of land to other retailing and franchising chains. Bargain Harold's Super Store Centers would act as the anchor store for each of these destination shopping, business and residential districts.

The next phase in the development of his brand involved the purchase of tracts of land off interstates, each between five hundred and one thousand acres. He was able to buy these properties for marginal amounts because they were on the outskirts of cities and towns, leading out of urban centers. Harold was skilled at rezoning these properties for retail, commercial and residential use. After doing so, he would approach other national retail chains to sign letters of intent to lease parts of these properties for 20 or more years, once they were developed. Harold then would go off to the bank and borrow on the future revenue that would be generated from these highly profitable leases. This formula allowed Harold to keep his company completely privately held. His business's internal cash-flows would fuel the company's future growth.

The growth in his business was phenomenal. From the 1960s to the mid-1980s, Harold oversaw the rapid expansion of his chain of stores and real estate holdings. He applied his formula successfully hundreds of times. He always set up shop away from major metropolitan centers. Eventually, the Menter retailing areas were receiving more foot traffic than the downtown shopping districts of the neighboring metropolitan areas.

A national business magazine picked up on what Harold was accomplishing in the 1960s and the trend he was creating, giving him his second nickname, which was to stick with him for the rest of his life. Harold had transformed the landscape of shopping patterns and main streets across America. Soon he was known simply as "The King of Main Street." But the name referred to so much more. It highlighted his influence on American culture. From that time on, Harold Bloom's name was interchangeable with "The King of Main Street."

To make his business model work, Harold emphasized saving money and time through logistics. That required him to locate stores within a day's drive of his regional warehouses. His large nationwide network of warehouses also allowed Harold to embark on other ventures, including a mail-order business. He created a popular mail-order catalog, which allowed consumers across the country to buy Bargain Harold's products. The mail-order business also had another benefit for Harold and his customers. Bargain Harold's wasn't required to charge sales tax on its mail-order interstate sales.

Harold was always trying to do things better and more efficiently. In fact, he was one of the first business leaders to see the potential of the

World Wide Web when it was created in 1989. Two years later, Bargain Harold's yet again innovated by creating one of the first online shopping portals to complement the Bargain Harold's stores and its catalog-distribution businesses.

By achieving success in several businesses, Harold became a connoisseur of buying into the best business models and enterprises. Outside of his main businesses (discount stores and real estate development), Harold used his highly functional and flexible corporate structure to excel at investing his extra cash directly into companies or the stock market. His investment philosophy in business was simple: Watch the store, not the market. His success did not come from some esoteric financial model or complex algorithm. Harold always kept his eyes wide open to the world he knew best, to observe what was around him. And by keeping an open mind, he saw many great business opportunities in which to invest, which he did. He followed the trends within his stores, noting which items flew off the shelves, and he kept up with the technologies that made it possible for those items to move efficiently into his customers' hands. It was this practical research that gave him his investment edge. It also gave him a stream of new ideas about which products, companies and technologies to buy and invest in. His choices made for good long-term investments to add to and hold in his investment portfolio. In a nutshell, his investment philosophy contributed to his finding great companies to invest in, at bargain prices. Most importantly, he had the patience to sit back and watch them grow and thrive.

By the early 1980s, Harold Bloom had more than excelled. He had gone beyond all his wildest expectations, and far beyond the dreams he'd had as a young immigrant kid. He had the Midas touch. He had fortune and fame, and his family was healthy. His two children were grown up—married with children—and well on their way to achieving success in their own right. He was most proud that his children did not try to use his clout, help or wealth. Rather, they were determined to make it on their own terms.

But as Harold became older, his inner voice began growing louder.

The more he ignored it, the more it made its presence known to him. It warned Harold that he needed to let go of the goals that had been important to him in his youth, the morning of his life. It told him that while his youthful goals had been mostly about building up and feeding his ego through the trappings of success, it was now time for Harold to put that all behind him in order to seek out greater meaning and do greater good.

In 1984, at age 52, Harold finally began listening to his inner voice. He made the conscious decision to embark on a new journey of seeking out and manifesting a greater meaning. He had committed himself to spending the rest of his days learning to let go of the goals that had once defined him. He was determined that in the afternoon and twilight of his life, he would become mindful of letting go of his attachments to his ego and, in the process, live for what really matters in life.

CHAPTER 5

THE APPROACH

ICHAEL WAS VERY hungry, but his first thought when he entered the diner wasn't about food.

"Mr. Bloom? Mr. Harold Bloom?" Michael asked the man he had mistaken for a trash collector just a few hours earlier.

Harold stared up at Michael for a good 30 seconds before saying, "Yes. Have we met?"

"No, sir," Michael replied. "We haven't formally been introduced. My name is Michael Stevens. I saw you earlier today as I was rushing to a meeting."

"Oh, now I remember," Harold said, reaching for his cup of coffee. "I saw you as you passed by with Richard's boy wonder."

"You know Mitch?" asked Michael. "And Richard Saunders?"

Harold gave a hearty laugh. "Richard and I have had our adventures together over the years," he replied. "All I can say about Mitch is, if you are keeping that boy's company, you are in good hands. I've met Mitch only briefly, but Richard has an eye for talent and a soft spot for that boy." He motioned to the empty seat at the table. "Take a seat, kiddo. How can I assist you today?"

Michael was slightly taken aback, but he already felt at ease around this seasoned warrior. He decided to tell Harold about his first impression of him, just hours earlier, and how mistaken he had been.

"I feel embarrassed admitting this, but I feel I owe you an apology."

Harold looked astonished. "We've never met before. Why do you need to apologize to me?"

"When I passed you earlier, I misread you," Michael told him. "You were picking up trash in front of those towers over there. I'm curious as to why. You are a busy and very successful man, and I can't see any reason you would be doing such work. Why would you choose to do such a menial task?"

It had been a long time since someone so young had been so bold as to approach Harold and ask such a pointed question.

"None of us is too high or too low in our station in life not to, at some point, feel a need to reconnect with the environment," Harold told the younger man. "I honor this reality by making sure my surroundings are in good order, even if it means getting my hands a little dirty from time to time. We never really own anything. Everything we would believe is ours in this lifetime is just on lease.

"When we take our last breath, and meet our maker, it all goes back to its rightful owner. And then it's leased out again. This cycle of life was here long before you or me. It will continue long after we're gone. I believe that our responsibility, while we're here, is to do our best to make the earth better than we found it."

Michael was awestruck. He was listening to one of the great captains of American business talk about his personal philosophy. But Harold wasn't finished. He was just warming up.

"I guess there is truth to the saying, 'Never judge a book by its cover,'" he said, an amused look on his face. "Have you ever heard the story about the roast beef?"

"Huh? Roast beef? No, I haven't," Michael replied.

"Then you are in for a real treat. It will help you the next time you are about to make another rash, uninformed judgment about someone or something. It's about questioning underlying assumptions. It is important for each and every one of us to question, from time to time, why we think or do what we do. When I think about questioning our underlining assumptions, I am often reminded of this story. It involves a newlywed couple, and it drives home the point I want to share. I believe it will be helpful in guiding you in your future."

Harold began to tell the story.

"One evening a husband arrived home as his new wife was preparing dinner. That night they were having roast beef. He noticed that his wife had cut off the ends of the roast and thrown them into the garbage. He found this puzzling, so he asked why she did that. His wife replied that this was the way her mother had always prepared roast beef.

"Now, this didn't really satisfy the husband's curiosity, but he wisely decided to follow some advice his father had given him on his wedding day. The advice was simple: Pick your battles wisely. So the young man didn't pursue it."

Where is this story going? wondered Michael. Harold continued.

"About a month later, the mother-in-law had the young couple over for dinner. She was preparing roast beef as the main course, and, true to what his wife had said, she cut off the ends of the roast and put them in the trash can. So he decided to ask her why she prepared roast beef this way. The mother-in-law replied that this was the way she, as a little girl, had observed her mother making roast beef.

"Several months later, his mother-in-law's mother flew in from Florida to visit the family. The husband, still puzzled by the roast beef preparation, saw his chance to get to the bottom of it. So he turned to his wife's grandmother and asked bluntly: 'I was wondering, why did you cut off the ends of a roast beef and throw them out when you cooked a roast? Your daughter and now my wife—your granddaughter—do the same thing.'

"The grandmother laughed, then told him that when she had first been married, she and her husband had been so poor that they hadn't owned a pot big enough to fit a roast. So she had had to cut off the ends, to make it fit in the pot. 'But,' she said, 'I never threw away the ends! I used them for soup the next day.'

"The grandmother thanked the son-in-law for asking the question, saying that she only wished her daughter and granddaughter had asked her it long ago, so that they wouldn't have wasted so much good meat."

Michael smiled, nodding to acknowledge that he understood the moral of the story. Harold smiled back. He knew there was more to this meeting than just a simple apology from Michael.

"Kiddo, it seems like you didn't come up to me here just to say sorry."

Michael looked Harold squarely in the eye. "You're right, Mr. Bloom," he said. "Today was a big day for me. Mitch took me to meet Richard. It was to discuss my options for taking my company to the next level. I needed to take some time to think afterward, so I've been wandering the streets, replaying the meeting in my mind, and trying to figure out what my next moves should be. Then, when I came to the diner to get something to eat, I saw you sitting here. I was hoping that you might give me some insight from your hard-earned experience into what I might do to achieve a fraction of the business success that you have earned in your lifetime."

Harold just looked at the young man. He then said something that shocked Michael.

"Do you know where success in business falls in the pecking order of living a full and meaningful life? I'll tell you. It falls after finding a worthy purpose, having a loving family, your health, having strong relationships that stand the test of time and, lastly, doing meaningful work that benefits the greater good of the community and society. Kiddo, you need to set your priorities straight. You came here for a lesson today, and I am going to give you an important one."

He continued by sharing that he had walked this earth long enough to know that people who blindly chase money and accolades will find their lives slowly slipping in the direction of disillusionment, sorrow and regret.

"An unquestioned life is an unlived life."

Michael was dumbfounded. Here was one of the most successful men on the planet telling him life wasn't just about the money and business success.

Harold then asked Michael a seemingly simple question. "Do you believe most people enjoy what they do for a living?"

"No, they don't, and I plan not to join those statistics," answered Michael.

"I have discovered by observing others and also by experiencing it myself that several things occur, consciously or unconsciously, at the end of our working lives," Harold said. "At the end of our careers, some of us might realize that the real goals are beyond our reach. Or we may find we have achieved our goals. But we realize that those goals turn out to be disappointments and meaningless."

He gave Michael a thoughtful look.

"Obtaining those goals, kiddo, may not match the movie that has been running in our heads when it comes to realizing and living a fulfilling life. You might achieve your goals and then ask, what's next? Or ask, what was all that work for? The saddest and most painful answer for an individual is to discover that his dreams were not truly his own, but someone else's."

Michael sat back, listening. He knew that he was where he needed to be, and this was what he needed to be hearing. Harold's words were beyond priceless.

"They tell me we have moved into the Information Age," Harold continued. "It seems that the only thing we can count on is change. We are just coming out of a recession in which millions of people's lives have been disrupted by corporate outsourcing, downsizing and re-engineering. People must come to the realization that relying on big government or big corporations to provide a living isn't enough. To succeed, they will have to take ownership of their careers and lives—like you are beginning to."

"I'm starting to understand what you mean," Michael replied. "I believe I am a part of a new generation, with a new view of our careers. I graduated during the last recession. The jobs I wanted weren't open to me, so I had to create my own. What that taught me was that, in the new economy, people in my age group and the generations that will follow have a better chance of getting a gold watch from a street vendor than we do from a corporation."

Harold let out a hearty laugh. He liked this young man, not much older than a kid, really, who had judged him at first sight.

"When I was young—before globalization and the Information Age that we now live in—people believed that success meant having a secretary, a company car and a corner office. You are right to think those are things of the past.

"Today we are all responsible for managing our own careers. Whether a person plans to own his own business or work for someone else in the modern economy, everyone must accept that all jobs, whether contract or permanent, eventually end. They should all be viewed as temporary. When I was young, the rules for achieving success were very simple for most people. You'd begin working for a large company after high school or college. From there you would receive incremental promotions every few years. That world is long gone now. If you want to do well in the new economy, you must be committed to being a continuous life learner."

Michael nodded. "I agree. I believe that our greatest assets in the new economy are the marketable skills we acquire. If a person's work becomes too easy to do, well, it's his position that is typically automated, or someone is hired to replace him for a lot less pay. I've seen a lot of factory and call-center jobs fall into that category. They can easily be done overseas or south of the border."

Harold could see that Michael sincerely wanted to understand more about life and business. He still had much to learn.

"Remember," he said, "in the new economy, don't ever sacrifice long-term growth for short-term gains that only benefit someone else and not you, or the greater whole of society. If I can recommend something of value now, never stop investing in yourself. This is how you will become invaluable to the whole.

"Ask yourself, if your own company were advertising your position and you applied for it, would you get it? Would you the employer be looking for the skill set that you the job applicant possesses?

"Do you know what the problem with most entrepreneurs today is? They don't know what they contribute to their company's bottom line. You have to know what you contribute to your company's success. You need to be able to describe what you do and how it benefits your company, clients, investors and your employees in the time it takes for a traffic light to turn from red to green. If you can't, most likely no one else can either. You're the boss; you need to know your value; you need to be able to express it in a positive and clear way."

Harold then asked Michael to think long and hard about what he would do if his company disappeared tomorrow.

Michael took his time before responding.

"I would have to be honest with myself and ask if I had invested enough in myself. I would want to know that I had developed marketable skills, built contingencies into my career plans and developed support networks to help me through a transition to new career opportunities."

"That is a good outlook to take," Harold said approvingly. "Success in the new economy means results. It means having had fewer job titles than you might have in yesterday's economy, but many, many more experiences. Have you ever heard of the Layaway Life Plan?"

Of course, Michael knew about layaway plans. But putting life on layaway? *What does that mean?*

"No, not exactly. Is it something like when someone pays a deposit to secure an item to be enjoyed later, once in hand?"

"Close. I borrowed the concept from my days working in the wholesale-retail sector." Harold explained how life is too short to live out the Layaway Life Plan—doing the things you don't like, in hopes that one day you will be living your True Life Plan. There are two major flaws with this type of thinking. One, will you know when it is time to switch over to living out your True Life Plan? If you have not taken the necessary steps towards making your dreams happen today, what makes you think you will embark on your true life path tomorrow?

And two, do you really have all the time in the world to make this change? Do you believe that you will be the only person in human history to live forever? Ask yourself: "Have I accomplished anything in my life that has real meaning to me, my family and the greater whole of society?"

Harold further explained that many people suffer from the delusion that by continuing in their Layaway Life Plan, they are earning a living and that this is the best they can hope for in this lifetime. "But if our hearts are not into our work," he said, "are we not actually making a 'dying' for ourselves? If each day you lose a little more of your dreams, your self-respect and yourself, what type of legacy will you create and leave behind?"

Michael knew that Harold was a man who knew business and numbers inside and out. No one knew how to make money better than the King of Main Street. But Michael now saw something much greater in Harold. Something he had been searching for. This was a man who understood what his true bottom line in life was. And he was at peace with it.

The conversation had confirmed for Michael that Harold was the mentor he had been searching for. Now the question was, would Harold take him on as his student and share his wisdom with him?

"Mr. Bloom—"

"Now you are calling me 'Mr. Bloom'?" Harold quickly cut him off. "Please just call me Harold."

Michael decided to lay his cards on the table.

"Harold, I feel that I haven't had any true guidance in how to become a mature adult since I was 11 years old. That's when my father died. He had worked almost his entire adult life at the Union Stock Yards, until he was killed in a workplace accident.

"That's how I feel right now—lost and without guidance. I know that I am over my head in my new venture, which will be a new phase for my business. But I know one thing now: I will probably blow it if I don't get proper guidance. Whatever it takes, I want to earn your wisdom."

Harold took a good look at Michael. He was genuine. He was a straight shooter. He was eager to learn. Harold remembered having a similar conversation with his Uncle Max when Harold had returned from Korea. He had asked for his Uncle Max's patronage. He fondly remembered the fraternity sweaters—and the invaluable life lessons his uncle had taught him while he built up his wholesale business. Harold had once been in Michael's shoes, and he knew how he felt—scared.

"This diner opens at 5:30 a.m. sharp every day. It opens when it's hot and humid, and it opens during the worst of Chicago blizzards. Meet me here next Wednesday and let's see where this goes. But I make no guarantees."

Michael couldn't believe it. The King of Main Street was giving him a shot at becoming his student. He had a million things he wanted to ask and say. But all that came out was a relieved "Thank you."

As they were departing, Harold left Michael with a final thought:

"Being who you are is not about being great. It's about being comfortable with your smallness in the grand scheme of life while still giving great self-expression to your full potential.

"I'll be seeing you next week, kiddo."

CHAPTER 6

→≫✠≪←

TORTOISE OR HARE?

T HE DOORS TO the diner opened at 5:30 a.m. sharp, just as Harold had said they would. Michael entered the restaurant, shaking off the chill in the breeze coming off Lake Michigan. Since Harold was a regular, and the owner of the diner had opened its doors a little earlier for him, he was already sitting at a table, enjoying his coffee.

"Good to see you made it," he said as he motioned for Michael to join him. "What would you like, kiddo? I'm having the usual"—he pointed to his coffee—"black, no sugar. And I ordered my regular—scrambled eggs and plain toast."

"Sounds good," Michael replied.

"He'll have the same," Harold told the waitress, and then turned back to Michael. "I have thought a lot about our first conversation," he said. "You're an intelligent young man. But you've still got a lot to learn and experience. So let's get started. I would like to begin this morning by asking you what might seem like a rhetorical question: Do you have more affinity for the tortoise or for the hare?"

Michael was taken aback by the question. But he knew Harold was being serious and that there was a point to be made by him asking this question.

"I'd like to say the hare, but I know the correct answer should be the tortoise—there's no such thing as a free lunch, and no shortcuts in life," said Michael.

"Wise. If you live long enough, everything eventually catches up to you," Harold said. "When I was young, I had a conversation with a seasoned business owner. What I remember most about it is his explanation of how the message contained in Aesop's age-old fable of the tortoise and the hare was not just for kids but also for adults—the universal truth that the slow and the steady always win the important races in life."

"So what you are saying is that, in the end, our quality of experiences always trumps the quantity of activity," said Michael.

"You got it, kiddo. One of my favorite presidents is Calvin Coolidge, and I believe he best summed up his thoughts on this subject." Harold paused before reciting the Coolidge quotation he had committed to memory:

Nothing in this world can take the place of persistence. Talent will not; nothing is more common than unsuccessful people with talent. Genius will not; unrewarded genius is almost a proverb. Education will not; the world is full of educated derelicts. Persistence and determination alone are omnipotent. The slogan "press on" has solved and will always solve the problems of the human race.

"I have failed plenty," continued Harold, to illustrate what he meant in quoting Coolidge. "Almost went bankrupt right at the start when I overextended myself by opening my first big-box store. Since then, I have narrowly avoided Chapter 11 bankruptcy protection another four times.

"Have you ever wondered what drives someone to soar to the top of his game in business? For my entire adult life, I have been asking myself this."

"Your question reminds me of the mythic Greek figure Sisyphus, who is condemned to pushing a huge rock up a mountain, only to find that it rolls right back down," said Michael.

"You have to have a sense of humor," said Harold. At my age, I still remain optimistic that I will find clues that move me closer to answering my question, and perhaps our morning meetings can help me achieve this."

That's interesting, thought Michael. "Does that mean we will make these early-morning meetings a regular occurrence?" he asked.

Harold chuckled. "We will see. We will see, kiddo. With years at the back of my sails, I have come to appreciate the *wisdom of Aesop, Coolidge and others.*

"Take Oscar Wilde's definition of what a cynic is: a man who *knows the price* of everything and the value of nothing. To be successful in any endeavor, we need to surround ourselves with the right people, those whose outlook on life and personal goals are in line with and mirror our own, who see our intrinsic value, not our price tag."

Michael was still in awe. He liked to constantly read and learn. But this was so much more, being schooled by a master.

"There are two kinds of lenses through which to view our subjective worldview of how we choose to play in the game of life," Harold continued. "One could be called finite, the other infinite. A finite gamer plays for the purpose of being the sole victor, while an infinite gamer's aim is to continue the play."

"I haven't heard those terms used that way before," Michael said.

"For now, let's agree to use the terms 'infinite' and 'finite' to refer to these two different worldviews that one could embrace," Harold suggested.

"It makes a huge difference which worldview we consider ourselves to have in this life game whose rules we call "reality." Are we pawns or players? If we are players, we should understand that rules are real only to the extent that we have created and accepted them as such. But here's what you need to know, kiddo. We can change these rules at any time if we choose to do so.

"But most people unfortunately don't believe this. They think that circumstances are the driving forces behind their lives. But if we step back, we will slowly realize that it is not our circumstances that create our outcomes. It is the underlying structure of our lives—our beliefs and mental habits—that determines the paths we take. I have learned that, by changing any part of that structure, we change our lives."

Another mental light bulb went off for Michael. He could not have received this kind of education anywhere else in the world. He had already learned more in this diner than he had from all his college professors over the years.

Harold explained that people must first understand that any relationship or process can be characterized in finite or infinite terms. The second step is recognizing that characterization is almost always a matter of choice, and that by choosing to see a relationship as infinite, you can redefine it in a meaningful and healthy way.

Harold had observed that when people see life as an infinite game and are living out their life purpose, they come up with more ideas, see more associations between ideas and people, and see more similarities and differences between things than do those who see life as a finite game. Infinite gamers are global thinkers and society's change makers and agents.

"So, what you are saying is that what emerges is more of an orientation towards family, friends, work, community, the environment and ourselves," said Michael.

Harold nodded in agreement—Michael was a quick study. "You are beginning to comprehend this important understanding about life," he said. "Infinite gamers take the long view in much of what they do. Their primary aim is to create a win-win environment in all of their activities, because anything less will impede their ability to truly experience and enjoy their life's journey."

"Last week we discussed the importance of questioning all our assumptions," Michael said, recalling his first conversation with Harold. "In my limited experience, I've learned that when I have one way of doing something, I get stuck. If I have two ways, I find myself in a bind. Only when I have three or more ways of doing something do I feel I have a true choice."

Harold nodded again. "Do you know what the Chinese symbol for 'crisis' is?" he asked.

Michael shook his head.

"I've been fascinated by the symbol since I was in Korea. It has a dual meaning. There is the meaning we are familiar with—crisis as something solely negative. But there is also a positive meaning."

Harold explained that the Chinese symbol also translates as "opportunity." Each player in the game of life who is perceptive enough to see that he is playing an infinite game has the ability to see crises as opportunities. He continues to play, no matter what the situation. So everything that happens to this kind of person is a part of the play, and there are no failures as far as this kind of player is concerned. There is only feedback so that play can continue and be improved upon.

"Take Warren Buffett. Most people don't know that a major influence on his investment philosophy is the legendary Philip Fisher, the author of the 1958 investment classic *Common Stocks and Uncommon Profits*. Fisher had adamantly believed in not investing money in a man who had never fallen flat on his face, broken some bones, knocked out a few teeth and failed miserably at least once in his life."

Harold shared Fisher's main points with Michael: Fisher had believed that people should invest only in someone who knew how to get up—someone who could pull himself up by his bootstraps through inspiration, sheer determination and perspiration. This individual is the kind of creative force to be reckoned with. A man who falls, gets up, dusts himself off and takes a step forward can be counted on as a leader.

Fisher had believed that this type of person has an indelible spirit, a moral compass and a strong defining character. He is an infinite gamer at his very best. This was the kind of person Fisher had wanted on his team, the type Fisher would have invested his, his partners' and his clients' time and money in—for the long haul. Because this type of person has faced adversity but does not allow himself to be counted out. He is a serious player in the game of life. Most people choose to sit in the stadium bleachers, watching others play in the game of life and wishing they were playing in it themselves. Fisher's serious player, on the other hand, has said no to merely watching others play. He has chosen to get on the field and play the game, the contact sport of life—and to play his heart out. And the only way the game will end for him is when his time on this earth is up.

Harold savored the last drop of his coffee. "Our lesson has come to an end for today," he said. "Let's continue next week—here again, same time."

Michael could not believe their time together had passed so quickly. He had a lot to absorb from their conversation. "You got it, Mr. Bloom. I mean Harold," he said. "Thank you. Thank you for giving me this opportunity and your time."

Before departing, Harold left Michael with one more lesson. It was a story of Don Juan, the Renaissance lover and warrior, who believed that the basic difference between an ordinary man and a warrior is that the latter takes everything as a challenge, whereas the former takes everything as a blessing or a curse. That is what makes all the difference between success and failure, between reaching one's goals and falling short.

"Remember, kiddo, the common denominator of all these sages' advice is this: all our failures in life are events, the full benefits of which we have not yet turned into our advantage.

"We'll expand on these concepts next week. Let's chat then about what it will take to be a leader in the 21st century."

CHAPTER 7

—⟫⟪—

BECOMING A 21ST-CENTURY LEADER

ICHAEL WALKED INTO the diner, having contemplated all that he had learned the previous week. He was still trying to absorb what Harold had shared with him. He felt it was incredibly useful and would help him frame his life going forward—how he would see the challenges ahead of him. And Michael knew he would face many tests as he expanded his business into unfamiliar territory. He now wanted to know what Harold had discovered—what it took to become an authentic leader.

Long before Michael had gone off to college, his love affair with secondhand bookstores and public libraries had begun. That's where he went in search of treasures that would expand his understanding of how the universe worked. He learned from authors who had spent a lifetime contemplating life's big questions. His visits to the bookstores were a sacred ritual for him. Every week he made his pilgrimage, to browse through the stacks of books on topics ranging from political science, psychology and business to philosophy, physics and biography. He had a deep appetite for uncovering the secrets of what makes an ordinary man become an extraordinary leader. He hoped that books would lead him to this holy grail, so that one day he could join the ranks of the business titans. Michael now believed Harold was much more valuable than even the greats who had written the classics. He was learning firsthand from a legendary leader who had absorbed life's most important lessons.

Michael was looking forward to another one of these lessons. He couldn't quite believe a whole week had passed so quickly.

"Hi, kiddo," Harold greeted him. "I took the liberty of ordering you a coffee, along with some toast and scrambled eggs."

Michael smiled, and then got straight to business.

"Thank you. Harold. I've been looking forward to today's breakfast all week. I have very little experience in the area of leadership, even given the running of my business. I know that if I plan to grow my company into a national enterprise, I must master key concepts and their applications. I cannot think of anyone I would rather gain a perspective on the important subject of leadership from than you. From where I sit, you have mastered it."

Harold looked at Michael. He had seen the seriousness in Michael's manner the first day they had met in the diner.

"Let's begin," he said. "And I'm glad you have such a high opinion of me. But I am still mindful that I'm just a novice in this matter. My journey to understand what is involved in becoming a great leader continues. I have found that many people will be happy to tell you what leadership is. Just ask them!"

Harold and Michael shared a laugh.

"Many have made at most a couple of observations about what they consider great leaders to be. But they too often miss the mark and focus on only the external successes and trappings, not the internal motivations that have made a man a great leader. Don't get me wrong. For some, the external is very important. But to be a great leader, you need more. So much more."

Harold told Michael that to master leadership, one obviously needs to go well beyond a basic understanding of it. "We live in a very competitive, unforgiving world," Harold said before taking a bite of his eggs. "We all share in the responsibility of what this world will look like when we hand it over to future generations."

Harold added that he believed that men in today's society want what men throughout history have always wanted. They want purpose, and a chance to strive towards a greater future and a bigger piece of the pie. A great leader can give them a vision and inspire them to take a path that will accomplish this.

"Each great leader needs to have an overarching vision from which he gains strength. That vision needs to be much greater than he could ever live up to or accomplish on his own."

Michael's mind was racing as he tried to take in what Harold was telling him. He thought about how comfortable Harold was in his own skin.

"Do you believe that acceptance of oneself is the first step towards becoming a good leader?" Michael asked.

"That's part of it," Harold replied. "Leaders are also rationally objective, well read, experienced and reflective. All these qualities endow them with the ability to respond to situations calmly, not allowing emotions to distract them from reaching their goals," he said.

Harold then told Michael about his Uncle Max, one of the great mentors in his life. "He told me long ago that the defining moments of leadership are not done in public. Rather, the defining moments of leadership reside in those times of solitude when you are all alone with the weight of a decision and the only company you have is your conscience."

"Do you believe that leaders are more willing to take risks and embrace challenges than most?" Michael asked.

Again, Harold responded quickly. It was as if he were anticipating Michael's questions.

"Yes. Those who command their emotions are powerful forces of nature. Most importantly, leaders are realists. These individuals first look at the world as it is, rather than as they would like it to be. In fact, it is essential to accept the world as it is if one is going to change it to what one believes it should be.

"When I started out in business, I built my first stores off the new Interstate Highway System. That was back in the late 1950s. I knew it was a big gamble. Urban populations were just beginning to move out of crowded cities and into the suburbs. I saw my first locations for what they were—wide open fields. My first stores were in isolated areas, but I had the vision that suburbs would expand and that one day these stores would be surrounded by huge metropolitan areas populated by millions of people who would need to shop."

In Harold's view, a great leader sees the need for a reformation in thinking before there can be resolve for action. Otherwise, it does not matter how innovative an idea is; if the wider population is not ready to accept a new concept, it will not spread far from the person who came up with it. It may even die with him.

"After the Second World War, I witnessed the postwar economic and baby booms, and the quick adoption of the automobile as America's preferred mode of transportation. But the growing middle class in this country was beginning to feel frustration with the status quo. Yes, there were the economic and baby booms, but people were still living in either overcrowded cities or sparsely populated rural areas. When I opened my first Bargain Harold's, I saw the willingness of many Americans to let go of the past and embrace a future by leaving the places that generations before them had lived in. They were ready to embrace suburban life."

These Americans had wanted spacious homes, Harold noted, and the new highways that had been being built across the nation had allowed them to live farther from the areas they had been familiar with.

"One develops the traits of a visionary leader by trusting and acting on intuition," Harold explained. "Visionary leaders and entrepreneurs are society's change agents. Many people want to be led and will rarely oppose men with clear visions for change. As I've said, after the war, Americans were moving into new territory. It was a new frontier, these rural and suburban areas—and these areas did not have many services. The time was ripe for Americans to change their shopping habits. These were my potential clients. They were the people who drove the skyrocketing growth my business experienced; they're what made it so successful."

Harold admitted that he had not been born an inspiring leader. At every stage of his business's growth and his own personal development, Harold had had to resolve critical issues before he could move to the next level. To succeed, he said, one must be committed to self-growth and self-correction.

Harold then told a story to illustrate all he had been sharing with Michael:

Once there was a man who dreamed of changing the world. After a long while, he realized that he could not change the world. So he set his sights on changing his nation. Before long, he realized that he could not change his nation. After some deliberation, he decided to focus on changing something he thought he *could* change—his family. This too ended in failure.

So, since everything else had failed, he turned to the one person in the world he could change: himself. Slowly but surely, over time he began to change. What he discovered by working on himself was incredible. It was what had eluded him when he had been aiming to change the world. By changing himself, he saw that his family, his nation and his world had changed.

"Kiddo, listen carefully. If you want to be a true leader, you are obliged to think. Yes, think, and think critically! You must know where you are going and why. You must also know where you are not going and why not. You need to continually probe deep into the distance, and be eager to see what may be lurking there. You need to search tirelessly for patterns that are not immediately apparent but that indicate what lies ahead. You will need to go where you have the greatest chance of running into what you need in order to take the next necessary steps—even if you don't quite know or understand what form the future will take. Much of this will be accomplished by having a well-thought-out vision and having an authentic intent behind that vision—the belief that, with hard work and determination, you will find what you need to turn your vision into your reality."

Michael contemplated for a moment what Harold had just told him.

"From what I've read about past visionaries, it seems they operated in the world at two distinct levels," he said. "First, they operated at a high-level perspective, which gave them a big-picture view of the world. Second, they peered deep beneath the surface, to detect the flow and counterflow of underlying currents. They were perfectly comfortable shifting instantly from big picture to detail and back again."

Michael wanted to know what Harold thought about it. "Would you agree from your experience that this is the case?" he asked.

"Yes, and I will add that, as a leader, it is not enough just to convince people of your competence and courage. Leaders must have faith in their own courage and their vision in order to make that vision reality. Leaders have a story to tell. Kiddo, are you prepared to tell your business story?"

"Not yet," Michael replied. It was an honest answer. He knew that if he was not sincere with Harold and with himself, all the lessons in the world would not make a difference, even if he truly wanted to succeed.

"I am working on crafting my business story. That is one of the reasons I'm working with Richard and Mitch right now—to create a more compelling story for my business, one that will inspire potential clients, partners, investors and lenders to actively participate in, in realizing my vision. I believe that a business leader will get better results by selling an inspiring narrative than by just being a salesman making a pitch."

Harold added that he had observed that the best stories are of no value when there is no one to listen to them, or when they are presented to the wrong audience. And the larger and more diverse a group is, the more important it is that the message be simple. That allows a man to be understood by the greatest number of people.

"That is why I stick to the KISS rule: Keep It Simple, Silly," Harold said, smiling. "A true influential, visionary leader taps into and shares a stirring narrative that inspires others to become visionaries in their own right. A visionary leader takes a story that has been latent and brings new attention or a fresh twist to it. He taps into stories that get us to see well beyond the present and prompt us to take action."

"That is a really important insight. Thank you for sharing it with me," said Michael.

"Please don't thank me yet," Harold insisted. "Right now, for you, this is all theoretical. It is you who will need to make it practical and real. Visions, and thoughts, need to be communicated. British Prime Minister Benjamin Disraeli instructed us that 'with words we govern men.' And almost all visionary leaders are life learners, well spoken and literate. They must be able to express their ideas clearly so that they are simple to grasp. People learn and act more quickly when the information they're receiving relates to their own experiences. But I can only speak from my vantage point. You will need to go out into the world and form your own opinion on the subject, rather than taking my word for it."

Harold then emphasized the need to unleash the power of speech: "A visionary leader needs to be conscious that *how* he says something is infinitely more important than *what* he says. Speech is a tool for us to break down barriers and connect with others, to create and maintain relationships in a direct and meaningful way."

Harold explained that he believed that what differentiates human beings from all other animals in the animal kingdom is our ability to express our thoughts, wants, emotions and insights through language. Language binds us to others by allowing us to share our experiences, enabling others to learn from us and vice versa—without their own direct experience.

The act of speaking has the power to change how we feel, what we think and how we act in the world. Simply saying something has the power to change our world and to change the realities of those who hear our words. Speech, then, does create reality. It affects connections between two people, and between groups of people.

Harold told Michael that if he became an empowering leader, he would dramatically increase his effectiveness—if he took the time to create a well-thought-out, informed vision of the future he desired for himself and for others. Leadership also meant taking responsibility for others' lack of motivation. A leader can move the unmotivated to action by speaking about a vision and a future that is worthy of their involvement.

"I know this to be true," Michael said. "I believe that leadership is a subject that can be mastered if a man is willing to invest heavily in its pursuit. The function of a leader is to raise questions that agitate, that break through the accepted patterns and paradigms."

Harold took the last bite of his toast and finished his coffee.

"Your lesson today reminds me of something the great physicist Niels Bohr said," Michael told Harold. "'Every sentence I utter must be understood not as an affirmation but as a question.'"

Michael began to ask another question, but Harold interrupted him with a laugh.

"Hold onto that thought, kiddo," he said. "Really think about what Bohr meant and what we discussed today. And I'll see you next week."

CHAPTER 8

—⟫⟨—

REACHING GOALS

MICHAEL ARRIVED AT the diner for his breakfast with Harold. He sat at their usual table, waiting in anticipation for his first cup of coffee of the day, and for Harold, who was a few minutes late, to arrive. He had been thinking a lot about what Harold had said about visionary leaders the week before. Michael intuitively believed his business was on the cusp of something significant when it came to going national and filling a societal need. Michael knew that this need was only going to grow, and that his residence homes would help tens of millions of people. Sitting there alone in the diner, Michael smiled as he remembered what Harold had told him the previous week—about how defining moments of leadership reside in times of solitude.

Just then, Harold walked into the diner. Michael waved hello, noticing a fly buzzing and bumping with all its might against a window near the door. It wanted to get outside, but despite its ferocious effort, its attempts were futile.

"Hi, kiddo," Harold said with a grin as he saw the two coffees on the table.

"Black, just the way you like it." Michael gestured to the coffee he had ordered for Harold. "I've been thinking a lot about our chats—and anticipating today's lesson all week."

Harold could see Michael was ready to start. "Imagination is everything," he said. "It's the preview of life's coming attractions."

Michael certainly felt that his imagination was running on overdrive these days.

"Is that a saying of yours?"

Harold chuckled. "No, I wish it were. It belongs to a man so much smarter than me. Albert Einstein.

"So, where do you want to start, kiddo?"

Before Michael could answer, Harold had guessed what was weighing so heavily on his mind. "Let's first begin with the question of what your goal is, and the intent behind it," Harold said in a reassuring tone.

"I suggest you remember that a question is infinitely more powerful and important than its answer. A well-formed question presupposes that there is an answer within the framing of it. Your success is founded on your ability and willingness to frame the right questions. And to have the fortitude to go down the rabbit hole to wherever your answer takes you."

Harold continued probing. He asked Michael to look at scenarios—that is, any and all scenarios that someone might be contemplating—not as predictions but as representations of possible alternative futures that would help someone navigate from the present to his optimum future. Harold explained that the setting of goals and planning is not a science but an art. It is a disciplined way for a forward thinker to see alternative outcomes and make difficult decisions. It's his ability to do that which allows him to adapt to the complexities he finds himself facing day in and day out.

"Harold, are you saying I should question my underlying assumptions about my business?"

"Not just your business but other aspects of your life too."

That raised many more questions for Michael. What is an appropriate range of alternative scenarios? What kinds of outcomes are effected by such scenarios? How do you know which decisions are better than others? Michael knew that the answers to these questions would help him develop appropriate goals and implement the right plan to fulfill his vision.

"From experience, I have learned that little decisions can make big differences in our end results and how we see and act," Harold continued.

He pointed out that our intent and the changes we make to the underlying structure of our lives shape the outcomes in life. Our personal and professional realities begin with well-defined intentions of what we want to experience in our lives.

"It has been said that if you don't know what you want, plenty of other people are willing and able to step in and gladly decide for you," Harold pointed out.

He could see that Michael was beginning to grasp what he was telling him. Then, to illustrate his point, Harold told him the story behind the retirement 401(k) plan. It started off with a simple question in 1980 by a Pennsylvania benefits consultant named Ted Benna. He wanted to know how American executives could save more money for retirement in a tax-efficient way.

Knowing what he wanted to accomplish, Benna turned to the American Internal Revenue Code. With his question in mind, he found an obscure provision within the code, the 401(k). By knowing what he wanted to know, Benna turned the 401(k) tax provision into an all-American tax solution. Today's 401k plans are America's most popular employer-sponsored tax-deferred retirement benefit plans.

"We can all benefit by learning the approach taken by Benna when it comes to reaching our goals," said Harold. "The 401k plan would have never materialized if Benna had not known what he wanted to create, if he had not begun with the end result in mind."

Similar examples can be found in all aspects of business, science, innovation and invention.

"Did you know that Edward Lindaman, the director in charge of planning the Apollo space program at NASA, had the same experience while working on plans for the first moon landing in 1969?"

Michael shook his head.

"He found that when people create a plan by working backwards from their desired future outcome, they end up taking less time to enact the plan than they otherwise would have. As well, the method increases one's enthusiasm for the plan and develops a more realistic simulation of the challenges ahead. In fact, this planning technique launched the discipline of project management."

Harold continued to explain that project management is a formalized and structured method of managing change. Project management focuses on defining future outcomes that are achieved by allocating resources effectively. These insights can be incorporated into the planning process both in one's personal life and in business. It was a process that had been successfully applied by project management professionals since the Second World War. Harold listed off the steps involved:

Step 1: Begin with the end in mind. Clarify why you plan to do what you do. To be successful at this step, you need to identify goals and objectives. In Michael's case, he also needed to clarify financial, business and personal values and attitudes. These considerations are important in determining the best planning strategy.

Step 2: Clarify your present situation by collecting and assessing all relevant personal and financial data, such as assets and liabilities. This gives you a clear understanding of where you are now and what you have to work with. It should create a tension between what you have now and what you want, pulling you from your present reality towards your desired destination.

"It is this discrepancy that will propel you forward," Harold noted.

Step 3: Work backwards from your desired goal towards your current circumstance. Identify what needs to be done to realize your end goal. During this step, problem areas will become clearer. These potential problem areas must be identified before solutions can be found and acted upon.

Step 4: Put your intent down on paper. Write out the path you plan to take to reach your goals. What it looks like will depend on the complexity of the goals. Harold noted just how important this step is to achieving ultimate success.

"If the plan is not written down in a tangible, formal document, the plan is not real," he emphasized. Then, to hammer home the point, he told Michael, "If you don't write it down, in all likelihood you won't act upon it and it will never happen for you."

Step 5: Take action, now. A plan is useful only when it is put into play. Implementing the right strategy will help you reach your desired goals and objectives.

Step 6: Consistently go back to review your goals and plans. Understand that this process should end only when you are no longer walking on this earth.

"Life is a journey, kiddo, so make the commitment to frequently review your intent and plan. This is crucial if your aim is to be successful in all areas of life," said Harold.

"The one congruent unifier about life is change."

Harold had known from his failures—and many successes—that situations and goals should be reviewed and reassessed at least once a year to take into account any changes in circumstances.

"When I adopted this process of seeing the end result in my mind, I found that I was trusting my intuitive assessment of my reality," Harold said. "Many of the great luminaries have adopted this process, which was eloquently stated by Napoleon Hill in his landmark book *Think and Grow Rich*, published back in 1937."

Harold had read the book in Korea.

"When I read Hill for the first time, I was on the front line of the Korean War. Hill's words were a constant companion to me."

Harold remembered how one simple line from Hill's book helped him during his darkest hours of the war and then also years later in business: "Thoughts become things," he said.

People who embrace this type of thinking and make it a way of life are not seeking social approval, personal advantage or a sense of absolute truth. They are seeking to find opportunities where they can contribute most and to live with purpose.

"If there's a secret," Harold said, "it's this: the more time you spend in this process, the more impact your end result will have on your life, on the lives of those around you, on your environment and, most importantly, on your legacy."

Harold recounted the legend of Alexander the Great's Gordian knot. ·

Upon leaving Macedonia to conquer Persia, Alexander the Great recalled the legend of King Gordius. Gordius had tied his chariot with a knot to the Temple of the Zeus Basilica. According to an oracle, the knot could only be untied by the one who was destined by the gods to become the king of Persia and the known world.

Alexander went to the chariot and tried to untie the knot, but he could not. Perplexed, he stood there for a moment, staring at the knot. He then pulled out his sword and with one bold stroke slashed the knot wide open. Soon after that, Alexander went on to countless victories and became the king of Persia and the known world.

"You too have the ability to take any intractable problem you face in your life or career and find your own solution," Harold said. "But you must be bold and determined. You must slash your Gordian knot. It is up to you and only you to make this happen in your life!"

Their time for the week was almost up. Michael had a familiar feeling, the one he always had after meeting with Harold. He was excited. But more than that, he was contemplative.

"Harold, thank you. This is something I really need to think about and put into action."

Ideas began swirling in Michael's head. Harold had given him a roadmap that he could begin to use immediately. He then noticed the fly again. It still hadn't made its way out of the diner but continued to bump furiously against the window.

"I've been noticing that damn fly too," Harold said, laughing. "Sometimes we all act that way, like that fly."

Michael raised an eyebrow, curious what Harold meant.

"We grind our way forward and then hit an invisible wall—just like that fly," Harold explained. "But unlike the fly, we can pause, step back and then decide the best way to move forward to avoid hitting any hurdles. If that fly would just move back from the window, it would see that there's an open door just a few feet away. It could easily fly out if it were able to pause, think and set out a plan. And the plan—at least for that fly—is simple. It could get outside if only it could work backwards from its goal and see what needed to be done to achieve it."

Michael laughed. It was all beginning to make sense. We can be tantalizingly close to achieving our goals, then hit an invisible wall—if we continue on a path without a plan or without readjusting our perspective when circumstances change.

"I'm meeting with Mitch and Richard on Monday," Michael said. "I have decided how I want to fund my company's expansion. And now you've given me a concrete method for planning the expansion in a successful way."

"Good stuff, kiddo. I will leave you with this: it has been said that those who fail to plan, and fail to act, plan to fail. I'm glad to know that's not you."

CHAPTER 9

—≫⊁⊰≪—

THE DEBT OPTION

MICHAEL WAS SITTING in the boardroom of Mitch's law firm. It had been awhile; the two friends were catching up. Michael also wanted to speak to Richard about how he planned to expand his business.

Mitch had been excited when he walked in. "Have you heard the good news?"

"No. What?" asked Michael.

"Wendy and Dawn found two rental properties right next to each other on Mackinac Island for us and the kids this summer."

Michael nodded. "Dawn mentioned sometime back that she and Wendy were looking into it."

"Northern Michigan in the summer—can't beat that. It's going to be great," said Mitch.

"There are lots of direct flights from Midway to Pellston, so we can commute back and forth and continue working," added Michael.

"Yup. I know you wouldn't have agreed to go unless you had that option available to you. You are chained to your work. But listen, we're going on this vacation to have a good time. Before we know it, our kids are going to be all grown up and will have their own busy lives. Then we'll wish we had more times like this with them."

Michael smiled sheepishly. "I know," he said.

"I hear it's a beautiful island. You can only get there by boat. Cars aren't allowed on Mackinac Island during the summer. I think Dawn and Wendy chose this spot to make sure we would take a break from work."

"I don't know what we would do without our wives," Mitch added.

"I know if it weren't for Dawn, you would forget how to tie your shoes—not to mention weddings, birthdays and just about every other important event in life."

Michael laughed. He knew there was some truth to what Mitch said.

"On another subject, last Wednesday I was coming into the office early and I walked past that 1940s-looking diner near Daley Plaza. I saw you sitting inside. I was going to go in to say hello, and perhaps grab a cup of coffee with you, but then I noticed you were not alone but in deep conversation with an older man. It took me a moment before I recognized who you were talking with."

Mitch had a million questions about the King of Main Street.

"Harold Bloom, what's he like? Is he going to invest in your seniors' residence business? If you get him on board, imagine the crowds of investors you will have to beat off with a stick."

Michael sat quietly for a few moments.

"I will tell you, if you promise not to say anything to anyone, or bring this subject up again." He wanted to keep his early-morning breakfasts at the diner with Harold private.

"In a word, he's a real-life Yoda. You are going to have to derive your own meaning from that."

Mitch smiled at Michael's *Star Wars* reference. And that was just like Michael: he was meeting up regularly with one of the world's most successful businessmen, but he wanted to keep it private.

"You have always been a hard nut to crack," Mitch said. "I wish I could be a fly on the wall listening. Do you know how fortunate you are to have met with him? Politicians and CEOs of Fortune 500 companies have tried to get him to meet with them to give them his advice but can't get him to give them the time of day. He's been a recluse for the past decade. I know of only one person who meets with him regularly and that's Richard. He keeps his meetings very hush-hush, just like you are now."

Just then, Richard walked into the boardroom.

"My ears are burning. Were you talking about me?"

Michael and Mitch laughed.

Richard dived straight into business. "We don't have much time—and there's a lot to discuss," he said. "Michael, I am going to come right out with it and ask. Have you made up your mind about how you want to fund the growth of your company? What's your preference, will it be through debt or equity financing?"

Michael had thought long and hard about this question since he had last met Richard, three weeks earlier.

"I started my business because I felt a need to be my own boss, to chart my future and create my own destiny," he said. "I don't want to become a fractional minority owner of my own company. Not yet, anyway. So I've decided that I want to grow it through leverage, by borrowing capital to invest in its growth. Perhaps in the future we can revisit selling off some ownership in my enterprise—when I'm ready to plan my exit."

Michael also let Richard know that there was already an investor in his company. Michael didn't know who it was. Mitch had set it up, and the investor wanted to remain anonymous.

"Your exiting your business is a long time from now," said Richard. "Let's talk about the option of using good debt. All that means is that you will borrow money to increase the value of your business. The key to borrowing other people's money wisely is to know your breakeven point. That's the interest rate charged for borrowing money minus the actual return on your investment. Good debt is where the return on the investment is higher than the interest you are charged for the use of that money. The breakeven point is where these two cash-flow numbers of return intersect with the amount of interest charged. I believe your company's past and future expected growth will far exceed the breakeven point for borrowing capital."

Richard then told Michael what he believed his role and that of his firm were when it came to advising their clients. "The role we play with our clients is that of the trusted advisor," he explained. "That means being the go-to professionals—the general problem solver."

Richard noted that this requires the mastery and integration of multiple specialties. A trusted advisor can take on problems that are of larger scope, scale and complexity than those addressed by specialists.

The trusted advisor must perform well in different areas of specialization to integrate them. By definition, a specialty is special, something set apart. Fiddling with specialties so as to integrate them is how a specialist becomes a generalist. The trusted advisors who work exclusively with business owners are also members of at least one specialty area, such as law, accounting, banking or financial planning.

"As such, trusted advisors who become generalists run the risk of criticism from their colleagues for deviating from accepted practices," Richard said. "My firm prides itself on being that type of disrupter. This is because, as your trusted advisor, we continually seek to advance a practice or specialty area, not simply adhere to the current view of accepted dogma. We will work with you to look for ways to fit things together."

Richard continued to explain why his firm excelled at being a trusted advisor for clients like Michael. It tackled problems that involved specialties beyond those that their clients have mastered. The goal of every trusted advisor should be to solve the problem at hand and to engineer a solution, making the unique value proposition greater for all involved.

"Assisting in debt financing of your business is an area we happen to focus on," Richard said with pride. "Many of our business clients use leverage and choose to incur corporate debt because they believe the risk is well worth it for the upside return potential. Borrowing to invest is appropriate only for business clients who have a plan for what they will do with these monies. They have a clear reason for needing it."

He explained that, in these situations, as a trusted advisor, it is essential that his firm make clients like Michael fully aware of the risks and benefits associated with investment loans. That's because the losses, as well as the gains, may be magnified.

Mitch jumped in as his mentor paused to collect his thoughts. "We believe that any client who is contemplating the securing of an investment loan must first be willing to invest for the long term," he said. "He should not be averse to increased short-term risk."

"Over the past 40 years, I have been privileged to be a member of a team that has been involved in quarterbacking the securing of financing for our clients," Richard added. "In many circumstances, the loan component was key to implementing business growth, succession and estate-planning solutions. When my practice started evolving into this area of expertise, I could not find a primer that would help me understand all the steps involved in the process of borrowing other people's money. This was frustrating, to say the least. So we created one—and our clients themselves have found it very useful for speeding up their growth."

Mitch smiled. He then asked Michael to imagine that he had decided to buy two additional properties for his immediate business expansion. In this hypothetical scenario, Michael would need to borrow $10 million from a lender. The lending institution would want to know how Michael, as the borrower, would be able to pay for the loan. Most lenders would need to see the positive before-tax cash-flow that was being generated by his company. In this scenario, Michael's cash-flow would need to be greater than or equal to the total amount of the interest on the loan.

"When these institutions give out large loans—like the one we want—the lender may demand that they have the right to retain direct control of all cash-flows generated by a borrower," Richard noted. "Provided the cash-flow is adequate, 100 percent leveraging may be possible in your situation.

"We are going to have to talk about this more a little later, but it is common practice for the lender to require a life insurance policy for the amount borrowed. It will have to be sufficient enough to eliminate the risk to the lender, just in case of your death."

"As with any loan, the interest rate is negotiable. The interest rate can be variable, variable with an interest cap, or fixed for a period. Generally, 10 years is the maximum period for which the loan rate can be fixed. There will be additional costs for the loan as well—such as your legal fees, the lender's legal fees, setup expenses for the lender and the lender's annual review fee.

"The lender will also conduct a preliminary review and may issue a discussion paper. The discussion paper is not a letter of commitment, but a tentative summary of the terms and conditions under which the lender is prepared to make the loan. The lender will require detailed documentation for the loan, including the following:

- Three years of business financial statements.
- Individual tax and business returns.
- Tax assessments from the past three years.
- Business valuations of assets.
- Information about cash-flow before and after taxes.

"Once the discussion paper is signed, the legal and setup fees are paid to the lender. Upon completion of the legal agreements, the lender funds the loan.

"In my experience, this can all take from three months to a year after the initial application before the loan is made," concluded Richard.

He had spent a couple of hours going over detail after detail with Michael. And he could have continued for several more. But he had given Michael all the information that he needed to make an informed decision.

"That's about it," he said, getting up from the table. "I am going to suggest that in the next two weeks you and Mitch meet separately to discuss the assets and collateral that most likely will be needed to secure your business loan. You must also discuss the best method for funding the life insurance that the lender will require for the loan."

And with that, the business meeting ended.

CHAPTER 10

MONEY TRUTHS

"OVER HERE," HAROLD called out to Michael as he entered the diner. This day, Harold was sitting at one of the booths, rather than at their usual table.

"What have you been up to, kiddo?"

"I met with Richard and Mitch earlier this week," answered Michael. "I've decided that for now I want to keep control of my company by taking on debt to fuel its growth, instead of selling off equity ownership."

"Are you happy with your decision?"

Michael didn't want to say he was feeling like he was about to take on the weight of the world. But he knew Harold would see through anything but the truth.

"I'm scared," he admitted. "I know it's the right move for now. But I will be borrowing a large sum of other people's money. It's a lot of responsibility."

Harold took a hard look at his young protégé before speaking.

"Business owners are in the business of making money and expanding the economy for everyone's benefit, including their own," he said. "But do we truly have a workable understanding of what money really is and how it operates in our lives? Can we consciously choose to use its power to achieve our full potential? Finding the answers to these questions has been a preoccupation of mine since I returned from Korea."

Harold explained that he wrestled with this subject because he strongly believed that by knowing what money means, we can apply universal principles of money to guide ourselves.

"I know the importance of understanding that currency is not money," Michael pointed out.

"Yes," Harold agreed. "Currency on the surface is a medium of exchange. It circulates from one person to another in the form of paper or coins. By itself, currency has no method of retaining its value."

Harold illustrated his point.

"If we were to sit on a bench with a $100 bill for 15 years, based on the inflation rate of the past 50 years, the purchasing power of that $100 bill would have halved by the end of that 15 years," he said.

They agreed that they would define money (not currency) as assets and property that retain and increase in value over time and enhance purchasing power. As their conversation continued they delved into the deeper meaning of "currency." They agreed that currency fostered relationships with others, and that it should stimulate a productive medium of exchange. Money at its core is what we choose to trade our life energy for.

"Benjamin Franklin had it right when he said 'Time is money,'" Michael quipped. The two men shared a laugh.

"And he did not say 'Money is time,' because he understood that money can never buy our time back once it's spent," Harold added.

"Yes, I get that when we spend our time wisely, we welcome new opportunities for creating money, foster long, productive relationships and increase the value in our lives," said Michael.

"Let's talk about some distinctions you may not have yet thought of," Harold said. "Through my journey, I have found it important to understand the difference between affluence and wealth. In this context, affluence means that someone has a great cash-flow. We all know people who make a lot of money but have little to show for it. Financial wealth, on the other hand, means the ownership of both tangible and intangible assets that generate positive cash-flow and give us the ability to seek out greater meaning."

Harold then shared something that had taken him a lifetime to understand and put into words. He called them the seven principles of money.

"I wish someone had taken the time to share them with me when I was your age so that I wouldn't have had to learn them by myself the hard way," he said, before carefully explaining them to Michael one by one.

Principle 1: Do What You Love

A person who lives this principle, accepting his life's calling, is a very attractive individual. His passion for life draws in the right opportunities and people. According to physics, an action causes an equal reaction. When this principle is truly lived, the universe can't help itself but compensate you for living out your true life's purpose.

Principle 2: Know and Apply the Rules of Money

"Remember this, kiddo," Harold said as he put down his coffee. "Money—more accurately, currency—is a creation of the human mind. It is not real—at least not in a physical sense. This is key. If you understand this, you'll understand that currency and money have rules. They have many rules. It's important to know these rules so you can master them, and achieve the optimum outcome."

Harold listed the universal rules that he had learned and adhered to.

"The first rule is simple: If you want to be financially successful, spend less than you earn and invest the difference in worthwhile opportunities that grow your options and experiences. The second rule is that money goes where it can reproduce itself." Harold noted that numerous studies have shown that if you spend $100 in the poorest parts of town, soon those same dollars gravitate to richer pastures, where they can reproduce themselves faster. "Other rules that keep money flowing towards you are the rules of accounting, working efficiently within the tax codes and investing wisely."

Harold went on to explain that capitalism is a simple system of voluntary purchases and transactions among individual players in an economy. Consumers reward businesses and entrepreneurs by purchasing their goods and services, if those goods and services serve the consumers' needs and wants. For example, imagine there is a big demand for deep-dish pizza in a certain area of Chicago. An entrepreneur sees this need and decides to open a pizzeria in that area to fulfill the need. In a free-market capitalist system, the shop owner earns a profit only if he serves a need by delivering a product desired by the consumer. The consumer does not make his choice because of manipulation or coercion. He makes his decision to purchase freely, based on the expected result or end product—in this case, the deep-dish pizza.

Harold next explained a concept that few people truly understood but which economists use to measure economic growth. He told Michael how the gross domestic product, or GDP, really works.

"The GDP system places a dollar value only on economic transactions. But these transactions occur in a society that includes things such as crime, environmental disasters, war, divorce, consumption and pollution. The GDP gives no value to things such as volunteering or caring for dependents—whether young or old. It gives no value to keeping rainforests pristine or water aquifers untouched."

Harold explained that, without these valuable human activities, and if people did not protect nature from being absorbed completely by the economic system, the social fabric and environment would break down and eventually cease to function.

"The current method for calculating GDP places more value on cutting down a rainforest than leaving it alone," Harold said. "With the current method used to calculate GDP, economists assign no dollar value to keeping the rainforest in its natural state. GDP ignores that the trees sustain a robust ecosystem that produces oxygen that we all need to breathe in order to stay alive."

As Michael shook his head in dismay, Harold continued.

"The way we measure GDP right now turns cut trees into transactions—basically, a bunch of ones and zeros. That means the GDP number shows only the economic value of the chopped-down trees. It does not give any value to leaving those trees alone."

Harold then explained how currency was created in our economy through what is called the fractional reserve banking system. "Governments allow lending institutions to magically create currency out of thin air," he said.

"The currency in an economy is created through loans. Let's say, for example, that a homeowner borrows $1 million from a bank in the form of a mortgage. That million dollars didn't exist in the economy before the loan was made."

Harold used the hypothetical example of a government printing $10 billion in currency and depositing it into a bank, to show Michael fractional reserve banking in action. The government requires only that the bank keep 10 percent, or $1 billion, in its reserves. The government then allows the bank to lend out $9 billion to borrowers. The new money that is lent out needs to be deposited somewhere. So, it is deposited into another financial institution. That financial institution is required to keep only $900 million in its reserves and can lend out $8.1 billion.

This process continues until it is not possible to divide up the currency anymore when the money is lent and redeposited in authorized financial institutions. That means that at the end of this process, $100 billion has been created out of thin air and placed in the economy in the form of loans.

"The human mind is incredible," Harold told Michael. "The number of rules that apply to money are limited only by our imagination. How we choose to apply these rules is entirely up to us and how we define success."

Principle 3: Money Is a Dream

"Another key concept," said Harold, "is that money is a dream." To ensure that Michael understood this concept fully, he began by asking a couple of rhetorical questions: "Do we as a culture ever have enough? And once we achieve what we have set out to reach, are we truly satisfied?"

Harold shook his head, then explained that, for most people, the answers to these two questions is a resounding no.

"Our consumer culture teaches us that we should never be satisfied with what we have, that we should consume more, desire more and acquire more," he said.

He asked Michael to think about all the times that he had really wanted something that was out of his financial reach.

"Chances are, when most people eventually get what they thought they wanted, they aren't satisfied, and trade it in later for something shinier, brighter and newer," Harold said. "I have found that the journey towards achieving a goal is often more meaningful than actually reaching that goal."

Principle 4: Money Is a Nightmare

"We have all heard stories about someone who lives on welfare winning the big lotto," Harold said.

Michael nodded.

"A few years later, they usually find themselves with less than they started out with," Harold continued.

"The truth is," he added, "you can't keep what you have not rightfully earned. If a person is not pursuing something greater than his immediate desires, having money for its own sake may result in his living out his greatest nightmares.

"The more money one has, the more responsibility comes with it. I learned this the hard way," said Harold.

As money grows, a wise person will learn to manage it, account for it, grow it through investments, secure it or give it away. The list of responsibilities is long. Only by having a purpose beyond money can we appreciate these responsibilities, knowing they will give us the opportunity to grow to our fullest potential and leave the worthiest of legacies.

Principle 5: There Is No Such Thing as Just Giving a Gift

"You might be thinking that this is a strange principle," Harold said. "But have you ever given to a charity that you were not so keen about? From then on, it called you continuously, asking for more donations."

When you give a gift, you are either starting a relationship or maintaining one.

Principle 6: There Is No Such Thing as Receiving a Gift

The flip side of giving a gift is receiving one. The law of reciprocity helps bind society together—meaning, if I give you something of value, you will feel the urge to give me something of value in return.

"So when you receive or give a gift, you have accepted a relationship, with all its rights, privileges, responsibilities and obligations," said Harold.

Principle 7: There Is Value Beyond Money

"Yes, we touched upon this in our previous talks," said Michael when Harold had told him the seventh principle. "There are things that are infinitely more valuable and important than money, such as the unconditional love parents give their children."

The truth is that the more you give to life and to others, the more energized you will become. If we are to truly get the most out of our life's journey, it is our responsibility to find those things in our lives that refuse to have a price tag placed on them. Hold on to them with dear life, and nurture them with love. Once you've achieved this, you will be compensated in ways beyond your imagination.

As usual, the time had flown by. Michael was amazed. He had been thinking about the concept of money all his life. Now Harold had shown him yet again just how much more he needed to learn and absorb.

Harold looked at his watch. "Unfortunately, I've got to get going if I'm to make it to an appointment," he said as he reached for the check lying on the table.

Michael got to it first. "Harold, please. I've got this one." He waved the waitress over.

Harold smiled and nodded in acknowledgment. "I'm off for a few weeks, kiddo," he said. "Let's meet in a month from now, once I'm back, to continue our lessons."

"I wouldn't miss it for the world," Michael replied.

CHAPTER 11

-->>><<<--

KNOWING THE VALUE
OF YOUR BUSINESS

THE LUNCH RUSH was in full swing at the Indian restaurant Mitch had been insisting Michael try, to broaden his palate. It was a stone's throw from Daley Plaza, just close enough for Mitch to slip out of the office between his morning meetings and afternoon conference calls.

Michael had a lot on his mind about how to run his premium seniors' residences while preparing for its rapid growth. Michael was glad Mitch had set up this business lunch, as he prepared to present his growth plan to potential lenders who might provide the capital for his expansion.

"Mitch, you had mentioned the value of a prospectus," Michael said, glancing at the menu. It was filled with words he didn't know. *What the heck is "biryani"?* he wondered.

"It's not enough to create a prospectus just once; you must continually keep it up to date," Mitch said, gesturing for the busy waiter to come over.

Mitch emphasized just how important the prospectus is for a business owner. It's basically a document that allows the business owner to objectively know what his company's financials and goodwill are worth in the marketplace, by providing an unbiased overview of its valuation. The valuation is made by professional appraisers for the purpose of obtaining debt financing or selling off ownership.

An updated document of this kind prepares the business owner for either negotiating the sale of ownership or arranging leverage financing on his own terms and with realistic expectations. Mitch noted that keeping this type of document nearby provides meaningful information for the business owner and his trusted advisors, such as lawyers, wealth managers, Certified Public Accountants, bankers and Certified Financial Planners. It is also useful when dealing with potential buyers and lenders.

It also helps ensure that when it is time for the business owner to sell shares and ownership, or to secure additional leverage financing, he will get the maximum price or the best borrowing terms. The prospectus adds value to the business simply through the organization of documents and information because it creates an overall picture of the financial position of the business in the marketplace. This allows the owner to anticipate the kinds of information that prospective buyers and lenders will request. Therefore, the business owner can frame the conversation on his own terms.

The waiter arrived and Mitch could see the confusion on Michael's face.

"Do you want me to order?" he asked.

"Sure, but I am trusting you won't order anything too spicy."

"I know, I know. You're a meat-and-potatoes guy. The most exotic thing you ate growing up was a spicy hot dog at Wrigley Field."

Michael laughed because his old friend knew him so well. Mitch ordered *naan*, a South Asian bread, for the two of them to share. For himself, he ordered the extra spicy beef and vegetable *biryani*, a deeply seasoned rice dish, which he had been craving all week.

"My friend here will have the tandoori chicken and *saag* paneer," Mitch told the waiter. "Please make sure it's mild—extra mild."

He then turned back to Michael. "Don't worry," he assured him. "The spices in the *tandoori* chicken are weakened by a yogurt mixture. And the saag paneer is just cooked spinach with cheese. And they're used to customers asking for their food to be mild."

They both laughed. Mitch then continued his explanation of why it was important for a business owner to have an updated prospectus on hand. A company, he said, effectively creates its prospectus by first completing a market valuation analysis of the company's value. Businesses generally do not need a valuation every year. However, most businesses will require an independent valuation at some point, for one purpose or another.

The market valuation analysis provides the company with the following scenarios to evaluate:

- Growth fueled by a capital or debt infusion.
- Growth through acquisition and/or capital infusion.
- Growth through merging with a complementary business.
- Sale of some or all of the shares of the company.
- Sale of a division or components of the company.

Michael listened intently as he waited for the food to arrive. Mitch had worked in mergers and acquisitions, and also transitions, at his firm for more than a decade, and Michael knew he had gained valuable insights. Mitch told him that, in his experience, when clients are creating, maintaining, reviewing and revising their prospectus, they need their trusted advisors to do the following:

- Review current financial statements and projections.
- Review the current business plan and financial model.
- Meet and assess key senior management.

- Develop detailed financial projections, using researched and documented market metrics.

- Develop a detailed methodology by which financial results are calculated for the pro forma revenue and expense model, and for cash-flow and balance-sheet statements.

- Develop the company's valuation range, using standard and accepted valuation methodologies.

- Document the internal capital structure.

- Document the scenarios that express the future for the company.

Mitch had come to realize that business owners' main driver is to grow their business's income enough so that they can eventually cash out, with the biggest payday possible. But because many business owners have not done their homework, they usually do not have a realistic picture of their company's value in the marketplace.

"Seeing just how unrealistic their expectations of their business's worth in the marketplace were was a real eye-opener for many of the business owners who went through this process," Mitch shared. "So many of these business owners and their advisors need to wake up to market and demographic realities. They need some cold water thrown in their faces!"

Mitch then told Michael about a scenario that is, unfortunately, all too common.

"Let's say I'm a buyer negotiating to buy a company. I begin by having my appraiser determine the worth of a business. I'll inform the seller, 'Mr. Seller, we've reviewed your financial statements and operations, and did a thorough analysis of your industry. We've calculated the worth of your business in the marketplace and, based on this, what our buyer is prepared to offer and pay is $1 million.' But no matter what the number is, the response is usually the same."

Michael was beginning to see the importance of having a proper prospectus prepared. It was the best way to gauge what his company was worth.

Mitch continued with his example. "That's right—no matter what the figure is, sellers who do not have an up-to-date prospectus usually have the same unrealistic expectation and response, which is: 'You have got to be kidding me.'"

Michael laughed softly as he visualized the scene.

"It can get quite heated," Mitch added. "I've had sellers tell me they don't care if my appraiser is an expert in business valuations. They are adamant that they know the value of their company, which is almost always much higher than its true value, set by the marketplace. If I say it's worth $1 million, the immediate response from the owner is 'No way, it's much higher.' And he'll pull out a number like $5 million, because that's the amount his financial planner told him he needs to retire comfortably."

The food arrived. Michael could smell the spices. "Did someone forget to tell the chef to make it mild?" he asked.

Michael took a tentative bite of the saag paneer. The taste was unfamiliar, but he liked it. And, to his surprise, it wasn't spicy at all. He looked over at Mitch, who had torn a piece off his naan and was using it like a spoon to eat his curried beef.

In between mouthfuls, Mitch continued his story about the seller who had not prepared a prospectus.

"I've actually had a seller tell me to stick it where the sun doesn't shine because the valuation did not meet his unsubstantiated expectations," he said.

"As they say, the first step to recovery is to admit you have a problem," joked Michael as he started in on the tandoori chicken. He was relieved to discover that its red coloring didn't mean it was extra hot. "It's tasty. Good choice," he said.

Mitch smiled at Michael in agreement.

"As one of your business advisors, my job and that of my firm is to help you create corporate value," Mitch said. "We want to make sure you won't suffer a life-threatening shock when you try to borrow or raise money, or—eventually—sell your business."

"What you're saying is I might have great revenue but that does not in itself translate into the company's true value, as seen in the marketplace," Michael said, beginning to comprehend the big picture.

"You got it. As I mentioned, part of the solution for you as the business owner is to submit to a corporate self-diagnosis from the perspective of a potential buyer or lender. You can do this by creating your own prospectus."

"This makes complete sense," Michael concurred.

"As a business owner, I accept this truth. At a certain point, the final customer I will have is the purchaser of my business when I retire. The value of my company will not be determined by me but by the marketplace and ultimately the buyer—that's all."

Mitch nodded, adding that risk is the prime determinant in valuing a business. "Let's now consider corporate risk and what is included in its composition," he said.

"From what I understand, business owners, lenders and investors segregate risk into specific corporate risk, economic risk and industry risk," said Michael.

"That's true. But for our purposes, we are including these risks under one umbrella. Within a business there are controllable factors, which we term your "company-specific risks." The other terms—"industry risk" and "economic risk"—are self-explanatory. These are the risks in the particular industry or in the general economy that affect the business owner's company and may be outside his control."

Mitch used an example of a trucking company to illustrate general economic and specific industry risks it could face. He asked Michael to imagine that there was a recession in the economy and the company was transporting less. "If fuel costs go up, the company's margins will shrink. That is economic risk," he said. "Industry risks, on the other hand, are things such as increased government regulations. In this case, they could be related to transporting goods across borders designed specifically for the trucking industry.

"Company-specific risk has to do with the business. For example, the age of the trucking fleet will have an effect on the capital expenditures in the near future."

"Many risks, whatever they may be, might not be in my direct control as a business owner," confirmed Michael. "However, my preparedness for them directly affects the risk inherent in my business, my industry and the economy. This readiness allows me to mitigate and lessen these risks if the economy is going into a recession."

"Let's talk about your specific scenario," Mitch said. "You are aiming to grow your business, so we have to ask if you have the right strategies to take market share from competitors. Are you well capitalized so that you can acquire struggling competition cheaply? What if there's a recession—can your company emerge from it as more valuable? Is your industry transitioning to new technologies? Have you identified untapped markets? These are just some of the many questions that your growth plan in your business prospectus must address."

Mitch explained that the corporate risk is in the range of 3 percent to 30 percent. "Realistically, higher-end corporate risk can be infinite," he said. "But in most commercial transactions right now, the value of a business is between 2.5 times and 7.7 times its income, not considering growth assumptions."

Mitch then gave another example of a company's financials. If its income is approximately $5 million, it can be assumed to be worth between $12.5 million and $38.5 million. Let's say it's worth $12.5 million in the marketplace. The business owner is given two options to grow the value of his company. He reinvests his $5 million of corporate income for one year by choosing either:

Option A: Doubling corporate income to $10 million

or

Option B: Reducing corporate risk by 25 percent

"Which option do you think yields the greatest one-year return on investment?" asked Mitch.

"Option A," answered Michael.

"At first glance, you might think so. The income increase of Option A would bring the business value to $25 million, a 250 percent ROI. The risk reduction of Option B would bring the business to a value of $33.5 million, a 420 percent ROI. Option B would yield a greater ROI of $8.5 million over Option A in this example. Now ask yourself, which is easier to do: increase revenue enough to double income in a year, or improve what you already have by reducing your corporate risk?"

"I like to control costs, so I would go with decreasing risks. But growing revenue is a close second," Michael replied.

Mitch had to get back to the office. As they were getting up to leave, after Mitch had paid the bill, Michael remembered something his wife had mentioned to him the night before.

"Dawn told me we are getting together with you and Wendy on Saturday night, to go out to dinner without the kids," he said.

A smile came across Mitch's face. "Yes, they want to plan out our summer vacation at Mackinac Island," he said.

"This time it's my turn to treat and choose the restaurant. I'll make the reservations at a good old-fashioned Midwestern steakhouse." Michael smirked.

"Perfect, we're on."

"See you and your beautiful wife at Gene & Georgetti at eight, then."

CHAPTER 12

---><<<---

KNOW YOUR ETHICS

"WE HAVEN'T SEEN each other for some time. Why the long face, kiddo?" asked Harold when he met up with Michael at the diner.

"I have a lot weighing down on me," Michael replied. "I'm feeling the pressure. I know that I need to grow my business to achieve my goals. At the same time, I must do it right, and in a manner that will match my values. Plus, I have to satisfy the expectations of both potential lenders and future investors. I need them to see the business's intrinsic value as clearly as I do."

Harold understood how Michael was feeling. He had been there himself many times.

"Over the last few breakfasts, I have alluded to the importance of knowing your values and protecting your ethics," he said. "We should have addressed this earlier. But there's no time like the present. Today is as good as any for us to dive into this subject."

A look of relief came across Michael's face. Not many people could understand the pressure he was under. Harold had been in the trenches and had come out alive. He was one of those rare individuals who not only understood Michael, but also could impart to him invaluable wisdom earned through his hard-won experience.

"I would like that," replied Michael.

"Perfect, let's begin," Harold said.

"Many organizations these days require their members to sign off on a code of ethics. The question I have often asked myself is, can a code of ethics be imposed on someone from external forces, or does it need to be found inside oneself? I have often wondered if a man would be happy if he had all the money in the world but had lost his family, friends and community because he had compromised his ethics. Knowing how to act ethically in whatever situation we find ourselves is not knowledge we were born with; it's something we learn through living and becoming more honest with ourselves."

"My father, unfortunately, did not live long enough to teach me everything he knew," Michael confided. "But *before he died, he told me that he didn't have much in the way of money or other worldly goods to give me. I was going to have to go after my goals myself. But what he had to give me was something much more valuable: a good name and a strong work ethic.*"

"Michael, I would have liked to have known your father. He sounds like a good man," said Harold.

Michael shared a look with Harold. It was the first time Harold had called him "Michael" instead of his usual "kiddo."

"Thank you, Harold. I appreciate that, especially coming from you. It means a lot hearing you say that. Looking back and learning more about my father's life, I truly believe he was one of the good guys. He was a part of what they now refer to as America's 'greatest generation.'"

It had been a long time since Michael had smiled while thinking of his late father.

Harold smiled also and asked, "Have you asked yourself if you are conscious of what your core values are? Are you game for a little exercise on how to flush out your value system?"

"Sure," responded Michael.

Harold proceeded to share that, over the years, he had discovered the importance of becoming conscious of one's values, and to then prioritize them.

"Let's put this to the test," Harold suggested. "Your exercise today is to write down what you value most. Then rewrite that list in order of importance to you."

It seemed like a simple exercise. But it took Michael a good 30 minutes to make his list. Harold didn't mind. He was content to read his copy of *Moby Dick* in the meantime. When Michael was done, he read his prioritized list of values to his mentor. It was the first time Michael had summarized his value system out loud. Not only that, but he realized it was also the first time he had become conscious of his value system.

Michael's Value Manifesto

1. I believe in living in truth, because when there are no lies, a man is not beholden to anyone or anything. He is then congruent with everything he does. The truth empowers him to do what is right and just. This allows him to take on ever bigger challenges in his life.

2. I believe change and success happens explosively and exponentially in one's life. To fully appreciate success, one must make the conscious commitment, prior to achieving that success, to become mentally, emotionally and spiritually prepared, so one will fully appreciate the success.

3. I believe in the importance of health. As long as I am healthy, the universe is open to me.

4. I believe that I should strive for personal control of my destiny. That will only come after I have taken complete ownership of

my own life, attitudes, dreams, hopes and actions. Life is not a dress rehearsal! If it is to be, it is up to me!

5. I believe my happiness and success in my life will be based on the quality of my relationships with others. Less is more. Quality is better than quantity. Depth not breadth.

6. I believe in living with appreciation for all that has been brought into my life and will enter my life. This is not just about the big triumphs; it's about the little things as well. Every day I say "please" and "thank you." I understand that life is a gift and that each experience, whether good or bad, is a part of the journey. I expect to get true value from this ride called life. By using "please" and "thank you," and practicing forgiveness, I have come to understand that these habits allow me to travel forward and are a powerful force in my life and the world around me. The purpose is to be an agent of good.

7. I believe that if money can solve a problem, it was not a problem to begin with.

8. I believe life is too short. A man should find balance with family, friends and work in a synergetic way. This way he can get the most out of the human experience. As the adage goes, "Don't sweat the small stuff, because in the end, it's all small stuff."

9. I believe in ongoing planning and continually putting my plans into action. Only then can I turn my dreams into my living reality.

10. Money to me is something I choose to trade my life energy for. I place no limit on that energy. Nor will I let outside influences and forces place a limit on me either.

11. I choose the role money plays in my relationships with others. It is to foster creative, stimulating and productive

exchanges. If not everyone in a relationship wins, it is not a relationship I want to be in. I believe true power is having the ability to choose my relationships and associations.

12. I believe that we should all strive to play a great financial offense in how we earn our living and to play an equally good defense in how we store our wealth, directing it towards achieving greater good.

Harold had been nodding approvingly as Michael read out his list.

"Bravo! Bravo! Bravo!" Harold applauded, then said, "Remember, it is one thing to be conscious of what you say you value. It is completely something else to always live up to those values. I, unfortunately, have disappointed myself on more occasions than I can count. What is important is to always aspire to the ideal and to never stop working towards it. We might be human, but that is no reason not to strive for the best."

"How did you deal with not living up to what you valued and believed was important?" Michael asked.

"That is a great question. I learned not to be too hard on myself and to move on after my missteps. I would promise myself that I'd learn from my mistakes and work my hardest to avoid making the same ones again."

To illustrate, Harold told Michael a story. One day, a man who was walking home turned down a familiar street. Oddly, this man always fell into the same deep hole whenever he was on that street. For some reason, he was always blind to it. He always managed to pull himself out of the hole and limp home, but not without cuts and bruises.

The man experienced this day after day after day. He always turned onto the street with the big hole, and without fail he always fell into it.

Finally, he made a decision that changed his life forever, and for the better. He decided to take another street home.

"One of my favorite quotes is from the late English Lord Justice of Appeal John Fletcher Moulton," Harold said. "He stated that the essential test of one's ethical behavior is 'obedience to the unenforceable.'"

"Does that mean one's willingness to go beyond the law and even the spirit of the law to do what is ethical and just?" asked Michael.

Harold nodded.

"How will I know what the right path is?" asked Michael.

"You have probably noticed that I find it best to make my point by telling a story, instead of just making the point."

"I have noticed that," Michael said, smiling.

Harold shared the story of the old Cherokee warrior. This warrior observed that his grandson, a high-spirited adolescent, was tense and anxious. The boy told his grandfather about his internal turmoil, mournfully describing the angst he felt over the discrepancy between what his parents and tribe had told him was right and wrong and what he desired. He wanted to have fun and be free of the shackles of his elders' expectations.

His grandfather reflected and then told the boy he had felt the same way when he had been his age. He told his grandson that he, like all human beings, had a battle that raged within him. The old warrior described it as a battle between two wolves. One wolf is good and brings us joy, peace, love, respect, humility, truth, generosity, compassion, faith and wisdom. The other wolf is evil and brings us anger, envy, greed, jealousy, hatred, arrogance, selfishness, false pride, self-possession, superiority, detachment from others and lies.

The boy thought about this for a moment. He then asked his grandfather, "Which wolf wins the battle?"

"His grandfather answered, 'The one you feed,'" Harold said, wrapping up his story.

Michael thought on this story and Harold's previous one for a moment. Then he shared that in his last year of high school, he had been assigned to read Robert Bolt's play *A Man for All Seasons*.

"All these years later, its theme has stuck with me," said Michael.

He recounted how this play was based on the real life and death of Sir Thomas More, the chancellor of England during King Henry VIII's rule. The king broke England away from the Roman Catholic Church, creating the Church of England. This allowed him to divorce Catherine of Aragon and marry Anne Boleyn. This was something that did not fit with what Thomas More believed. He refused to go along with the king and would not be moved by bribes or threats. Because of this, More was convicted of treason—and eventually executed—for not giving his outright consent to the king's actions. Before the verdict came down, More put it simply: "No temporal man may be head of the spirituality."

"I have always believed that the meaning of these words was that authentic truths are eternal and they are not at the discretion of men," said Michael.

Harold had been in similar situations during his long ascent through life. He quipped that this was why he was a fan of Emiliano Zapata, one of the leaders of the Mexican Revolution, who once said, "I'd rather die on my feet than live on my knees."

Michael laughed. "The reason Bolt's play has stuck with me all these years is because it portrays More as a principled man who would not yield in his beliefs simply for the pleasures of physical comforts and social acceptance. He died for his principles," he said.

"A lesson for the ages," Harold added.

Harold told Michael not to expect his having high standards to make him popular. Excellence did not come for free, not in this day and age, where fame, wealth and expediency were valued.

"I have learned this the hard way, kiddo," Harold shared. "On my trip through this life, I've been cut and scarred on many occasions while striving to achieve the highest standards without compromising what I knew was just and right. You are on your way to discovering this yourself."

"So what you are saying is that a good way to live ethically is to think long term as I make my way through life, including my career choices?" Michael asked. "That I should at all times take the long view in considering my actions and behavior?"

"Yes, you are beginning to see the bigger picture. I have learned that one might find acting in the moment beneficial in the short term.

But without weighing the consequences, one may be mortgaging one's future," Harold answered.

"I want to live an ethical life," Michael said emphatically. "I know that requires living by high standards, because nothing else will satisfy my desire to get the most out of life. This, I believe, is what my father was trying to communicate to me that time at the museum. I was just too young to understand that at the time."

Harold told Michael that if he chose this route through life, it would mean making a conscious choice not to tolerate immoral behavior and low standards—not from himself or anyone around him.

"Are you prepared to let everyone know that you won't allow yourself to be associated with low standards and immorality?" asked Harold.

Michael said that he was beginning to understand why his values and ethics should not be compromised by anyone—not by his colleagues, not by his lenders, and not by investors, employees or clients. And most importantly, not by himself.

"By no one," said Michael.

"Good," said Harold. "It is said that you are what you eat—and that you are seen to be that which you associate with or what you permit."

As their lesson came to an end Michael remembered a line from Shakespeare's *Twelfth Night*: "Be not afraid of greatness: Some are born great, some achieve greatness, and some have greatness thrust upon them."

"I could not have said it better," Harold said with a laugh. "I would add that you can't put anyone else in charge of your morals. Remember the words of President Harry Truman: "The buck stops here!" You have to take total ownership of and responsibility for the choices you make, and not blame others or circumstances for what you do or don't do. Your conscience is your greatest guide to living a life based on your ethics, values and vision."

Michael could not believe another breakfast with Harold was almost over. The time had flown by. As usual, over a simple meal of coffee, toast and scrambled eggs, Harold had given him a lifetime of advice to contemplate. And then Harold surprised him.

"I want to say thank you, Michael."

"You're thanking *me*?" Michael asked, slightly astonished.

"You have made me think of my own father. We did not have much to say to each other. But one thing he did instruct me when I was young and more daring than he liked was this: 'Don't do anything you would not be proud of if it was written about in the *Chicago Tribune*.'"

CHAPTER 13

IDENTIFYING THE NEXT STEPS

IT WAS TIME for Michael and Mitch to have their regular meeting with Richard. Every single one of these meetings was important, but this one had an added significance. It would focus on their progression in preparing Michael's company for its next steps in its growth and development. Richard hadn't yet arrived in the boardroom, so the two of them used the time to recap the weekend.

"That was a great steak dinner," Michael said, almost salivating at the thought of the 16-ounce tenderloin he had ordered at Gene & Georgetti.

"Wendy couldn't believe how quickly you got it down your gullet—and that you were able to walk out of the restaurant still standing," Mitch said, laughing as he remembered the scene.

"You're funny. My ribs are starting to hurt from your wise cracks. Funny guy, I thought you were a lawyer, not a stand-up comedian. You might be in the wrong line of work," Michael said, smirking. Then he added, "Dawn and I are really looking forward to this summer. I mean, can you beat summer at Mackinac Island with our families? It's tough enough finding quality time together these days, but to be able to share it with your closest friends …"

"You're not going to believe this," Mitch said, shaking his head, "but I heard Wendy making bets with Dawn on the phone yesterday."

"Bets?"

"They're actually betting on which one of us will be ready to climb the walls first and try to escape back to Chicago to work."

"Say no more," Michael said knowingly. "Dawn thinks I work too much and that I have tunnel vision. Sometimes she tells me that my business is the other woman in my life. But now I'm trying harder to find balance with family and work, to be there more for her and the kids. I don't really know what I would do without them. I'm hoping our summer vacation will show them they are my rock. I work as hard as I do so that we can afford to spend quality time together, like we are planning to do this summer."

"I know that, and so does she," said Mitch. Then he got down to business. Mitch wanted more details about what Michael and Harold were meeting about. But Michael had already said the topic was off limits. Mitch persisted anyway.

"I have to know," he said. "What is Bloom like at those early-morning breakfasts you're always having at that diner?"

"Mitch, we spoke about this already."

"I know, I know. I'm not supposed to ask. I can't help but think how your surreptitious breakfasts with Bloom are like the times you used to sneak off in college to volunteer at that seniors' residence. You never said a word—not a peep. And in the end, you built a successful business around that volunteer experience."

Michael understood Mitch's curiosity. "Okay, I will tell you this," he said. "I can't put it into words, really, but I believe Mr. Bloom is preparing me for something big."

"Does it have anything to do with your business?"

"I don't know what it is, not yet. I think he has something much bigger and bolder in mind for me. But I can't put my finger on it."

Now Mitch was even more curious, but just then Richard walked into the boardroom. He shook Michael's hand.

"Mitch has been keeping me in the loop about your progress, Michael," he said, sitting down at the head of the table. "I understand that the two of you have been working hard to put together a prospectus we can take to potential lenders. Simply put, that is great progress!"

"It has been a full physical and mental workout running the day-to-day operations while planning to expand the company into its future facilities," said Michael.

"I understand. Okay, let's begin, boys," Richard declared. "First things first. Your prospectus should help us communicate how your business can easily grow in a practically competitor-free environment. I mean, you'll have to explain your plan of building off the Interstate Highway System, near small cities and towns with aging populations.

"It must identify your market niche and show how it has not been well developed, or been overcrowded by competitors. This document needs to show the potential lender or investor that you're in an untapped market space, with the opportunity for highly profitable and groundbreaking growth for those who have the courage to step forward and take the plunge with you."

"As trusted advisors who assist with the creation of this type of document," added Mitch, "we have learned that having a well-defined prospectus frees up our time, so we can find the right partners. By that I mean partners to form deep relationships with. These relationships done right earn greater income for everyone, income that will power growth for the business owner, with far less effort in the future."

"Party now or party later," agreed Michael. "I have always been a firm believer in putting in the time and hard work up front so that eventually I can enjoy the benefits of that groundwork later on."

"Plus, having this document in place will allow us to quickly identify qualified potential lending partners for your venture's growth," Mitch said.

"Look, here's the upshot," Richard said. "Basically, a good prospectus will allow you to present information about your company in such a way that it answers any objections investors or lenders may have, before they even ask the question. Remember, people pay for value when that value has been demonstrated to them. They will be willing to pay a premium in order to participate in turning a well-crafted vision into a living, profitable reality."

Michael understood this. "As a business owner, I've learned that a financial asset is something that puts money in the pockets of the business, with minimum labor. For example, a business can buy a car. But a car cannot buy a business. Therefore, a car is not an asset but a liability. This is because, in most cases, the value of a car depreciates the moment you drive it off the lot. The exception to this rule is if you are in the business of buying and selling cars, that is, to earn a profit. Liabilities are things that take money out of my business's pocket."

"You're right, and that leads us to another area we need to address," said Richard, "which has to do with the stage your business is at in its development. Companies are like human beings. They are born, they reach adolescence and then they grow into adulthood. And, unfortunately, most at some point begin to decline and eventually cease to exist. Companies fail because they are not built to last. Their founders did not invest enough in putting into place a sustainable infrastructure."

Richard continued to clarify that there are four ways in which individuals can choose to make a living. They can be an employee, working within a business system. They are a cog in the wheel, so to speak, and are replaceable. At the next stage are the self-employed. They are the business system. If they stop working in their business, the business doesn't make money and fails.

"This is where you are now in your business-development stage, Michael. We need to work to get you to the next level," he said pointedly.

Michael told Richard that because he had grown up in a working poor family and become an entrepreneur, he had a clear perspective on what differentiated an employee mindset from that of an entrepreneur. He had discovered that most people with an employee mindset fear not having a weekly paycheck, whereas many who are self-employed fear having only one source of income.

"That is a keen observation. We want to get you to the third level, where you own and operate a business system and where your business runs by itself. Many who are self-employed are mistaken, believing they own a business system, but really what they have created is just a job. You will own a true business system when it makes money even when you are not actively involved in the day-to-day running of it. That's the third level, and as I said, you're not there yet. We are all working together towards getting you to that stage," Richard said.

Michael loved Chicago. His hometown had given him his sense of place. It was where he had grown up; it was home. It was at the center of many of his memories, and of his business successes. But then he thought about the cold, windy winters. He liked the thought of delegating responsibility so that he had more time to enjoy himself with his family and community. Perhaps by creating a business system he could take up a hobby other than work.

"That sounds like a great idea," he said. "Maybe one day I won't have to worry about the day-to-day running of my company. I'll be able to live anywhere I want, maybe relocate to the West Coast and enjoy golf in December. Try doing that in Chicago's cold winters!"

Mitch interjected to say that highly successful individuals often make a lot of money, yet fall short of their true potential. "I see it all the time," he said. "They lose it all, or they fail to grow their business properly to reach *its* full potential. Most entrepreneurs like you, Michael, have everything tied up in their companies. Everyone is focused on planning for their business—their banker, their lawyer, their CPA, their CFP and other financial advisors. But who plans for the business owner? You need shrewd financial planning that will separate your company from your personal interests, needs and wants."

"Michael, Mitch is absolutely correct," Richard said. "Growing your business by building it on a sturdy foundation and with the right structure will give you financial freedom, with many advantages and benefits when it comes to your financial affairs. This is the beauty of the American democratic republican capitalist system. This is why our country is envied and emulated by the people of the world."

Calculated risks, creativity and the fortitude to do something on one's own, Richard told Michael, is well compensated in such a system. This had been the American way since its founding, and America's promise to each of its citizens. If you work smart and work hard, you will be handsomely rewarded. Richard explained how the brilliant incentives found within the tax codes worked to remunerate entrepreneurs who chose to become builders of the economy.

As an employee, the equation for earning an income goes much like this:

- You earn.

- You're taxed.

- You get to spend what is left over.

If you're a business owner in America, the US government allows you to adopt a much more favorable equation for earning and spending your income:

- You earn.

- You spend and/or income-split and/or defer your taxes.

- You are taxed on what is left over, usually at a favorable tax rate.

As economy builders, business owners are treated differently from everyone else in a free market capitalist system.

"That's true for many reasons," Mitch said, "but a big reason is that the tax code favors people who work for themselves."

The biggest expense business owners pay in a year is taxes. Reducing taxes legally is not only not unethical, it is smart. Michael had understood this intuitively. He had three easy rules that he followed in order to keep money in his own pocket so that he could do greater good. Both Richard and Mitch listened intently as Michael recounted these rules:

1. Find the right business structure so that the business pays the least amount of tax possible and that what you have built is protected.

2. Learn to make more money by using wise tax strategies that have been applied in the past and are being used in the present. Always be on the lookout for new and innovative strategies. Hire only the smartest and most creative trusted advisors to implement these strategies and solutions.

3. Pay less tax legally and sleep well at night.

"These are areas we will investigate with you, and we can assist you in implementing them for your company and for yourself," Richard said.

"We are going to bring in other professionals to advise you in developing your strategies and come up with new ones. You have built a well-run and successful business. Once you have gone through this several times, you will have honed your skill at identifying other well-run business systems and know when to invest your money in them and when to avoid troubled ones. This is the fourth and last way that a successful entrepreneur earns and increases his wealth."

"I know why I'm here," Michael acknowledged. "The experience your firm brings to the table is not *expensive*. It is *priceless* to a business owner like me."

Richard smiled. He had seen too many business owners hit a wall or outright fail because they did not want to learn or integrate new information and ideas. He was glad to see that Michael "got it."

"I'm excited about the future," Michael said as they wrapped up the meeting. "I'll keep you updated on the development stages of my business as it progresses. That way I can be sure that I have all the information I need to make successful decisions."

CHAPTER 14

—➤➤➤❮❮❮—

WHAT IS YOUR UNIQUE VALUE PROPOSITION?

MICHAEL HAD BEEN meeting with Harold for several months, and he was making good headway with his business plan, with Richard and Mitch's help. He had been spending a lot of time developing a thorough prospectus to raise money, a prospectus that would be used to expand his retirement homes and senior care facilities. He was now zeroing in on the value proposition that he would use to take his company to the next level. He had also been thinking about what Richard had said about creating a self-sustaining business system. He knew there was a growing need in his industry, and he envisioned being the nation's premier provider, serving seniors across the country. A tsunami of aging baby boomers was coming, and he wanted to be ready to provide proper care when they retired almost en masse in the first few decades of the 21st century.

At their meeting that morning, Michael didn't even wait for Harold to take the first sip of his coffee before diving in with his questions.

"Harold, I have been wondering this for some time now. How did you stay encouraged? How did you remain positive in those early days when you were building Bargain Harold's? There must have been so many naysayers and forces working against you. How did you carry on implementing your vision?"

Harold took a long pause to think about Michael's questions.

"Perhaps with age I have become set in my ways," he finally replied. "In the early days, it all came down to trial and error. But I was led by the vision that I would eventually overcome all the obstacles standing in my way, that I would revolutionize the American shopping experience. It's like we discussed earlier.

"Look, Michael, I had a plan, and I knew what I valued. I have discovered that a person who is conscious and stays true to his core values and mission is a very attractive person indeed. Yet, these individuals are rare."

Harold reflected on his statement for a moment. He then restated a concept that they had discussed during a past breakfast. Harold explained that once an individual truly knows himself by accepting who he is, he has to believe that the right business relationships, customers and opportunities will show up in his life when needed.

"Those things happen at just the right time, when they are needed most," Harold said.

He felt that when he stayed true to his vision, an invisible hand would guide him to circumstances and his success. But when he went off course, that's when things would begin to disintegrate and mayhem ensue. Things got back on track only once he returned to the path leading him towards his goals.

"The question you are really asking me now is 'How do you get people to share your core values and vision?'" said Harold.

That is exactly right, thought Michael.

"How do you do that?" he asked. "I really want to know. I need to know."

"The quick answer is you can't," his mentor replied. "It's impossible. But here's what you can do. You can find those people who are predisposed to sharing your values and purpose. Attract and retain them. Let go of those who don't or won't share your vision. When you stay true to your core values and your authentic purpose, the right people will show up, at the right time and at the right place. The same holds for circumstances. The universe works in mysterious ways, as they say. I promise you that it will both surprise you and defy all reason."

Men who are self-actualizing, Harold explained, are aware of the unique value they bring to their environment and to the world. Each one of us has a unique value proposition to offer. But not everyone is able to recognize and appreciate our value. Indeed, it's the rare person who can immediately recognize a unique value proposition, and when he does, he acts upon it. Others may not recognize it at first. But through time and experience, they will eventually come to see it and then act upon it. But there will be times when someone will never see the value in another, no matter how much time passes or how much is done to try to prove it.

"Have I told you the story of George?" Harold asked.

"No, I don't think so."

"It's a story that beautifully illustrates this concept of knowing your unique value proposition. The fact is, the right people pay for your value when you know your worth and will not accept anything less. Back in the early 1960s, a CEO of a multimillion-dollar business wanted his company's logo to be redesigned to express the values the company stood behind. He visited more than a dozen design studios, but none of them could come up with a logo that truly expressed what the CEO had in mind.

"After several months of what was turning into a futile search, he was directed to a boutique studio. It had a reputation for its design 'miracles.' The CEO decided to visit it for himself. When he arrived, he was met by the marketing team, which asked him what he was looking for. As soon as the CEO explained his vision, the vice-president of marketing quickly responded, 'This sounds like a job for George.' He then picked up the phone and asked George to come into the room.

"George had been the head of the studio's design department for over 20 years. He listened intently as the CEO described what he wanted in the new logo, the message he wanted it to convey.

"The CEO watched as George pulled out his sketchpad," said Harold. "It didn't take George long. He was done in just a couple of minutes. He then showed the CEO the rough sketch. The CEO took one look at it and jumped up in amazement.

"The sketch was exactly what the CEO had been looking for. The sketch reflected the values that best described his company. The CEO asked George how much it would cost for the logo. George replied, '$100,000.'"

Michael raised an eyebrow.

"That was the CEO's initial reaction too," Harold remarked. "He thought the asking price was crazy. The CEO told the marketing team that he had watched the entire process with his own eyes. It had taken George only two minutes, he said.

"George turned to the CEO and calmly replied, 'It took me 20 years to learn and master the skill to draw your logo in those two minutes.' George had put a lifetime's worth of experience and talent into those two minutes. In that moment, the CEO understood George's expertise and acknowledged that the price was fair.

"That CEO was me. That day, George taught me an essential lesson in value. He was to become one of my great mentors in life and in business. I have come a long way in my belief system since I neglected to see or understand the true value of a man and to appreciate what he had spent a life time learning and mastering."

At that moment, Michael understood his mentor a little better. Harold's experiences had taught him the meaning behind value, that which comes only with life experience.

"Son, you are asking the same type of questions I was asking myself at the beginning of my career. Back then, I believed that the world was falling apart around me. When I thought I might not meet my goals, I reminded myself of the story of Nehemiah."

Michael smiled. "Harold," he said, "your stories are always relevant and they perfectly illustrate your points, setting me in the right direction."

"You are beginning to know me well," Harold said with a smile that was followed by a laugh. "Just the name Nehemiah is enough to give me the strength to stay the course, to achieve my life goals, no matter what obstacles are in front of me. Nehemiah reminds me that the important things in life are not easy but that they are worthy of our efforts."

Michael recalled the name from a biblical story but was unsure what Nehemiah had done or why he was significant.

"Who was Nehemiah?" he asked point-blank.

Harold liked the directness of his young student and told him that Nehemiah was from the Old Testament. Michael had been right.

"It's the most inspirational biblical story of them all for me, and it best illustrates the point I am making in today's lesson," Harold said by way of introducing the tale.

Nehemiah's story begins in Persia around 446 BC. He held a key position as the king's royal cupbearer and advisor. One day, Nehemiah met up with some travelers from Jerusalem who were visiting the palace. They told him that the city of his forefathers had fallen into disrepair. His heart filled with sadness upon hearing this. For many days afterward, he couldn't eat or sleep, nor could he stop thinking about Jerusalem. Seeing the state Nehemiah was in, the king asked, "Nehemiah, why have you been so sad these last few days?"

Nehemiah explained that he had learned that Jerusalem had fallen on tough times, and that he wanted to do something to help it. The king honored Nehemiah for his loyal service by giving him permission to move to Jerusalem, where he would serve as the governor of Judea. Upon his arrival, Nehemiah began to survey the city secretly at night. He then formed a plan for its restoration, a plan that would be practical while also being innovative. And he wanted it to unite the people of Jerusalem.

Nehemiah saw that there were great holes in the city's walls. He decided that fixing the walls was the project that would unite his people and begin the restoration of the city. So Nehemiah went before all of Jerusalem and proclaimed that he and all who would join him would work to fix the walls. This, he announced, would begin the rebirth of Jerusalem and unite its people.

Some of the residents saw the value of what Nehemiah planned to do and joined him in his efforts right away. Others were ambivalent, and some even felt threatened by Nehemiah's goal. "Nehemiah, you are crazy! It can't be done. Why even bother to try?" they asked, with some simply laughing at his grand plan.

Nehemiah's reply was to simply restate his goal. He wanted to fix Jerusalem, its spirit, by restoring first its walls. He did not let his critics deter him; he remained focused on his goal. His vision was more than about the walls: he wanted to resurrect an entire people. But he had powerful forces and foes working against him. There were many who had a vested interest in keeping Jerusalem in disrepair. Those negative forces tried to sabotage his and his supporters' worthy mission. But Nehemiah would not let them discourage him or his supporters in this goal. In fact, these obstacles they faced made them even more determined to reach the goal. When he thought of all those who supported his goal, he knew that the goal was much greater than any one person.

He was so determined, most of his critics soon realized they wouldn't be able to deter him. He was going to fix the city walls with or without them. But some of his critics wouldn't let up. They kept calling on him to halt the work. Some even suggested a meeting to discuss their differences. But Nehemiah saw no need in meeting with people whose aim was to distract him from his goal. He remained focused. His supporters also remained steadfast in their belief in the importance of the vision. While faced with brutal opposition, many had taken great personal risk, but they still used all their skills, might and unyielding determination to get the job done. The project was completed just six months after Nehemiah had first publicly voiced his goal.

"It is critical for us to set goals that are greater than ourselves, goals that inspire and unite others, and result in accomplishments that live on for generations to come," Harold said. "But understand that although there will always be people who support us in achieving our goals, there will always be others who are threatened by them. Those people may at first try to discourage us, and then they may attack us. After they come to terms with the fact that we cannot be put off our chosen path, they may pretend to have accepted our goals. But don't be fooled. Their real aim is to distract and destroy us—however misguided this might be."

Michael nodded that he understood. The moral of the story was burned into his brain: he should never allow himself to get distracted from his goals, values and vision. He would remain focused, vigilant and committed until he turned his vision into his living, breathing reality.

"I will always appreciate, honor and show my gratitude to those who support me on my journey towards my goals," he said.

"Nehemiah," Harold said softly, ending the week's lesson with Michael.

CHAPTER 15

---❯❯❮❮---

EVERYONE NEEDS TO
BE PROTECTED AT A
REASONABLE COST

MICHAEL WAS SITTING in Mitch's office in the Sears Tower. They were going to discuss the risk mitigation that lenders would require as Michael sought funding for his company's expansion. But Michael's mind wasn't entirely on his business when he sat down with Mitch.

"Are you packed yet for Mackinac Island?" Michael asked. He didn't even wait for Mitch to reply. "I still have a ton of stuff to do before we leave. I've been working around the clock to knock items off my to-do list. The trip's just a week away, but I haven't had a chance to think of anything other than the daily operations and expanding my business."

Mitch shook his head. He hadn't had much time to think about the trip either. He knew Wendy would take care of everything, even if he kept working right up until the last minute before their vacation. He got down to business.

"You are a key man in your business and are responsible for a young family," he said, looking at Michael across the large oak desk that had been his great-grandfather's. It had belonged to Justice James Wilkerson when he had sat on the bench of the US District Court for the Northern District of Illinois. It was now a treasured family heirloom, given to him by his mother to honor his achievement of being made a law partner at his firm.

"Every interested lender and investor wants to know that their capital will be protected with you and your business. They want to know their money is safe in a worst-case scenario, just in case of an untimely death."

"They don't have a thing to worry about," Michael responded. "I spend almost every waking moment working on my business. When I am not doing that, I'm thinking of ways to streamline costs while improving the quality of service—I really value the residents at my facilities. And when I'm not focused on that, I'm trying to figure out the best practices to implement in order to grow my company."

Mitch had known Michael long enough to know that he was obsessive about details when it came to his business.

"I can see in my mind's eye every element we are putting into the prospectus and the why behind it," Michael continued. "No one wants to see my business succeed more than I do, and I plan to be around for many more years to realize my vision."

"Michael, I want to assure you that I am not wishing you dead any time soon," Mitch said. "I love Dawn and your kids so much that I want you to live to be 120 years old. I want them to suffer a pain in the ass like you for a long, long time, like I plan to myself."

Michael laughed, but he was also a little confused.

"Mitch, you had mentioned the need for my company to take out life insurance on me—and for a significant amount. Why are we talking about my untimely death?"

This situation was familiar to Mitch. As a mergers and acquisitions lawyer, he had witnessed many business owners grow uncomfortable at the thought of their death. They disliked talking about the need for life insurance to protect their business interests and their family.

"I'll tell you why this is necessary by giving you an example of what happened at another M&A firm," he said.

"A senior partner—a healthy man in his early fifties—was killed in a car crash. His firm could have been gravely impacted financially. Instead, it transitioned smoothly, and his spouse was paid handsomely for her husband's interest in the firm."

"Okay, I'll bite," said Michael.

"How did that firm manage to stay financially healthy after one of its senior partners was gone? Why did his wife and kids not end up on the curb?"

Mitch explained what happened. A year before the car accident, all the partners at the firm purchased keyman, disability and critical illness insurance policies to insure two years of profits and to pay a deceased partner's estate for his equity interest in the firm. They did this in the event that any of the partners became disabled or critically ill, or died.

"No one wanted to think of these worst-case scenarios, but it was one of the best decisions the firm ever made," Mitch said. "The life insurance provided for the deceased partner's family, and today the firm continues its practice."

"So, what does keyman insurance achieve?" Michael asked.

"It's simple. This type of insurance provides enough cash to replace lost revenue due to the death of a key member of a company. And in your case, I can't emphasize this enough: the key member in your business is you, my friend.

"If you die, the life insurance payout will cover the repayment of business loans, and the recruitment and training of your replacement—and take care of Dawn and your children financially. Future scenarios aside, for you, keyman insurance will improve your chances of loan approval. Lenders look favorably on a company with keyman insurance, since having it shows responsible financial and strategic planning, and makes it more likely, should you die, that creditors will be repaid."

Michael thought of his company's bottom line. "That sounds great," he said. "But I know that insurance for the amount I would need to be covered for would be expensive. We are planning to obtain $30 million worth of loans over the next year, and more if needed. I know that I can put those premium dollars to good use by investing the money back into my business instead of paying them to an insurance company."

"Our most successful clients are often the most frugal," Mitch joked. "That's why they have tons of money in the first place—because they followed the oldest financial rule in the book: Spend less than you make, and invest the difference in worthy ventures. So these types of clients—to be absolutely frank, my friend, people like you—don't like to or won't spend money unless it is absolutely necessary."

"Oh, I don't mind, Mitch," Michael replied. "I'm glad that after all these years of knowing each other, you really know who you are dealing with. I didn't get to this point in my business by spending like an idiot with a monkey brain."

Mitch wasn't surprised at Michael's response. "I didn't forget that you would want to do this with the least amount of cost," he said. "I understood this before I even brought up the subject today. And that's why I want to tell you about a concept known as premium financing. I know that a life insurance policy is a key component for you to cover off on tax, financial and estate liabilities in a worst-case scenario."

Mitch explained that premium financing is an important tool in a trusted advisor's tool kit for helping clients manage and cover off on their risk. Premium-financed life insurance involves borrowing money to fund the premiums for a life insurance policy. It makes sense in many situations, no matter how wealthy the clients. Large life-insurance premiums could end up eating into cash-flow they would rather not have to pay or direct towards paying those premiums, or into assets they would rather not have to liquidate just to have the adequate amount of insurance on their lives.

"Opportunity costs are not the only reason premium financing makes sense," Mitch said. "Business owners can avoid forgoing life insurance or obtaining the appropriate amount of coverage by exercising this option and employing this very useful financial strategy."

"Are you telling me that premium financing will eliminate the strain and drain on my company's cash-flow, and it can also affordably fund buy/sell and keyman obligations?" asked Michael.

"Yes, absolutely," Mitch replied. "With all premium-financing scenarios, there are some basic drivers—the insured client, the policy and a loan to pay premiums. In a nutshell, premium financing is where an individual or business borrows money from a third-party lender to pay life insurance premiums. The money is paid back later through the death benefit. This strategy eliminates the expense of insurance."

"When we go after the loans for my business expansion, can we use some of that money for a life insurance policy?" asked Michael.

"The simple answer is yes, but we're jumping ahead," Mitch answered. "We'll get to that discussion a little later."

According to Mitch, this was a way to obtain "cash-free" life insurance. The life insurance policy is issued only after a thorough underwriting process looking into the applicant's health, financials and appropriate insurable interest has been completed.

Mitch explained that there had been abuses where premium financing with questionable insurable interest had been used. In essence, that meant that someone, or a legal entity, did not have an invested interest in the insured person staying alive. There had also been abuses where policies had been purchased with the intent of selling the policy to secondary markets for a quick profit.

"Fortunately, recent oversight—along with pressure from insurance carriers, regulators and lenders—stopped this practice," Mitch said.

Mitch then explained that premium-financed life insurance would benefit both Michael as an individual and his company overall. He noted that this solution works best with someone who has a net worth of at least $5 million—it's a solution for individuals who have large estates and who need large amounts of insurance.

"I am the ideal candidate, then," Michael said with a wink. "I meet those criteria. I just want you to remember that."

Mitch laughed. "Of course," he said, "general good health and insurability come into play too, so you will need to undergo a medical evaluation. As such, it's important that you understand the idea behind financial leverage and be at ease with the concept of premium financing."

"It works for me if it's going to allow me to get insurance while eliminating a huge cash-flow drain," Michael said. "I want to invest as much money back into my business as possible. I'm comfortable with this approach."

Mitch explained that there are a number of sources for premium financing. Among them are the traditional national banks, private investment groups, brokerage firms and, in some cases, insurance companies themselves. These lenders have requirements based on the size of the loan and the financial profile of the borrower, as well as on the net worth of the individual and the term/funding schedule of the lender.

"These are areas that you and Richard covered when you explained to me the concept of smart leverage," Michael said. "No need to go over this again right now. I got it."

Michael gave Mitch an exaggerated wary look. "Just don't go into cahoots with Dawn and kill me to get my insurance payout," Michael said with a smile. "It looks like I will be worth more dead than alive, at least for a while."

Mitch burst out laughing.

"First off, you know that Wendy would throw me to the curb if I didn't protect your family's interests, as your friend and as the godfather of your children," he said. "But that's also my role as a trusted advisor—to educate you properly about your options, and to protect the interests of your family."

Michael turned serious again. "Okay, let's move on this right away," he said. "I'm looking forward to knocking one more item off my to-do list. Let's arrange to meet the right insurance professional, and we can begin the paperwork."

CHAPTER 16

—➤➤⤸⤹⬅—

WATCH WHO YOU INVITE
TO YOUR PARTY

HAROLD HAD ALREADY ordered his morning coffee by the time Michael arrived at the diner.

"Black, just the way you like it," the waitress told Harold as she put down a menu for Michael.

"I'll have the same," he told her, pointing to Harold's breakfast.

It was what Harold always ordered. Black coffee, scrambled eggs and plain toast.

"Good morning, kiddo," he greeted his protégé. "How have things been shaping up?"

"I feel more popular than ever," Michael answered. "I've been receiving phone call after phone call from business brokers across the country—completely unsolicited. They're telling me they have interested buyers and investors for my company."

Harold laughed. Business brokers could sense a good opportunity when they saw one.

"You must feel really great about that," he said. "All your hard work and investment in your company seems to have paid off if you're being approached unsolicited."

Michael wasn't sure what to make of all the attention. "It does, sort of," he said. "It's kind of like the high school dance. I was always the guy too shy to go up to the girls to ask for a dance, and now they're approaching me. That's a switch."

Harold wasn't surprised, but he was concerned that not all of the attention Michael was receiving would end up being a positive experience; he'd have to be extremely careful. He remembered what his Uncle Max had told him when he was just starting out in the business world. He remembered the words almost verbatim.

"Harold," Max had said, "If you want to make it in any professional endeavor, you must quickly identify both time wasters and true partners. Your real partners will help you achieve concrete and enduring success. But be prepared to eliminate time wasters from your life."

Harold liked Michael's example of the high school dance. "Michael, always try to go home with the date you brought to the prom," he said. "There are a lot of sharks out there. Trust me, I know from experience. I have the scars to prove it."

Harold told Michael to be careful whom he invited to participate in his business vision. He explained that he was sadder but wiser after being used and abused, having made some wrong choices. "We learn from the darker side of human nature," he said.

"A man must learn to control his impulses. Otherwise he is a slave to his appetites and can be easily manipulated and used by others. There are and have always been spiritual vampires, in all areas of one's life, including professional."

Putting down his knife and fork, he looked Michael straight in the eye. "What are spiritual vampires?" he asked rhetorically. "They are individuals who will drain you of all your life energy and even of all your resources if given the opportunity."

Harold said his hope was that Michael wouldn't have to learn life's lessons the hard way, like he had. He wanted Michael to be better prepared to identify and so avoid the sinkholes. He then recounted the story of his own experience with a spiritual vampire.

Decades earlier, he had found himself in a situation in which he ignored logic, and the telltale signs that the trappings were too good to be true.

"I was just starting out in the business world," Harold told Michael. "I was introduced to a man named Valentine. He told me he was an excellent business associate and had great influence on the decision-making processes of many of the state's top business and government people. I took him at his word. Boy, was that a mistake."

Harold had met regularly with Valentine over the course of four years. But despite his big talk and promises, their business relationship had spun towards "destination nowhere." Instead of giving Harold a firm yes or no to the business opportunities Harold had been offering, Valentine had remained evasive. He would always imply that he would respond soon. But a firm response never came, despite Valentine having been given many opportunities.

"It wasn't his fault, it was all mine—for allowing myself to be blindsided by glitz and the prospect of glamour, for letting this painful game continue for as long as it did," Harold said. "But one day I made the conscious decision to get up from the table, cut my losses and not look back. I was thankful for the experience—I had learned some valuable life lessons—but glad too that it was behind me."

Harold explained that his indecisiveness had finally come to an abrupt end after seeking advice from his Uncle Max. Harold had told him about his frustration with Valentine.

"I still remember Uncle Max's exact words," Harold recalled. "He said, 'It looks like you have been sitting on a Fabergé egg with that one.' At the time, I thought it a puzzling statement."

Michael had just seen a Fabergé egg at the Virginia *Museum* of Fine Arts. He was in Richmond, Virginia, looking to purchase a property for one of his projects—he wanted to expand into America's southeast. The exhibit card had said that Peter Carl Fabergé had created the jeweled eggs for the czar of Russia.

"I know they sell for tens of millions of dollars at auction these days," Michael said, wondering where Harold was going with the story. "What about them?"

"In sales lingo, sitting on a Fabergé egg is when you won't leave an opportunity because the upside and financial potential is so big... if the deal is actually inked," Harold explained. "Every realistic indicator could be telling you that the egg won't hatch. But you ignore reality because you think you're about to hatch a priceless Fabergé egg. In truth, it is not a real opportunity at all and probably never was. Your energy would be better spent investing in activities with a greater chance of coming to fruition."

Michael nodded; he understood. "Unfortunately, valuable life lessons need to be first experienced and endured," he said. "Only then can we learn from them. Sometimes the most valuable life lessons come from really painful experiences. It looks like we should avoid these spiritual vampires at all cost. But how? How do we identify them before they sink their teeth into us?" Michael asked.

Harold laughed. He had learned the hard way. But over the years, he had eventually learned too how to identify time wasters quickly.

"Conduct this simple test," he said. "Identify those individuals for whom you don't want to pick up the phone when you see their names pop up on your caller ID. Recognize those people with whom you would rather not speak, or those who make you cringe when you hear their voice after picking up the phone. That is a quick way to identify a spiritual vampire."

"And remember this: to achieve longevity—in a profession, activity or relationship—you must strive to be surrounded only by spiritual angels, those individuals who give you positive energy, and those whom *we* want to be around and who want our companionship as well. You're both genuinely invested in each other's success. Spiritual angels want success in all their relationships and dealings."

Michael nodded in understanding. Harold sounded like he was giving a powerful sermon.

"We want to run to the phone when we know a spiritual angel is on the other end of the line," Harold continued. "Owning and running a profitable business means being responsible when dealing with those who act responsibly towards you. Don't give credence to those who intentionally—or worse, unconsciously—drain you and waste your time and life energy. Many people we meet in our day-to-day activities—clients, employees, suppliers and, unfortunately, even professionals—walk this earth making others feel responsible and even indebted to them, without cause."

"The spiritual vampires." Michael sighed.

"Yes, you know you are being drained spiritually if you are incessantly called upon to do favors for someone who does not return them. He doesn't acknowledge that you also have needs. And when you need him most, he always has other, 'pressing' obligations."

Michael was starting to see that spiritual vampires exist because they cleverly choose responsible individuals as their victims. "They seem to seek out people who are dedicated to their relationships, their business, their profession," Michael noted. "That takes us back to where we started—those unsolicited phone calls I've been getting from those business brokers."

Harold could see Michael was again proving to be a quick study. He told his young student to be wary, saying that there are basic questions to ask.

"Where were they when you were struggling to make it?" Harold asked.

Michael shrugged his shoulders.

"Over the years, I have observed that spiritual vampires always select people who are relatively content and satisfied with their lives," Harold said. "They seek out those who are happy with their lives and careers, and those who are generally well adjusted to the world around them."

"That's their nourishment," Michael agreed. "That's whom they feed upon." Thinking back, he realized that the spiritual vampires he had met usually had no long-term relationships, either professionally or personally.

"When you meet them, they tell you that they are very selective in their choice of networks and friendships because of their high standards," Michael said.

"That's their excuse for having no real long-term relationships. But it's a lie."

Harold clarified this by pointing out that to develop and keep a long-term professional or personal relationship, one must be willing to give of oneself. "Spiritual vampires are incapable of doing this—but they will hasten to add that you fulfill every quality lacking in others, that you are truly an outstanding exception. In essence, they will constantly remind you of your duty to them."

"You're right!" exclaimed Michael. "I've never thought about it like that before. And when they feel you are falling from their clutches, two things may happen."

"Go on, I'm listening."

"First, they will act crushed, hoping that your old feelings of duty will return, and if that doesn't work, they will show their true colors and become angry and vindictive."

Harold nodded. "Fortunately, when you ignore a spiritual vampire, he usually will release you from his clutches. He then moves on, setting his sights on his next unsuspecting victim. But not all of them will release their grip. Some will do everything to torment you."

Michael asked if that was what happened with Valentine.

"Yes, for this reason, it was both financially painful and time-consuming, taking my attention away from my family, from building my business and from my general well-being," Harold confided.

"It is best to avoid these kinds of relationships from the get-go. Sure, the attention they throw on you is initially flattering. They also make you believe they want to work with you to achieve success—financial or otherwise."

Harold put down his coffee cup. "Michael, if you are not selective, you will eventually find yourself paying for these types of relationships many times over. With time, you will learn how to quickly identify them and push them out of your life. When you have lived long enough, you learn that everything in this world has a price, whether you pay it now or later."

"Are you still angry with Valentine for duping you?" asked Michael.

"No, I have come to believe that holding onto anger towards another person for how you perceive he has wronged you in the end hurts you the most. Holding a grudge is tiring because it makes you the judge, jury and jailer. Anger and resentment only age you and deplete your life energy, which could instead be directed towards achieving your goals."

Harold pointed out that relationships can be classified into three distinct groups:

Group 1: Individuals who want only to win in their relationships. All that matters to these individuals is that they win and you lose.

Group 2: Individuals who want to win and don't care if you win or lose from the relationship. If you win, great. If you lose, they don't care.

Group 3: Individuals whose primary goal in all their personal and professional relationships is to create a win-win situation for everyone involved. The main goal of these individuals is for everyone to come out a winner and for each party to strive for success in their dealings. These are your spiritual angels.

Michael understood spiritual angels very well.

"I know that I could not have come this far in life without the assistance of good, smart and giving individuals like Richard and Mitch, and others I have met so far," he said. "And Harold, I am fortunate enough to include you in that category now."

"Thank you, kiddo, but you are being too kind," Harold said sincerely.

Michael shared that he had been thinking a great deal about collaborative relationships. He had come to realize that the best working relationships and friendships are those that enhance one's competencies, opportunities and career—that is, one's well-being, but, most importantly, that of others.

Harold said he couldn't agree more. "The aim of all our professional and personal collaborations should always be to make one plus one equal infinity," he noted.

"There is a simple law I have learned in business that can be applied to all aspects of life. If everyone in your business does what you do, you can't both make a living. No two species can coexist if their 'niches' are too similar. This basic law of nature applies, of course, to two business-people who offer the exact same service or product to the same types of customers. So, when finding the right people to collaborate with, make sure you and your partners add true value to the relationship."

Harold suggested Michael always ask himself three key questions: Where are you going? Who will you invite with you on your journey? And why? "The important thing is to get these questions in the right order," he emphasized.

Michael felt like he had just finished a master-level crash course in life. "Thank you for sharing your insights with me," he said.

"It's time to go, kiddo," Harold said. "Next week our breakfast will have to be briefer. But it'll be an important lesson about a concept you may not be too familiar with: synergy groups."

CHAPTER 17

SYNERGY: THE KEY TO SUCCESS

MICHAEL HAD BEEN looking forward to his breakfast meeting with Harold all week. He was curious about what Harold had meant by "synergy groups." He didn't even wait for their coffees to arrive before he got out his question.

"What's a synergy group?" he asked.

"You're right to be so direct," Harold replied. "It's an important question, especially for you at this early stage of your career and when your business is in development. So I'll get right to it. But it's about so much more than just a mere definition."

Michael nodded.

"A synergy group is composed of likeminded individuals," Harold said. "It's based on the mental and emotional connections among them. Each member of the group acts for the benefit of all involved. The ideal synergy group consists of 2 to 10 people. That number tends to create an atmosphere of trust and harmony, conducive to providing mutual support and encouragement. A synergy group will also seek to create opportunities for its members to work together on projects that will help both the individuals and the whole group."

The waitress brought their breakfasts to the table. Harold took a sip of his coffee and set the cup back down. "My Uncle Max and his buddies were the first to show me the value of synergy groups, though they didn't put it as directly as I am now," he said. "For as long as I can remember, I met up with Uncle Max for breakfast at Manny's. It was his favorite place."

"That deli on Jefferson Street?"

"That's the one, kiddo. It's been there since just after the Second World War. Anyway, that's where I was schooled firsthand that it's not what you know but who you know that makes all the difference. I've mentioned my Uncle Max to you before. When he was young, he was the black sheep of the family, my father's side. He didn't have much of a formal education and that was frowned upon by my father and many in his family."

Harold shared how his Uncle Max had been an immigrant, just like the other men in his group of friends. They hadn't let their lack of formal education and training stop them from reaching their goals and obtaining success in both life and business. Instead, they had filled in the gaps in their knowledge and experience by making it their duty to pull each other up.

"Their results were spectacular," Harold said. "With each other's help, they all built tremendously successful businesses. Pooling your resources with those of likeminded people is one of the most valuable elements of achieving enduring success. Fortunately, I observed this behavior by watching my Uncle Max and his buddies do this for each other again and again over the years.

"I can't understate the importance of this to you. Michael, the right synergy group will ignite an ordinary life—and that includes your career and business—and turn it into an extraordinary—and profitable—venture."

Almost all successful business system creators and owners understand this principle at their core, Harold said. If a man achieves true and enduring success in life, he will have learned to focus on his ROR, that is, his return on relationships—not his ROI, or return on investments.

"It should always be about the people you choose to surround yourself with. I have learned that it is never about objects or money."

Michael had also learned to appreciate how important this was in his own life. "That is so right," he agreed.

"The wise man knows that no one is an island unto himself. He is a member of a wider community. Have you heard of the British anthropologist Robin Dunbar?" he asked.

Michael shook his head.

"Dunbar determined through his thorough research that each person is involved in a webbed community of 150 people. These are the 150 individuals with whom we feel comfortable enough to invite for coffee if we bump into them on the street. For most people, this group is constantly shifting, some entering the community as others leave," explained Harold.

"I would like to believe that I have made it into your 150," Michael said with a smile.

Harold smiled back. He then noted that most individuals, especially businesspeople and professionals, are unaware of their or anyone else's community of 150 people. "Not knowing your web of connections or that of another is a risk you take; it can short-circuit your career and perhaps even your life," he said.

"That sounds similar to six degrees of separation," Michael said. "You know, the theory that says we are only six handshakes away from any person on the planet."

"That's exactly right," acknowledged Harold. "I've been fascinated with human social network theory for over three decades now, and I believe that applying my knowledge in this area was a big part of my successes in life."

What social network theorists have discovered can essentially be organized into four principles. By consciously applying these principles, one will make meaningful connections with the right people, thereby creating serendipitous—and profitable—opportunities. Harold described the four principles to Michael.

Principle 1: Know Thyself

Harold explained that it is important to know who you are, what you love doing, what you stand for and what your boundaries are—the lines in the sand that you will not cross.

"We've talked about this before," said Michael.

"Yes. I can't emphasize the importance of applying this principle enough," said Harold. "It's one of the most important things a man can do to help himself succeed in his life. How can you expect to reach a destination if you're not sure where you are going and who you are?"

Michael responded with a question of his own. "What's your secret to doing this?"

"You have to be brutally honest with yourself," Harold quickly responded. "Know your strengths and weaknesses. This can be accomplished only through great introspection. Identify what your life has been telling you about what you are really meant to do, and then go out into the world and do it."

Harold illustrated his point with an example from his own life. He had grown up in Skokie, Illinois, and had been no academic star. But he had learned much from watching his mother and Uncle Max. They had been constantly working and hustling, as they had been running their own businesses. This had had a huge influence on Harold's mental filters and how he processed the world around him.

"Look, I was no genius in the classroom," he said. "Like I said, I had to be honest with myself. I wasn't my brother, David, who was always studying. It's a trait he inherited from my father, who was the same way growing up. I loved working at my Uncle Max's scrap yard. I also loved assisting my mother at her dress shop. They were just like you, Michael. They were in the business of finding a consumer's need, acting on that opportunity and fulfilling those needs. I knew at a very young age that I wanted to emulate what they were doing. It was a drive within me that I needed to fulfill."

Michael recalled Sun Tzu's *The Art of War*:

> If you know the enemy and know yourself, you need not fear the result of a hundred battles. If you know yourself but not the enemy, for every victory gained you will also suffer a defeat. If you know neither the enemy nor yourself, you will succumb in every battle.

"By recognizing your strengths and weaknesses—coming to know yourself," Harold summed up, "you will be able to identify the characteristics and skill sets of potential partners you will need to invite on your journey, to enhance your vision and to compensate for any of your shortcomings."

Principle 2: Leverage

Harold continued by sharing a poignant quote from George Orwell's *Animal Farm*: "All animals are equal, but some are more equal than others."

"What this means is that every man has the ability to be equal, but only a few choose to commit to their passions in order to bring their vision to fruition," he said.

"A man with purpose in his step is always found attractive. Once he is clear on what he wants, he can then identify individuals who can help him find shortcuts to where he intends to go. These are the only people he should search out and invite on his journey."

Harold explained that in the famous 1960s experiment that had spurred the concept of six degrees of separation, social psychologist Stanley Milgram identified those people whom he called "super connectors." These individuals were the human hubs, connecting everyone else who participated in the study. In a nutshell, what we can learn from Milgram's findings is that if we know what we want to achieve, we can quickly identify the people who can help us achieve it—we can identify those human hubs that can lead us closer.

"Wouldn't it be nice to have a lens with which to identify these individuals whom we can help and who in turn can help us?" Harold asked rhetorically.

"Having a well-formed vision and knowing what types of people can assist you is extremely important in achieving your goals. But it is not as crucial as you helping them on their journey as well. Also, keep in mind that you never know whom someone might know. Even if a person is not able to assist you directly at that moment, someone he knows may be able to help you. By having a clear vision and sharing it with the right people, you are empowering others to know what you want to achieve. This helps them bring the right opportunities to you when the time is right.

"People can fast-track their success," Harold noted, "by finding patrons or mentors who are well respected and well connected—often people who are higher up on the ladder of life, or in the field in which you want to succeed. It is important to be selective when choosing a patron," Harold again emphasized. "You will have to spend a great deal of time scouting for those people who have the power to help you jump social network levels in order to achieve your goals. Then you must convince your potential patron to help you."

Listening to Harold confirmed what Michael had been thinking about several months earlier, after his first meeting with Richard and Mitch about his planned business expansion: it was his desire for a mentor that had prompted him to approach Harold in the first place.

Principle 3: Reciprocity

"No one likes a chirping bird," Harold said.

"A chirping bird?" said Michael, his voice rising in question.

Harold laughed. "A chirping bird is a taker, always asking for favors but never offering anything you'd find of value," he explained. "We all have had those types of people in our lives. The person with a clear vision can quickly identify them so that he can either avoid them or get rid of them from his life."

"Reciprocity," Harold said, "is the glue that holds society together. It's the system of give and take. Reciprocity may not occur right away, which is why, in most cases, the long view is a man's best course, as it typically results in the optimum return.

"Everything you do that supports your goals will eventually return value back to you a trillionfold," Harold said. "All that the principle of reciprocity means when applied in the real world is this: never show up at someone's doorstep empty-handed. You should have something he places value upon and is willing to trade for. If you have nothing worth trading, even if he has something you really want, wait until you have something worth trading and he also sees value in possessing."

In game theory, the most successful strategy is that of "tit for tat." This is where you always give and see if the other person is a giver or a taker. What happens again and again is that the givers of this world end up surrounded by other givers, while the takers are surrounded only by other takers. People who play this game best are infinite game players who have mastered the deep understanding that when the watermark rises, all their boats rise together.

"These are the *only* people you want on your team, Michael," Harold said. "Even better is to always give more than the other person expects."

Principle 4: Compensation

"I know you're familiar with Ralph Waldo Emerson," Harold said, finishing off his breakfast.

"His writings were a constant companion of mine while I was growing up," Michael shared. "He was not just a poet but someone who really understood life—relationships among things *and* people. And most importantly, he knew himself."

"I couldn't agree more." Harold nodded. "He's also the author of a masterpiece of a work that has served me well throughout my personal and business life."

Harold then went on to summarize the essay "Compensation." It can be boiled down to the notion that for everything that is gained, something is lost.

"If you really understand the meaning of the principle 'Know thyself,' you will be prepared for the mental, physical, emotional and spiritual toll some losses will have on you," Harold said. "Take those big lotto winners. Many of them are worse off only two or three years after their big win than when they started out. Not only have they lost all their unearned money but their entire social support network has been destroyed. They are just not properly prepared for the big financial change in their lives, nor did they have the proper support network to handle that change."

Harold explained that their social and financial decline could have been avoided if they'd had a strong synergy group in place.

"Avoid individuals who knock you down and do not build you up," Harold stated.

"In that case, I'm on the right path," Michael said. "I have you, Mitch and Richard. I also have a few other trusted advisors to rely on for wise counsel in legal and other matters."

Michael remembered his previous week's discussion with Harold on spiritual vampires: don't bring into your midst anyone who sucks the life blood out of you. As they were winding down their breakfast, Harold noted a few key questions one should ask oneself when creating a synergy group.

Key question 1: Do the people in the group share the same values and goals?

If not, avoid working with those individuals at all cost. For potential candidates for your synergy group, ask yourself these qualifying questions:

1. *Can you trust them?* Trust means that an individual is doing what is right for himself, the group and you.

2. *Is this person committed to excellence?* Is the individual doing his very best and has he made the conscious commitment to continuously improve himself?

3. *Does this person care about you?* It does not matter what skills an individual might bring to the table if he doesn't care about your well-being. Without that, you won't fully benefit from his expertise.

"When you can answer these three questions in the affirmative, then and only then should you seriously consider inviting the person into your synergy group," Harold said.

Key question 2: Can you work together?

A person may share your values and goals, but that does not necessarily make for a smooth business relationship. If there are major differences in personal or work styles, you may not be able to work well together.

Key question 3: Is there opportunity for members of the group to work together?

Even if you answer yes to the first two questions, the timing may not be right for working together on a project. However, if someone who shares your values and goals genuinely wants to create an opportunity and you believe you can work well together, invite that person into your synergy group. Together you will create the opportunity.

Harold reminded Michael that members of a properly formed synergy group feel compelled to make your problems their problems, your solutions their solutions, your opportunity their opportunity, and your successes their successes. Members of a synergy group have an invested interest in each and every member's success. The mindset of a synergy group is that when one member succeeds, all do.

"This is how real miracles happen every day, everywhere, all the time," Harold said. "There is a limit to the number of quality relationships we can have at any one time, especially when we're busy with our careers. So, it's imperative to know whom we can best serve and who can help us at the same time.

"Those are the people we should invite into our lives," Michael acknowledged.

"One of the best investments of anyone's time," Harold said, "is to sit down with a pen and paper and categorize each relationship, whether it be professional or personal. Place each into one of three distinct groups, based on the three key questions I just laid out," Harold said. "Remember—it only takes two to make a synergy group.

"There is nothing more empowering than becoming conscious of how you evaluate the people you have unconsciously surrounded yourself with. Very few people ever take the time to be honest with themselves, to consciously take stock of their relationships—of their true nature. Those who do this have a real chance of exercising their personal power for good.

"This way," Harold said, "a man does not waste his time with people who will drain his energy and may ultimately destroy him. Instead, he will be left to concentrate on those people who appreciate their responsibility to lift people up."

"So what you're saying is that writing this down is more than just an exercise," Michael said. "You can determine which relationships will move you closer or farther from your goals. Prosperity is more than money. We tend to feel wealthy when surrounded by the people we've chosen to be in relationships with, and when doing the activities we love. We need to find them meaningful."

"Amen to that," said Harold. He looked at his watch and saw that the time had flown by, as usual. "Let me grab the bill this time, kiddo," he said, "and we will continue next week."

CHAPTER 18

-->>><<<--

NEGOTIATIONS ARE ALL ABOUT PEOPLE AND TRADING IN VALUE—DON'T FORGET IT!

MICHAEL WAS AT the law firm, waiting for Richard and Mitch. Just a short time earlier, he had completed his prospectus, with their assistance. They had since sent it to lenders and private equity funds to secure the funding Michael would need to expand his company.

"We've had a very favorable reception to your prospectus," Richard said as the two walked into the boardroom. "The lenders are looking for well-managed companies, and they like what they have seen of your past performance. They are excited about the upside potential your business expansion offers."

Michael thanked Richard and Mitch for all their hard work. They had put in a lot of time and effort to make sure lenders and possible investors realized that they would be investing in a premium service provider.

"We're not at home plate just yet," said Mitch. "We've received some really good offers that are being vetted even as we speak."

"Mitch is right," agreed Richard. "We've received good offers from interested parties that want to lend you money. But they also want to take part ownership in your company, to directly participate in your business's growth."

Michael had been through enough negotiations to understand there was still a long way to go before inking a deal. But he also understood his limits. He was the best at what he did on a daily basis—working with senior citizens and their families at his seniors' residences. He knew how to get the best value from his suppliers. He also knew exactly whom to meet at local and state governments when it came to rezoning property or other bureaucratic matters.

"So, we negotiate for the best deal," he said. "However, this is not an area I'm too familiar with. I don't have your experience when it comes to going out into the marketplace to raise money. This is where I'm going to have to rely on you for your expertise."

Richard assured Michael that he was in good hands. Negotiating with suppliers of capital is not so different from what Michael had done in the past to create his successful business, Richard said. The business of raising or borrowing money is just another form of human interaction. Every time we deal with another human being, we are negotiating. The successful businessperson has mastered the art of negotiation.

Business is all about trying to convince someone of something, trying to get him to adopt an idea, belief, service, action or thing. Research suggests that only 1 in 50 business ideas that are adopted by a qualified prospect were given the green light from the get-go. If you don't follow-up and engage in a meaningful dialog, there is no opportunity to build the trust needed for a rewarding relationship and the implementation of the idea. Furthermore, only 2 percent of qualified prospects purchase a service or product during the first meeting with the seller. The other 98 percent who don't buy in at first contact may eventually buy in if trust is established between the buyer and seller, and the seller demonstrate that what he is selling satisfies the buyer's needs and/or wants.

Anyone who wants to promote something successfully—whether it's a service, a product or a vision—in the 21st century must first come to the basic understanding that *timing* is rarely a key factor in the sell. Rather, success is the result of how much *time* you invest in your relationship with the prospect. And the more you invest in the *right* people, the greater the success. Acceptance springs from continual engagement and ongoing dialog. It's that simple.

"Finding the right people to adopt your vision is key to any business deal," Mitch noted. "But it doesn't matter how great your ideas are if you don't persevere in finding the right kinds of people and then committing to converting them into clients and, subsequently, advocates of yours."

Michael understood this intuitively. He had always succeeded because of his perseverance. It was how he had built his business, one brick at a time, from the ground up, no matter what obstacles stood in his way. He never let anyone or anything hold him back; he continued to move forward, guided by his vision.

"Mitch tells me you're an avid reader," said Richard.

"He's always devouring books," Mitch said, nodding. "I don't think I saw his face for the first few years after meeting him. His nose was always deep in a book."

"Then you'll like this." Richard looked over at Michael. "Have you read Dr. Seuss?"

"I read them often to my kids at bedtime," said Michael, curious about where Richard was going with this.

"Exactly," Richard replied. "I was reading *Green Eggs and Ham* to my grandkids last night. It's a great children's story, but it has a moral that we can all learn from and apply in our lives. It has to do with exactly what Mitch was talking about: perseverance."

The story has two main characters, Sam-I-Am and a skeptic, who is set in his ways and doesn't want to try anything new. Sam-I-Am is determined to get the skeptic to eat green eggs and ham. The skeptic doesn't even want to taste them. In fact, he is so against the idea that he rejects it more than a dozen times. But Sam-I-Am does not give up. He asks and asks and asks. The skeptic finally says yes. But he doesn't stop there. After eating the green eggs and ham, he is willing to try many of Sam-I-Am's other recommendations.

"They had built a relationship based on trust, thanks to Sam-I-Am's perseverance," Richard said.

"And on green eggs and ham," Michael added with a laugh.

"That's right. By the end of the story, our skeptic had turned into one of Sam-I-Am's biggest advocates," said Richard. The lesson was that if you want something—a product, a service, an idea or what have you—adopted by the right people, you must learn not to take rejection personally. Potential partners (in Michael's case, investors and lenders) can't really know who you are. If they reject your proposal, what they are rejecting is their *perception* of what you are selling.

"That doesn't mean don't polish your shoes," Mitch joked. "First impressions still have a lasting effect. Research shows that, to sell something successfully, one must be committed to making at least five follow-ups after the initial contact with a qualified prospect. Most people who try to sell something give up before that."

"I intend to be a part of the percent who do at least five follow-ups, because my vision is much greater than me," Michael noted. "There really is a societal and consumer need for these retirement services, and that need is going to grow exponentially. People may know they don't need these services right now, and may think they won't need them in the future, but believe me, eventually they will expect these needs to be fulfilled."

Richard nodded in agreement. "When you persevere, you will join the successful 8 percent, and they create 80 percent of all the business transacted in this country," he said.

"Here's what we're going to do, Michael," Mitch said. "Your concept must meet lenders' criteria before they will even consider lending to your business. We need to give them something they value, something that meets the potential lenders' core financial needs—perhaps even a solution to a problem.

"We don't need to get everything we want all at once—not even by the end of our negotiation," Richard interjected. "Massive bold moves that turn into big successes exist only in our minds. In the real world, these types of moves just scare off the right partners. I have learned that success in negotiations of any kind comes down to the amount of time invested. Rarely, if ever, is it about 'perfect timing.' I'll be the first to admit that, when I was younger, I sometimes failed to close a deal because I asked for way too much at first. I reached too far and acted too impulsively. When we go back to negotiate for more favorable lending terms with the capital firms and financial institutions that have shown a serious interest in your company, Michael, we must keep this understanding of investing time top of mind."

Being too emotionally attached to your strategy or an immediate outcome, Richard said, destroys your chances of arriving at a positive result. Oversized egos kill deals. You must remain as emotionally detached during a negotiation as possible—that makes for a rational discussion that honors the other party's needs, along with your own. If you make demands and take everything at once right at the start, the people on the other side of the table will likely avoid dealing with you in the future.

"All businesspeople who aim to be successful will work in partnership with others to create long-term trusting relationships," Richard said. "We want you to be able to have a successful relationship with the same people if you choose to raise additional financing. That's why we are carefully vetting each offer we've received so far, before we go over them with you. We want everyone involved to see this as a lasting venture."

"That's why I put so much emphasis on creating the prospectus for your company," Mitch noted. "If you don't know what you stand for and want to accomplish from these negotiations, we can't expect the other party to either. That's why we needed to invest so much time and effort up front. When the other party doesn't have a clear goal but you do, it's more likely that they will accept your vision of what is an equitable result."

Richard explained that, in his experience, a good deal provides an emotional payment—the feeling that the needs of everyone involved in the negotiating process have been met. "It's the principle of reciprocity," he said.

"It involves trading items of unequal significance," Michael noted.

"That's right," Richard said. "And it's worth recapping that individuals give different weight to things—the values they place on those items are often unequal. It's always important to think creatively of ways to enlarge the opportunity for all involved. It's important to find out what the other party places value on, so that you can offer things that are not already part of the negotiations."

Michael understood this clearly. But, he said, he believed the negotiations in his case were rather straightforward. He had a well-running, profitable business, and he believed that lenders and private equity funds wanted to find good companies like his to lend to or invest in, to grow their money. Both he and potential lenders had items of unequal significance that each wanted from the other. Each would want to negotiate and make an exchange.

"It sounds like a more than fair trade," he said.

"Smart-ass," Mitch said.

Much was involved in the best and most successful negotiations, Mitch noted, giving the example of an investment manager he knew. This investment manager was trying to turn a very wealthy business owner into a very satisfied and paying client, but his prospective client was already served by highly qualified advisors. One day, the investment manager learned that the prospective client's wife loved to listen to Barbra Streisand. Seeing her perform live was one of the items on her bucket list.

The investment banker made it his mission to make that happen. He called in some favors, pulled a few strings and managed to get front-row tickets to her upcoming, sold-out concert, plus backstage passes. He presented these to his prospective client—who then had a wonderful night out with his wife of 40 years. The wife was overjoyed—and so appreciative that she insisted her husband hire the investment manager immediately. He eventually became their go-to and most trusted advisor.

"Success does not have to come at someone else's expense," Richard said. "Good negotiations always end in win-win agreements. Relationships are created on the foundation of trust and honesty. Trust does not mean both sides agree with each other on every issue. But both sides should know where the other stands. We have built our firm's reputation on this belief."

"I couldn't agree with you more, Richard," Michael said. "The aim of every negotiation should be to create an ally. Life is so much more worthwhile when you're working with the right people, those who need and appreciate you and who are invested in your success—and you in theirs."

Richard told Michael that he would go back to the capital firms and financial institutions with counterproposals. He and Mitch would then present the best offers to Michael, along with their recommendations.

"I have been saving this for last," Richard said. "There is potentially one more offer we are waiting on. It may be the best offer of all, but the private equity investor is still evaluating the deal."

He told Michael that the firm would let them know soon if it would be making an offer. "Let's see what happens."

CHAPTER 19

→→»→«←←

THE LONG BREAK

"NO, SHE DIDN'T," Michael said, speaking into the phone. "I can't believe I missed that."

He was speaking to Dawn, who was at Mackinac Island with Wendy and the kids. She was telling him about a frog their youngest daughter had caught on a day hike. They were having a blast horseback riding and taking long swims in Lake Huron.

Michael and Mitch found time to join their families for the vacation on weekends, and once even took a week off, getting away from the bustle of the city. They'd hop on a plane at Chicago's Midway, landing at the airport in Pellston. Then they would take a short bus ride, followed by a ferry ride, to join their families on Mackinac Island for some well-deserved rest and relaxation. And almost every Sunday, they'd hop back on the ferry, bus and then plane, leaving northern Michigan to return to Chicago. They wanted to be back at work first thing Monday morning.

It was Wednesday, and Michael wanted to quickly catch up with Dawn before his breakfast with Harold. It was the beginning of another long day that would be filled with the routine but grinding tasks of running his business. On top of payroll obligations, paying suppliers and making sure his residence homes and his clients were taken care of, he was still also constantly thinking about his expansion plans for the business. He knew there was only one constant in life—and business: everything must innovate, change and grow or it will decline, decay and cease to be a viable enterprise.

"Okay, I have to run; I love you, and miss you and the kids lots. Please give them kisses and hugs from me, and tell them Daddy misses them so much," he said, "I'll call you again in the evening."

A short time later, he was at the diner, sitting across from Harold at their regular table.

"You look like you've been getting some sun," Harold said.

Michael nodded, then quickly turned the subject to his business expansion. "It looks like I'm about to secure the necessary financing for my business," he said. "I have my eye on acquiring several new properties across the Southeast and on the West Coast."

"Is that a good thing?" Harold asked. "Is that what you really want?"

"Of course. It's something I have been striving towards for a long time," Michael responded without hesitation. "Can I ask you something, Harold? I've had this question on my mind for a while."

"Ask, kiddo," Harold said, putting down his knife and fork and giving Michael his full attention. "That's why we have these conversations. What's on your mind?"

"We've been having our early-morning breakfasts together for a while now," Michael began. "I've enjoyed our talks about how to make one's way through this life and in business. Your lessons have been invaluable. I don't know what I would have done without them."

Harold interrupted. "I feel like there is a big 'but' coming," he said.

Michael was tired and feeling overworked. Being away from Dawn and his children didn't help his mood much. "Yes, there is a 'but' coming," he said bluntly.

"During this entire time we have been meeting for breakfast, you've never asked me what I am doing with my business. You've never given me advice on specifically what I should do with my company. You've never offered your help with my business venture. Why?"

"Is that what this has all been about?" Harold asked, taking a sip of coffee. "You want me to get involved in your business affairs?

"I can tell you this. If I had thought for a moment that that was your true intention, we would have never had these early-morning breakfasts. If that is what you wanted from the start, you would have been placed at the back of the line, turned away like the countless others who have tried to make business pitches to me over the years.

"And frankly, you would have had to go through dozens, if not hundreds, of my people first. And even then you would not have heard directly from me. You would have been given a firm no from one of my representatives."

Michael waited before speaking again. He knew that once something is said, it can never be taken back.

"It's so easy for you to say that, Harold.

"I believe in speaking truth to power. I am no sycophant—I don't try to win favor by kissing someone's ass. I have never been one, nor will I ever allow myself to become one. You have everything. I was born on the wrong side of the tracks. I had to fight for everything that I have ever earned in this life. I have struggled every day. No one has given me anything that I have not worked hard for and rightfully earned. I was not born with a silver spoon in my mouth. When I was in college, I was surrounded by these so-called P-H-Ds. They had everything given to them from the day they were born. These P-H-Ds didn't have the ability to appreciate the privileged life they were born into."

"What's a P-H-D?" Harold asked, a perplexed look on his face. "I don't think you're referring to doctoral students."

"'Papa has dough,'" Michael replied sharply. "It's irrelevant. You get my point."

Harold calmly listened to his junior, then took a long pause before he spoke.

"Old age gives us a collection of experiences and insights that are beyond the ability of youth to understand and fully appreciate," he said gently. "Many truths that we cling to depend on our own point of view—our reality—and we must understand that these truths are not likely to be someone else's truths. That's because they don't share our vantage point. I have learned that I can't tell anyone what to do or how to do it well. It is impossible to command someone else to do something well if their hearts and inner drive do not command them to do so for themselves.

"I have not interfered in your business affairs because you won't—and shouldn't—listen to me about business specifics at this stage in your life. You need to go out into this world and fall flat on your face again and again. And when I say fall flat, I mean fall hard. And you need to fall often. You will need to test your limitations in order to discover if they are real or imaginary, and then break through them either way.

"When you have the tenacity to bounce back from all the setbacks life throws at you, only then can you choose to come back to me with an open mind. Only then will you be ready to really listen to what I have to say."

Michael interrupted Harold before he could finish expressing his thoughts.

"When I first saw you near Daley Plaza, the day I first approached you at this diner, I thought to myself that I had never seen a man so content with himself, that he needed nothing but the sun and a good cup of java," Michael said.

"I wanted nothing more than to find that majestic calm that's been eluding me all my life. I felt that a person only looks that way when they have conquered both the world and their inner demons. I wanted to learn from you how to conquer my own demons and discover that same serene feeling and satisfaction in life.

"I am not the same person who introduced himself to you that day. I admire you and value your teachings. I now know one truth for myself. I can never, ever lower my eyes for another again. I want to thank you for your time and instruction. But I can no longer continue with our early-morning breakfasts. It's time for me to write my own melodies, not read off the pages of someone else's music sheet. From now on, life and experience will be my principal teachers."

Michael got up from the table, reached into his wallet and put down money for their meals, plus a hefty tip.

"Goodbye, Harold," he said, heading towards the door.

But even as he was walking out, he had a lingering question, and a moment of doubt came into his mind. *What have I just done?*

But he was too proud to go back and apologize for his insolence. Not even after this man, this mentor, had shown him so much patience.

Harold sat back after Michael had left and finished his breakfast. He reflected on what had just happened. He understood that Michael needed to take this break. He needed to find his own way. Harold would not chase him. Harold believed that when a man has learned to control himself, he doesn't need to control others. Every man needs to voluntarily separate from his mentor's influence, to differentiate himself as a unique and independent individual so he can become a healthy and well-equipped adult. Only then can he return as an equal and eventually a successor to his mentor.

Harold wished he had the words to communicate this truth to someone as young as Michael. He knew that his protégé had much to experience and learn on his own. Only then would he be ready to return for his final lessons, so that he could then pass into the final stages of his personal journey.

It had been over a decade since Harold had had his own life-changing epiphany. He had been 52 at the time. He had realized that he would have to voluntarily adjust his goals beyond just the somewhat aimless accumulation of money, belongings and accolades. Only after doing that would he be able to transition successfully into his later stages of life. He would have to let go of his ego's demands before he would be able to find and then fulfill the true meaning of his life.

To know that we are wounded is half the battle. Every man must find his own response to his personal questions and the challenges posed by life. The worthiest quest in a man's life is to know how to find his wounds so that they may be healed.

Finding the answers to life's great questions are rites of passage that mark a man's transition from one stage of life to the next. During his own quest, Harold had clumsily stumbled upon six questions that a man must ask himself. *When* he asks each of these questions is typically linked to his age, experience and maturity.

Life Question 1: *Who am I?* This is an identity question, usually first asked when a person is young. When we are born, we have no real identity of our own. We are born into a certain place and culture, we are given our names by our parents and we assume the religion of our parents.

A boy answers this question by taking on different labels that describe who he believes he is. This is how he identifies himself in the external, sensory world—the world of sight, sound, touch, smell and taste.

Life Question 2: *How will I fit in?* This question is usually asked in the teenage years, when a boy is trying to find his place in his social and physical environments. At this stage in his life, he is deeply influenced by his friends and is susceptible to peer pressure.

Life Question 3: *What will I do?* This question often arises during a man's early 20s, when the young man is searching for a career and life partner. This question is different from Life

Question 1 because it concerns actual actions a man will take in his life.

Life Question 4: *Who have I become?* This question usually arises when a man reaches his 40s. He suddenly realizes he is no longer planning his life, dreaming of what he will become when he grows up—he already is grown up. Some men ask themselves this question gracefully; others do not, which may lead to a midlife crisis. This is a time when a man becomes serious about planning his personal and financial affairs. He is becoming conscious of the fact that he is mortal and one day will not be around to enjoy life.

Life Question 5: *What have I accomplished?* When a man is young and believes he has nothing but time, he focuses on *doing*. Later, when he understands that time is finite, he must learn to focus on *being*. A man is always yearning to be something more. A healthy man aims to become whole. This question about accomplishments usually arises when a man reaches his mid-50s. He realizes that his working career is coming to an end, that there are more working days behind him than in front of him. A healthy man asking this question realizes that a new stage of life is about to begin for him. At this stage, he's getting ready to transition from work to entering his last stages of life. A man addressing this question is putting his financial affairs in order, ensuring he has enough money to support himself when he is no longer earning an income. This is the time when a business owner starts planning and implementing a succession plan for his business and begins to think about his legacy.

Life Question 6: *What will my legacy be?* A man starts to ask this question as he nears the end of his life. He often finds himself becoming less ambitious and less aggressive, seeking to replace dreams of unlimited success with opportunities for nurturing, mentorship and friendship. He begins to think beyond his mortal existence, contemplating what he will be remembered for and what his positive legacy will be. He begins to ask what he will have passed on once he is gone from this life.

Those asking this question are quite serious about gifting their time and money to people and causes they care deeply about. It has been said that the sooner a man begins to ask this question, the larger his parting impact will have on his family, community, society and the world in general.

Harold knew that an overemphasis on power at any stage in a man's maturing process is often a defense against feeling vulnerable. He could not interfere in the process that Michael was about to go through. Harold understood what he had to do. He reached into his bag, pulled out a pen and a pad of paper, and began to write.

Dear Michael...

CHAPTER 20

~->>>≫≪<<-~

THE ONLY CONSTANT IS CHANGE

"TRY THIS ONLY if you think you're flexible enough to do it," Michael heard someone say as he walked by the fitness room of his Naperville, Illinois, seniors' residence. The home was a short distance west of Chicago, and he was about to meet Richard and Mitch there. Mitch had called earlier that morning, saying they wanted to drive in to meet with him immediately. They wanted to share some great news they had received the night before about the money Michael was seeking for his expansion.

Michael peeked into the room and saw a fit young woman leading a yoga class for half a dozen residents.

"This pose is called Lord of the Fishes," he heard the instructor say.

"Take your left leg and step it over to the outside of your right thigh. Now, don't force this. If you're not able to do it easily, just bend your leg and leave your foot on the floor on the inside of your right thigh. Take a look at Beckie and James—they've got it. Great job, Andrew, just leave your left leg where it is."

The residents all wore big smiles. Andrew waved a friendly hello to Michael. Michael waved back before heading towards the residence's main dining room. He had made it a point to visit all his residence homes on a regular basis, and he knew many of the residents by name. He would talk to them frequently, and the one thing he heard over and over again was that they wanted to live as independently as possible, with dignity. They needed assistance as they grew older, but none of them wanted to step out of life and sit in a rocker for their remaining days.

Each of Michael's seniors' residences had assisted-living areas, which were fully staffed by on-call nurses and doctors, available at a moment's notice. Seniors who wanted to live more independently could choose the option of their own apartments. These were secure, furnished units, with their own kitchen and balcony. These residents had full freedom without the hassle of doing chores, or their own cleaning and cooking. The residents could even choose to keep a pet if they so desired. And everyone, whether they lived in the apartments or assisted-living quarters, had access to the fitness areas, sauna, pool, common dining rooms and lecture hall, and to the staff and medical care. Michael had created a community, and many of the residents were as much family now as they were neighbors.

Michael took a seat at one of the corner tables in the dining room. It was almost 10 a.m. and he could hear the kitchen staff preparing for lunch. He wanted to say hello to two residents who were leaving as he walked in, but they were already out the far door. Ordinarily, Michael would have gone to the indoor pool, where there was always a number of residents sitting on lounge chairs, participating in aquatic aerobic classes or just enjoying the water on their own. But Richard and Mitch would be arriving any minute. And, indeed, as soon as the clock struck 10, a staff member was escorting them to his table. *Just like them*, he thought—*right on time*.

"I would love a tour of the facility," Richard said as he shook

Michael's hand. "But first, we have pressing business we need to go over. We have an offer. But there is a strike date for your signature, if you decide to take it."

Mitch told Michael that the largest private equity investor in the Southwest had couriered the firm an offer the night before. "It'll lend you $30 million in two separate tranches of funds—when you meet certain growth hurdles," he said.

"Mitch will go over the specifics with you a little later," Richard interjected. "But you should know that this private equity fund has its fingers on some of the most successful growth businesses across America and around the world. If you are agreeable to the terms, this firm is prepared to make available additional monies above the first $30 million and on the same lending terms, for even further corporate expansion."

"What are the terms and conditions?" asked Michael. "Do they want to have their hands on the strategic development, or to pick my management team? If that's what they're interested in, I want no part of it."

The private equity investor was prepared, Mitch said, to lend the money at 1 percent more than the London Interbank Offered Rate, more commonly known as Libor, which is the rate banks charge each other for short-term loans. However, there was a caveat.

"It's a unique stipulation that it's put into the loan agreement," said Richard.

"Unique?" Michael asked with some suspicion in his voice.

"It put in a clause that it says is nonnegotiable," responded Richard. "To tell you the truth, this is the fairest offer I have ever been involved with negotiating in all my years in the M&A field. The condition is that if you decide not to transition your business to your children sometime in the future, it wants to have the first right to make an offer to buy out all your shares in your company, as it would like to add it to its portfolio of businesses."

Michael agreed that the offer was more than fair. Plus, he knew that he wouldn't have to worry about a succession plan for a very long time. He had plans for expanding his company even further. Ultimately, he wanted to dominate the country's seniors' residence market. He understood the demographic tsunami that was about to hit over the next few decades. He also knew that the best way, the only way, to dominate the market and help prepare the country for the coming reality was by becoming a premium provider in this area.

Richard knew that Michael was sincere, and he had no doubt that he would succeed: what Michael was saying was reflected in his actions.

"Youth is truly fleeting, Michael," he said. "Time will fly by in the blink of an eye. It feels like only yesterday that I was getting out of the army after serving in the Second World War and starting my career in law. Yet I look in the mirror and see an old man looking back at me. But you know what? I still feel like I'm 18. But tell that to my body. Every fiber of my being wants to go along with you on this quest. I want to directly help implement your vision."

Michael sensed a change in Richard's tone. His voice had become more serene.

"I've been holding off from making this public," Richard continued. "But next week, I'm going to announce that I'll be retiring. It's time to make way for the next generation at the firm. This is the last transaction I will be actively involved in. But I'm leaving you in the best of hands. Mitch is ready to take the lead on your project. No one has my trust more than he does. And I know he loves you like a brother."

"You knew about this, Mitch?" Michael asked.

"I was shocked at first, like you," Mitch answered. "Richard has been more than a mentor; he has become a second father to me."

He turned to Richard. "Michael is the only one who knows how long I have looked up to you, Richard," he said, choking up. "What I'm going to miss most of all is being able to just pop into your office whenever I need your counsel."

"Hold on," Richard replied, "I'm not dead. Not yet. I'll be just a call away.

"I've been doing mergers and acquisitions for more than 40 years. I loved every minute of it. But now I want to enjoy quality time with my wife, and our children and grandchildren. There are so many items on my bucket list that I want to do before I depart from this world."

Richard turned to Michael. "I've learned that each generation's obligation is to nurture and guide those who will succeed them," he said. "I need to thank both of you for allowing me to do this by allowing me to work with the two of you."

"It's been our honor, Richard," Mitch and Michael said in unison.

"Now," said Richard, "how about that tour, Michael?"

CHAPTER 21

---><>>><<<---

TIME WAITS FOR NO MAN

DESPITE BEING FLUSH with cash thanks to the money he had received from the private equity investor, Michael couldn't help but wish things had gone differently with Harold. This feeling was even more intense after he had witnessed the smooth transition of leadership from Richard to Mitch. Richard shared a deep connection with Mitch. Michael had hoped he was on his way to establishing a similar bond with Harold. But it was not to be. *Not right now*, he thought. Instead, Michael had walked away from Harold's teachings and guidance in defiance.

However, Michael wouldn't let it prevent him from turning his vision into reality. He was now, more than ever, fixated on a singular mission: to put his company on the national and international map. Hearing the hero's call to adventure, as had entrepreneurs before him, he embarked on a unique quest.

Over the next two decades, he underwent many tests, trials and tribulations. He had many successes and also the inevitable setbacks that
accompany being an entrepreneurial trailblazer. He eventually over-
came many of the obstacles placed in front of him by just doing what
needed to be done and staying true to his vision. That gave him even
more valuable knowledge and experience. Through sheer determination
and perseverance, Michael reached heights that were unimaginable for
him as a poor kid growing up fatherless on Chicago's South Side.

He had matured into a master treasure hunter, becoming an expert
at locating hidden assets that others failed to see. His sharp eye and a
keen sixth sense for acquiring undervalued assets allowed him to push
the value of his company upward year after year. He knew how to
acquire land and buildings that he could then develop into retirement
facilities. He knew how to accurately measure the intrinsic value of a
business, property or opportunity.

Michael's keen eye for detail also allowed him to identify companies
that planned to spin off their retirement residence divisions or hotel properties. He knew how to identify companies that faced short-term quar-
terly return pressures when their parent companies needed to demonstrate
short-term profits to their stakeholders. So Michael would find companies experiencing cash-flow problems. Then he would ride in to save the
day: he would purchase flagship assets at deep discounts, allowing their
parent companies to take them off their balance sheets—and pay down
their debts, meet looming payments or honor payroll obligations.

Over the next 20 years, he had many ups, downs, misses and mishaps. He often worked 18 hours a day straight, with very little down-
time. Building his business was his dream, and he was not about to let it
slip through his fingers because he wasn't committed enough to it. The
hard work paid off in spades. He built up the largest chain of seniors'
residences in the Southeast and Midwest, and on the West Coast.

But his singular focus on his business, including its expansion and
success, nearly cost him everything. He overextended both himself and
the company resources, including its finances. Despite all these trials,

he eventually persevered, coming out on the other side. But he was also emotionally and spiritually starved and scathed. He had been working such long hours and his vision was so focused on his business that he was in complete denial about how it was affecting his health.

The human body is not a machine; it has its limits. If you ignore this fact, eventually your body will refuse to cooperate. And when your body wants to send you a message, it will—and it will be very blunt. In Michael's case, it was a physical collapse from exhaustion. He was at his office at one of his facilities, and even though staff were milling about, no one knew he was lying face down, unconscious and in his own excrement, until the next afternoon. He was a workaholic and his staff were used to him pushing himself, so they had just assumed that he didn't want to be disturbed. When the janitor found him, he was rushed to the hospital. This left him no choice but to take time off from his business. It took him nearly a year to fully recover.

Michael's collapse forced him to come to terms with the paradoxes in his life that he had tried to ignore. He was both weak and strong. He had a young spirit but an aging body. He was materially rich but had become spiritually and emotionally poor. He had built a successful company but had become self-destructive. He was one of the smartest men you would ever meet in business but a fool when it came to knowing himself and his limits. He spent hours and hours selflessly helping the residents in his facilities but was neglectful when it came to spending quality time with his family and friends.

When Dawn and Michael's children had grown up and left home, Dawn realized just how much she missed the old Michael, the Michael she had fallen in love with. They had been married for 30 years, but he had been working so hard for decades, and she felt that they had grown apart. She had devoted her life to helping and supporting him when it had seemed like it was the two of them against the world.

But she was sick and tired of being alone most of the time now. Dawn told Michael after his collapse, "I love you so much; that's why I can no longer just stand by and watch you kill yourself with work. All the money in the world does not mean a thing to me without you." She threatened to leave him right then and there if he didn't reprioritize his life. "No ifs, ands or buts," she told him in no uncertain terms.

That was the wake-up call Michael needed. Nothing mattered if his life partner was gone. He thought of just how much Dawn had sacrificed over the years so that he could build his business empire. And he realized that he had ignored the most important things in his life, the things he had once claimed were critical for him—his health, family, relationships and community.

Michael rose from his own ashes like a slow-moving phoenix. He learned how to let go and delegate his responsibilities. He knew he had to reclaim control over his most precious asset—his time. To do this, he lessened his daily workload in his business affairs by learning to find the right relationships to nurture and grow. He allowed experts both within and outside his business to manage his wealth and grow the company. He did this by implementing a well-thought-out plan. He set the criteria he would employ when appointing trusted individuals to greater responsibility:

- He ensured that he tasked only those individuals who had performed better than their peers for an extended period. These were people like him—committed, driven and focused. They were goal- and people-oriented.

- He ensured that his selected experts had good combat experience, meaning they had worked in both the boom years of the 1990s and the bust years of the early part of the 21st century.

- He selected experts who were in it for the long haul, people invested in the success of the company and the growth of his investment portfolio. Michael accomplished this by designing incentive compensation plans that his people actively participated in.

As Michael crossed the threshold into late middle age, he began to reflect even more on the morals of the stories he had read and heard over his lifetime. He was now an extremely successful businessman, an American success story. He had earned more than he or his family could spend in 10 lifetimes. But something was still missing inside him, and he felt an urgent call to do something, but he didn't know what exactly. The story that he couldn't get out of his mind after his collapse was one about a Brazilian fisherman. It kept popping into his mind over and over again because he knew its moral directly applied to him:

A successful fortysomething New York stockbroker worked a hundred hours each week. His compulsion was to earn more and more. He was driven purely to grow his bank account. But one day he came home to find his house empty. All that was left was a note from his wife saying she'd had enough, that she could no longer take being left alone all the time. He had ignored her, so she had packed up the kids and moved back to Nebraska. And just to put an exclamation point on her exit, she told him in her note not to come looking for them.

The shell-shocked stockbroker broke down. He couldn't stay another minute in his luxurious but empty home. He drove straight to the airport with nothing more than the suit he was wearing, his wallet and his passport. He bought a ticket on the first plane going anywhere, as long as it was heading south. Ten hours later, he landed in Brazil. The next day, he took a walk along a desolate beach, trying to figure out what had happened and how he had gotten to this place in his life. That's when he came across a man catching fish with only a fishing rod.

"What are you up to?" asked the stockbroker.

The fisherman looked up casually, a contented smile on his face. "Looking for my dinner," he responded serenely.

Just then, a fish tugged on the fishing line. The stockbroker watched as the man reeled the fish in and grabbed it with his bare hands.

The stockbroker shook his head. "Why don't you buy a net?"

The fisherman answered the question with a question of his own.

"Why would I want to do that?"

"Because then you would be able to catch more fish."

The fisherman repeated his question.

"Why would I want to do that?"

"Because then you would be able to catch more fish than you need. Then you could go to the market and sell the extra fish to earn the money to buy a small boat. With your small boat you would be able to go farther out into the ocean and catch even bigger and better fish."

The fisherman smiled again. He asked the same question yet again.

"Why would I want to do that?"

The stockbroker was amused. Did this fisherman not understand anything at all about business and the benefits of economies of scale?

"You would be able to catch and sell even more fish and then you could buy a bigger boat," he said. "By working hard and earning more money, you could buy a fleet of ships!"

The fisherman asked the same question again.

"Why would I want to do that?"

"By doing all that, you would have enough money to have all the time in the world to do whatever you chose to do."

The old fisherman took a good hard look at the stockbroker. He had another question. But this time the question was more like an answer.

"Who says I am not already doing what I want to be doing right now?" he asked. "Is the desire to have more and more and more yours or mine?"

Michael was beginning to understand why that story was constantly on his mind. He kept on working on it until he figured out what it meant for him personally. He realized that his old dreams of creating a successful business were no longer giving his life meaning. Those dreams were now leading him to despair and the slow death of his soul. He had known for a while that he had been chasing a mirage. He had been living life on the layaway plan for the past few years.

He had attained huge business success and received many accolades. Yet one question remained unanswered for him: How would he share his good fortune and hard-won insights with the rest of society? It was time for him to redefine and reorient himself so that he could set out on a new path.

He believed that his life's mission was no longer in line with his youthful desires, which had already been more than fulfilled. His past successes had forced him to confront his inevitable appointments with old age and mortality. He was beginning to understand his need to consciously mature into the last stages of his life, to travel on the path towards greater meaning in his life and that of others. He knew that men who didn't make this transition gracefully would remain prisoners of their youth, no matter how successful they appeared. He feared that if he continued on his old path, the one he had set off on in his youth, he would eventually suffer physical decay, emotional bankruptcy and spiritual death.

As Michael was emotionally and mentally preparing to embark on the next stage of his journey, he was reminded of the ancient sage Hillel the Elder. In the Ethics of the Fathers, part of the Musar literature, he said, "If I am not for myself, who will be for me? But if I am only for myself, who am I? If not now, when?"

Michael was now more determined than ever not to remain a prisoner of his youthful passions and appetites. As these thoughts crossed his mind, Michael picked up the phone and made the call he knew he needed to make. It was to Mitch, his oldest friend and one of his most trusted advisors.

"Just the other day, Wendy told me that Dawn is so glad you two moved to California," Mitch said.

"Yes, she's been loving it ever since we moved here last year. Why don't you and Wendy come join us, maybe sometime this month? The weather's perfect, plus there are a lot of important things I would like to discuss with you."

"I like that idea," Mitch said without hesitation. "You've given me a great excuse for taking some time off work—and it'll be a nice break from this Chicago winter. I think I can clear up my schedule in a couple of weeks. We can fly out to see you then. Let me just check with Wendy."

"That's a plan," Michael said. He hung up the phone, feeling both relieved and apprehensive about meeting with Mitch to discuss what he had decided to do next.

CHAPTER 22

THE GRACEFUL EXIT

A WARM PACIFIC BREEZE swept across Mitch's face as he swung his golf club. His eyes followed the ball as it shot into the air, where it seemed suspended for a moment against the backdrop of the perfectly blue sky. "I have to hand it to you," he said, turning to Michael as the ball landed on the green, just yards from the eighth hole.

"You really picked the perfect location to live. This sure beats wearing a parka. Right now, back in Chicago, it's snowing up a storm. I could get used to this. I know Wendy loves it."

Mitch and Wendy had arrived in Rancho Palos Verdes just that morning. After lunch, Wendy and Dawn went off shopping, giving the two men a chance to catch up and get in a few holes before dinner.

"Can you believe it's been almost 38 years since we were paired up as roommates back in college? It feels like just yesterday," Michael said.

Mitch laughed. "Yeah, it's hard to believe! My parents would help cover only my tuition, books and board. They were afraid of spoiling me. They were determined to teach me to have an appreciation for what I earned. I remember when the two of us had to scrape together quarters for beer money. And now look how far we've come."

"I almost forgot about that," Michael said. "You still owe me two dollars."

"As I recall, it's you who owes me a couple of bucks," Mitch said, nudging Michael's elbow.

"Okay, winner on the 19th hole buys drinks in the clubhouse."

"You're on," Michael shot back.

"Can you believe that was 38 years ago? Back when kids could drink when they were 18."

"Please stop reminding me how old we're getting," Mitch replied. "You are beginning to sound like my four-year-old grandson. He keeps asking me what it was like 'in the olden days.' Can you believe that? 'The olden days.' He says it like it was a million years ago. Anyway, it's good to know that we can still stand each other's company after nearly four decades."

Michael had known Mitch so long, he could sense every nuance in his tone. "You sound like you're surprised," he said.

Mitch hesitated.

"Out with it, old man," said Michael. "What are you getting at? I know it's something. No holds barred."

"You asked for it," replied Mitch. "If it's no holds barred, then I have to tell you that I couldn't stand the sight of you for most of our freshman year. I even asked to change roommates or be moved to another dorm. But they told me it was a long process and to just suck it up."

Michael let out a huge laugh. "I've been holding back from something as well," he said.

"Oh. We're coming clean about everything now, are we?"

"I was told the same thing," Michael replied. "Those first few months, you were a real pain in my side. And looking back, I was a real ass to you too."

"Then it was providence that we never were separated," Mitch laughed just before taking a swing.

"In all seriousness, Mitch, I'm glad we ended up sticking it out as roommates," Michael said earnestly.

"I wouldn't have had it any other way. Who knows what would have become of me. I was so darn lucky to be paired with you. I have to tell you, I've depended on you so much for guidance over the years. You really have looked out for me. You've always had my back.

"I don't get around to telling you this enough, but I really feel blessed to call you my oldest and dearest friend. I value our friendship with my life. I couldn't have ever asked for a better soul brother."

Michael began to choke up. But he wanted to get his thoughts out.

"You've done more than well, my friend," he said. "Look at you, the managing law partner of one of the nation's leading M&A firms. You really have brought honor to your family's already impressive lineage. Best of all, you did it on your own terms—all with skill and class, and without stepping on anyone's toes."

Mitch was taken aback. But he wanted Michael to know how he felt as well.

"Wait, Michael," he said. "You should really take a good look at yourself in the mirror and see the man who's staring back at you. Butterflies might be beautiful, but what makes them really interesting and impressive is that they used to be caterpillars. You're like a caterpillar that transformed into a Monarch butterfly.

"I've had a front-row seat, watching you work day in and day out to change the bad hand you were dealt in childhood. You've built it up into a beautiful and impressive life. You turned it into a royal flush. You've taught me that none of us is controlled by our past or our circumstances. We are what we choose to become."

"Hey," a voice came from a distance. It belonged to another golfer who was wanting to play the hole. Michael and Mitch looked at each other and burst out laughing.

"Those young guys behind us must think we've lost it," Michael said. "Let's move on—and let's stop being so sentimental before we both begin to cry. But before we put this conversation behind us, I just want you to know that I'm glad we were able to get this all out before it was too late."

"Me too," said Mitch, then smoothly transitioned the conversation. He told Michael that the last time he had been in Manhattan, he had heard through the grapevine that the owner of the golf course they were playing on was considering a presidential run as the 2016 Republican nominee. "Last I heard, he was a Democrat. I read that he had even made a number of large financial contributions to Hillary Clinton's political campaigns. If he wins the Republican presidential nomination for 2016, he'll be running against Hillary."

"Nevertheless, can you imagine if he pulls it off and gets himself elected?" asked Michael.

"Got to hand it to him. That man is a ball of fire. If he is elected president, he would be older than Ronald Reagan was in 1981, when he first took office," answered Mitch.

This conversation was reminding Michael of what he had been thinking about a lot recently—what it takes for personal growth, especially when you move into your twilight years. He believed that true growth occurs when a man no longer feels the need to be king or receive praise from others. What was once important in the first half of his life has little value for him in the second half.

"I have found that surrendering my youthful optimism has been the most difficult task as I travel through my middle age," Michael said. "It has forced me to confront many of my weaknesses, pains and regrets. I can no longer afford to ignore them. The one thing that I know is true is that change is just another sign that we are still players in the greatest game of all—life."

Mitch looked at his friend. He realized he wasn't surprised that those words were coming from the guy he once roomed with. Michael had always had a spark of understanding of the greater meaning of life. He just needed time to fully comprehend and express it for himself.

"You're becoming a sage, old friend," Mitch said.

"Well, no one is at exactly the same leg of their life's race. And by some miracle, if this man is elected president, we'll just have to wait and see what type of legacy he creates and leaves behind for the rest of us mere mortals," Michael said.

Michael's sentiments reminded Mitch of a story that Richard had told him long ago, about a traveler who asked an old man about the town he was approaching. The old man asked, "What was your last stop like?" The traveler responded enthusiastically, "It was a great town. Good times, friendly people. I was sorry to leave." The old man replied, "You'll find this place much the same." The next traveler the old man encountered asked the same question, he too wanting to know about the town he was approaching. The old man asked him about his previous stop. The traveler said it was horrible—an extremely negative experience. "The town you are approaching," the old man said, "is much like the town you just left."

Michael understood why this story encapsulated not only Mitch's field of mergers and acquisitions but also his own journey through business. They had both once set out and approached their careers with youthful exuberance.

Mitch had helped Michael at every stage of his business. He had watched him slip away at night during college to help seniors. Mitch had been his moral support—and had found the initial funding—when Michael had purchased his first retirement facility. And he had gained intimate knowledge of Michael's business when he had helped Michael expand it and turn it into one of the most successful enterprises in the United States.

Mitch told Michael that he felt that, much like Michael's business—which focused on providing dignity at the end of a person's life—his mergers and acquisitions business focused on people planning and then executing the last and largest transaction they would ever make: selling their businesses and transitioning into the last third of their lives. If done well, it would be the best third. If done poorly, it would be the biggest regret of their lives.

Americans are aging, Mitch agreed. Over the next decade, more than half the owners of the country's private small and medium-sized companies are expected to retire. But, according to all the studies he had read, business owners are generally not adequately prepared for all the business succession and personal estate matters that need to be addressed.

Currently, there are millions of family-owned and privately held businesses, worth tens of trillions of dollars, that are ripe for business succession transitioning. The timing is right for people looking for new opportunities. Tens of trillions of dollars in private equity, investments and pension funds are waiting to be invested in these well-run companies. Investors are looking to buy up profitable, well-positioned and well-managed private businesses. In fact, there's more work to be had helping entrepreneurs do their succession planning properly, Mitch believed, than there are trained professionals to do it.

Mitch pointed out there are huge obstacles when matching potential buyers with private corporations. It doesn't help that more than 60 percent of business owners aged 50 to 70 have yet to start discussing their exit plans with their families, business partners and professional advisors. Whether these businesses are sold, liquidated, wound down, passed on to heirs or recharacterized in some other manner, a proper exit plan must be put in place and then executed. Owners of these companies will require leadership in taking their active illiquid business assets and transforming them into secure liquid personal financial assets to ensure financial security for themselves and their families, and to benefit the causes they care about most.

In addition to the demographic challenges this aging population will present when it retires en masse are other factors that need to be considered. These include increasing global competition, ongoing international and country-specific economic risks, and business consolidations.

All are important issues that very well might cause business owners and their trusted advisors to stay up well into the night.

Michael agreed with what Mitch was saying. He knew that if a business owner hadn't executed a well-thought-out exit plan by the time he was 70, in all likelihood he would not do it at all. Every time he had tried to buy the business of someone older than 70, the deal usually died on the vine.

"Many of the business owners I know who are over 70 wouldn't know what to do with themselves once they're no longer the boss," he said. "Their identities are so tied up with being the commander-in-chief that they would prefer to die with their boots on, sitting at their office desks, rather than sell their business and confront the important things in their lives—usually things they have neglected to deal with."

Mitch agreed. "The best time for a business owner to sell is after he's discovered what his personal financial independence number is. This 'magic number' is the amount of capital the business owner will need to live the rest of his life on his own terms. The number is 'magic' because once this number has been achieved, it can turn a business owner into an open-minded potential business seller."

"Can you be a little more specific on how you identify someone who is ready to sell his business?" asked Michael.

Mitch explained that there are five key indicators that a business owner is ready to sell the ownership of his company:

1. **Age:** The business owner is between the ages of 50 and 70, or he has been in the business 20 or more years. At this stage, the business owner is ready to do something else or wants to enjoy the fruits of his labor.

2. **Fatigue:** The owner demonstrates a lack of daily enthusiasm for the business. The owner has traveled across the globe, building his business too many times, and has dealt with too many employee and marketplace issues. He is just too tired to continue on.

3. **Money:** The owner wants to take some or all of his equity off the table. Most of it is usually tied up in the company. He wants to secure his family's financial future.

4. **Partners:** The long-term arrangement has finally hit a major snag, and the business owner wants to part ways with his business partners.

5. **Future:** The future of the business is not as bright as it once was because of competition, currency exchange, technology, globalization or other factors.

Mitch explained that there are three primary categories of potential buyers to consider in any exit- and succession-planning exercise:

- Family members, whether active or passive in the business.

- Key managers and senior employees of the business.

- Third-party purchasers. These are buyers looking for mature and well-managed companies that are leaders in their defined markets and have significant upside in their growth potential. Third-party purchasers include public and private entities, pension plans, major universities, insurance companies, investment banks and high-net-worth individuals. A subset of this group includes strategic buyers, such as competitors, key customers or suppliers of the business.

"Personally, I believe a third-party purchaser is the best option—if a business owner can find one interested in buying him out," Mitch answered.

A third-party-purchaser transaction usually gives the owner what he really wants. It completely cuts all his ties to the business, and puts plenty of cash into his pocket once the keys have been handed over. These types of buyers have substantial financial resources and expertise, giving them the latitude to structure the purchase of a company in such a way as to accommodate the unique requirements and objectives of the various shareholders in the business. Unfortunately, most employees and family buyers do not have the same means—or skill set—as a third-party purchaser.

When selling a business to either employees or family members, the business owner usually continues to have a close connection to the business and to those who have taken it over. Usually in these types of purchases, his money is still tied up in the business because the purchaser doesn't have the proper financing to pay the owner out quickly or at all.

Michael had read *Every Family's Business: 12 Common Sense Questions to Protect Your Wealth*, a book written by Dr. Thomas Deans, a successful third-generation business entrepreneur. Michael was so impressed, he even went to see Deans speak on the perils of gifting a business to family members.

Deans points out that children who are gifted shares in an operating company often stay for the wrong reasons—usually because it's easy to. Deans discovered that a second- or third-generation family member often runs the business as they found it—which does not typically equate to maximizing shareholder value. If selling a gift is difficult, fundamentally changing a gifted business is equally or even more problematic. Consequently, this is seldom done by succeeding generations. And it usually spells doom for the company and a family's long-term financial wealth—and the family's health.

Deans suggests that the best way to determine whether a family member is capable of taking over a successful family-run business is for the business owner to conduct a simple test. Offer the family member a living gift with the proviso that it can be used for anything the recipient desires. At that same moment, tell the family member that the business is for sale and that they can return the gifted money in exchange for shares—in other words, the family member can purchase the family business with the gifted money.

Deans says that the answer to this question speaks volumes about that family member's attitude towards independence, ownership and their own capacity to build the business and grow their gift. Family members who invest their gifted money by returning the gifted cash in exchange for shares in the family business are prepared psychologically to be an owner—they have in effect risked their inheritance to purchase the family business. It is the act of taking risk that gives the next generation the authenticity to drive change and innovation. Some call this having "skin in the game."

When the shares of a business are simply gifted to the next generation, it is nearly impossible for the recipient to change that gift, drive innovation or sell that business (how do you sell a gift?). In truth, most family members fail this cash test, taking the gifted cash instead of exchanging it for shares in the business.

"Deans provided powerful information for owners like me to seriously consider," said Michael.

"If children don't want to purchase a business, key employees don't want to purchase it, and neither competitors nor private equity funds want to purchase it, the business owner has simply waited too long to exit and monetize what is typically his largest asset. The fact is that most family members are not purchasing ownership of the family business. Most are taking gifted cash to use it, invest it or start their own business."

Is the discontinuation of a family business failure? Deans asks. Or is it the secret to preserving family wealth—you know, finding the end before the end finds you? For Deans, it's clear that while businesses don't last, one's wealth and family relationships can and should. Too many business owners are chasing the wrong legacy."

Mitch said that he couldn't agree more with Deans' observations. That is exactly why he had found selling to a third-party purchaser the preferred option for the vast number of business owners whose aims are wealth preservation. They would rather pass on their legacy by sharing their values and work ethic with their family than risk the nightmare of handcuffing family members to an existing business that they don't really care to operate and grow.

Mitch went on to explain that to increase the probability of a successful business transition, a responsible exit-planning program requires enlisting the assistance of many outside professionals in different areas of expertise, such as bankers, valuators, Certified Public Accountants who are income tax specialists, attorneys, Certified Financial Planners, management consultants, investment advisors, insurance professionals, employee benefit specialists and estate planners. Although each specialist on the succession-planning team has a different role to play, one lead advisor needs to be appointed. This trusted advisor will quarterback the entire exit-planning process for the owner and other team players.

Michael took a long pause as he stared down at the 18th hole.

"I always enjoy spending time with you and Wendy, but I have to tell you that the real reason I asked you to come visit is because I want completely out of my business," he said. "I want to sell all my financial interests and relinquish all control in my company to a third-party buyer. The only person I can trust to do this correctly is you, Mitch. I want you to quarterback the entire process to make sure it's done properly. I have thought long and hard about passing my company onto my children. I have come to believe it would be very unfair of me to have my children constrained by continuing to work on my dreams.

"They should be free to follow their own ambitions and shouldn't feel they have been chained to mine. They have their own goals. I intend to be behind them 100 percent in whatever they choose to do in their lives. On this decision, Dawn and I are on the same page. We want our children to have the satisfaction of having created their own identities. As a parent, the last thing I want for them is to live in my shadow."

Mitch was silent for a moment, then told Michael that he would be honored to assist. "Many business owners underestimate this challenge and the time it will take for them to make a smooth exit," he said. "Are you sure you're ready for this?"

"I am both mentally and emotionally prepared to commit to getting it done," Michael responded.

"For a while now, something greater has been calling me towards it, though I don't know fully what it is yet."

Mitch told Michael that he would have his assistant arrange for

Michael to come to Chicago as soon as two weeks from then to begin the succession process.

"That works for me. Let's do it," said Michael.

"Now I want my damn beer. You are down by two strokes. So take your shot already, slow poke," Mitch said, smiling.

CHAPTER 23

THE SHOEMAKER

MICHAEL WAS BUSY getting ready for his trip back east to Chicago—his hometown—for his Monday meeting. Mitch had assembled a team of key professionals who would assist in the succession-planning process and the selling of Michael's business. It was Friday morning, and Dawn was with their daughter down in Orange County, watching their granddaughter's pre-school dance recital. Dawn had woken up early, determined to be off the grid for a few hours. True to form, she was already packed and ready for their trip back to Chicago, excited about reconnecting with family and friends.

That morning, Michael had instructed his staff not to disturb him or his assistants while they collected the documents he would need for his meetings at Mitch's office. It wasn't until early afternoon that Michael noticed that his cell phone was set to silent mode. He told his team to take a break, then checked his voicemails. All these messages, he thought. Most of them were routine, but one was marked urgent. It was from Cathleen, Mitch's administrative assistant, asking him to call the firm's office in Chicago immediately.

Michael felt an ominous cloud descend over him as he left the boardroom for his office. But he tried to reason with himself. After all, it was just like Mitch to call at the last minute to give him more instructions and pile on to his rapidly growing to-do list.

"Hi, Cathleen, it's Michael Stevens. May I please speak to Mitch?" Michael asked.

"Mr. Stevens," replied a soft voice. "We have all been waiting for your call. Please hold for a moment."

A feeling that something was very wrong gnawed at Michael. Then he heard a voice on the other end of the line. It wasn't Mitch. Instead, it was Adam Boson, one of the senior partners at the firm. Mitch had handpicked Adam right out of law school 15 years earlier, mentoring and grooming him to one day become his successor at the firm.

"Michael, we've been trying to get a hold of you for the past several hours," said Adam.

"Sorry, I just got the message a few minutes ago, and I called right away. I've had my head down, preparing for our meeting this coming Monday. What's up?"

"I don't quite know how to say this, Michael, but Mitch is gone," Adam said.

"Gone?" Michael asked in a loud, joking voice. "Where the hell has he gone this time? Are you guys planning on canceling our meeting? Does Mitch think he and your firm have grown too big for me? Don't need my business anymore?"

"No, Michael, Mitch is gone," Adam repeated. "He died."

The words hung in the air. He's dead. Michael's mind went blank.

"Michael... Mike?"

Michael, dazed, tried to focus on Adam's voice.

"Michael, are you there?"

Michael was in shock. "Yes, sorry, Adam," he said. "What happened?"

"He was playing racquetball at the club. Apparently, he was having the game of his life but then began having chest pains. I was told he just brushed them aside and kept playing. He just thought he was a bit out of shape. And then all of a sudden he collapsed in the middle of the court. They rushed him immediately to Mount Sinai Hospital, trying to resuscitate him in the ambulance, but it was too late. He was pronounced dead on arrival at the emergency room. They say it was a major heart attack."

Michael couldn't believe what he was hearing. He couldn't make any sense of it. He had been golfing with Mitch just two weeks earlier.

"Mitch and Wendy had just visited us here in California," he said, not sure if he was telling this to Adam or himself. "I just spoke to him the other day. He was telling me he had arranged for us to meet with the team of transitional experts he had selected to work with us on the execution of my succession plan. I was just getting my papers ready for Monday. This is impossible, Adam. I can't believe what I'm hearing. It just can't be. Mitch can't be gone."

"Mitch was special to me and everyone else at our firm," Michael heard Adam say as he tried to regain his composure. Adam was choking up.

"He was loved. I wanted to get a hold of you as soon as I could. I know how close you two were."

"I apologize, but I can't talk now. I've got to go," Michael said. "Please have someone notify me as soon as you know the arrangements for the funeral. I am sorry. I've got to go now. Thank you."

Michael hung up the phone. All the energy had drained from his body. He walked back to the boardroom, opened the door and tried to keep his composure in front of his staff. They were back at work, gathering the documents for his meeting.

"Thank you for the good work you've done today," he said. "Please take the rest of the day off."

He then went back to his office, closing the door behind him.

About half an hour later, Dawn arrived. Wendy had called her, crying and disoriented. Michael too felt disoriented.

"He was just here," he said, looking up at Dawn, tears running down his face. "He was just here visiting us two weeks ago. We played golf, drank beers, retold each other old war stories." Michael hadn't felt this much anguish since his father died, when he was 11 years old.

"Let it all out. I'm here for you," Dawn said, holding him tightly in an embrace. "He was more than your friend. You grew up together. You confided in him. You trusted him. And he trusted and loved you. Everyone who knew the two of you knew this."

There was a long silence as they reflected on how much Mitch had meant to them.

"I need to come to terms with the fact that if we live long enough, everyone we love will eventually leave us, and if we die too soon, we will leave everyone we love," Michael said.

He straightened up and wiped the tears from his face. "We're all mortal—our lives are finite," he said solemnly. "And I must learn to come to terms with mortality."

That Sunday he and Dawn flew to Chicago, but it was not the weekend either of them had been anticipating. Michael was making last-minute touches to the eulogy for the following morning instead of to his transition plan.

As he stood at the podium that Monday morning, he surveyed the massive crowd that had gathered for Mitch's funeral, then began to read the eulogy he had prepared.

"One individual life may not seem that important in the big scheme of things," he began. "What is important is the meaning that we draw from witnessing that life well lived. I am proud to have witnessed and been a part of Mitchell Meadows' life. We were best friends since we were 18—just kids at college. Almost 38 years ago. For me, it feels like just yesterday.

"I have to be honest with you; we got off to a rough start. But

through Mitch's perseverance—which was one of his great strengths—
we became more than brothers. We grew up and became men together.

"Mitch was loyal to a fault. He was always open to lending a helping hand and sharing his ear, giving guidance to those who were smart
enough to ask for it."

Michael looked over to the open casket and at his departed friend's
still body. He felt one tear after another roll down his cheeks.

Regaining his composure, Michael took out a note from his pocket.
"This is Psalm 23," he said. "I would like to read it to you now."

The Lord is my shepherd; I shall not want.

He maketh me to lie down in green pastures: he leadeth me
beside the still waters.

He restoreth my soul: he leadeth me in the paths of righteousness for his name's sake.

Yea, though I walk through the valley of the shadow of death, I
will fear no evil: for thou art with me; thy rod and thy staff they
comfort me.

Thou preparest a table before me in the presence of mine enemies: thou anointest my head with oil; my cup runneth over.

Surely goodness and mercy shall follow me all the days of my
life: and I will dwell in the house of the Lord forever.

He was about to wrap up when he caught a glimpse of the crowd.
Hundreds of heads were bowed in respect for Mitch. He could hear
sniffling as people wept, some openly, others trying to hide the pain and
the great loss they were feeling.

"It is said that a dying man never wishes he had spent more time at
the office," Michael continued. "Mitch's life was cut short. He was so
much more than his work. He had so much more to give to this world.
We needed more time, we needed more of his love, we needed more
of his gentle guidance and we needed more of his wisdom. He had so

much more to share, so much more to give those who were fortunate enough to have him in their lives.

"Mitch, your beautiful wife and soulmate, Wendy; your family; your friends; and your entire community will miss your loving spirit. It truly knew no bounds, my friend.

"There are two types of people we meet as we walk this earth: givers and takers. Mitch, you were a life giver. Not just to me but also to countless others. You helped us, you guided us and you helped shape our lives. We are better people because you were a part of our lives. I will miss you for the rest of my days. I love you, brother. Until we meet again, my friend."

Michael turned, wiped the tears from his face and walked back to his seat. The room was silent and still.

After the funeral and the burial, Michael and Dawn headed to a hall near Mitch's home in Arlington Heights, northwest of Chicago. Michael reflected on his lifelong friendship with Mitch as he watched the Lake Michigan coastline pass by. He thought about all those summers he and his family had spent with Mitch and his family—those long summer nights on Mackinac Island, sitting by the beach bonfire, talking into the wee hours of the morning.

How young and optimistic they had been then, he remembered. The thought of death back then had not even entered their minds. And now he could think of nothing else. Michael thought about what it meant to have a peaceful death. He realized just how important it was to be prepared, because the way we die gives meaning to our lives. He believed a peaceful death meant that a man had put his life in order, both emotionally and in practical terms.

Michael believed that there should be as little unfinished business as possible at the end of a man's life. As they age, some men may believe they can simply continue on the same path as when they were young, but the wise man knows how to leave a worthy legacy. Mitch's death had come so suddenly, Michael wondered if he had taken the time to put his own affairs in order. For instance, was his will updated? Mitch was always busy helping others; had he made time for himself?

Michael thought of the story of the shoemaker who had holes in his shoes. Of course, he knew that his shoes needed repair. But he continued to procrastinate about repairing them, all the while taking care of others who needed *their* shoes fixed. As if him ignoring his own shoes wasn't bad enough, his family's shoes weren't faring any better than his. The point of this story is that none of us has control of what happens in the world around us, but what we do have control of is how we choose to react to what has happened.

Michael didn't have to wait long to find out that Mitch wasn't like the shoemaker at all. At the hall, which was just large enough to fit the large number of people who had come to show their respect and honor Mitch's life, he saw just how many people Mitch had touched with his life. The atmosphere was almost jubilant. Wendy, her children and her grandchildren, along with their friends, laughed and cried, and shared stories.

When he and Dawn were finally able to speak with Wendy alone, he was relieved to learn that Mitch had all his affairs up to date—he had plugged all the holes in his estate plan. He had updated his will. Mitch had ensured that if he died suddenly, got sick or became disabled, his family would be taken care of. He had made sure they would be able to continue on without compromising their quality of life and personal goals.

Michael listened to story after story about how much Mitch had touched people's lives in important and meaningful ways. It was then, really, that Michael finally came to terms with the idea of his own mortality, an idea he had been wrestling with for the past few years. He knew that an active youth is no guarantee of a healthy old age. In our modern society, we are constantly schooled in the art of achieving while being entirely unschooled in the art of being. Michael realized that when we cut ourselves off from our pain, we deplete ourselves of the energy needed to complete our life's work.

He had a strong feeling that he was being called to do something very different with his life, something greater, something more important, something more meaningful than what he had ever embarked on before. He felt compelled to listen to what life was telling him to do. In that moment, it was telling him to continue on the path that he and Mitch had discussed on the golf course and set into motion so that he could transition smoothly through to the most productive and meaningful years of his life.

With this revelation, Michael approached Adam Boson. The two looked each other straight in the eye, each understanding the pain the other was feeling.

"Mitch would have wanted me to complete the work we were about to begin with your firm," Michael said. "When things settle down, I want to start the exit process from my business—with your help."

Just as Michael said this, he noticed a familiar face. It belonged to a man he had not seen in more than 20 years. There he was across the room, now looking elderly and frail, supporting himself with a cane. It was the King of Main Street, now in his 80s.

"Adam, we must continue this conversation later, once you are back in the office," Michael said, keeping his eyes on Harold. "I need to say hello to an old and dear friend. I look forward to working with you and completing this project."

Michael excused himself and walked over to his old mentor. The two looked at each other, then hugged.

"It's been too long, kiddo," Harold said.

"I wish this could have been a better occasion," Michael replied.

"Mitch was a good man, a good friend," said Harold.

"Much too young. I'll miss him. After Richard died, Mitch stepped up and more than filled his big shoes. I came to rely on him for his good counsel in the years since."

Harold reached into his blazer jacket and pulled out a worn, sealed envelope and handed it to Michael. "Son, we did not leave on good terms," he said. "Can we meet again this week at the diner—you remember the one?"

Michael was tearing up as he nodded.

"At the usual time, if that's okay with you," Harold said. "I have so much I need to say, to ask of you, and there isn't much time."

"The diner near Daley Plaza," Michael confirmed. "I would love that. I need that. I wouldn't miss it for the world. It's a date, Harold."

CHAPTER 24

THE LETTER

DEAR MICHAEL,

Moments ago, you rushed out of the diner with one hell of a fire in your belly. You would think I would be angry. But I'm not. I am proud. What you've done is very good and very right. You wore the expression of a man who was about to go out into the world and accomplish great things. I've witnessed this in young men before.

You should think of your life as if it were the planning of an adventurous trip. You first need to determine where you intend to travel. Once you've chosen your destination, you must decide on your mode of transportation—a car, a train or a plane? If you decide to travel by car, say, you must determine the route you will take, along with the necessary items, such as maps to ensure you are on the right road and don't get lost. Most importantly, you must be selective about the companions you invite on your journey with you.

Let's say that during your travels, one of your companions decides he doesn't like the destination you have chosen. It is your responsibility, because it is your trip, to stop the car and get out to discuss, to see if you can find a compromise. If you can't, let that companion go his own way, wishing him well. Perhaps there is an opportunity for him to rejoin you in the future. When you reach your chosen destination, enjoy it and plan for your future trips, of which there will be many.

I want to state for the record that I give no apologies for the beliefs I hold. I have learned a thing or two on my life journey. I wish you nothing but many worthy experiences on your travels. Many times you will ask yourself, "What should I do?" You will find your answer. It will be your own answer. I could never have answered the question for you, and it would have been wrong of me to try to do so. I truly believe in the notion "If you meet the Buddha on the road, kill him." Your life must be your most trusted teacher. You must become your own Buddha.

I wanted you to think about our Wednesday-morning meetings. I spent the year making sure that I provoked thought, caused you to reflect and take action. In the end, only you can define your important life questions. Only by answering your own life questions will you find your true path. Learning comes only after many years of making your own choices and charting your own destiny. You cannot learn it through a book or be taught it in a Chicago diner.

Only after you have made the decision to commit will you be able to live a full and complete life on your own terms.

There are, in my judgment, two main reasons most people are reluctant to have a well-formed belief system, one that would guide them through their personal lives and in their professional pursuits. One, having such a belief system requires coming to terms with one's mortality, and two, it requires having an inner compass, having clear convictions, making judgments and having an opinion about what is right—and only then can one believe in something so deeply that one would be willing to die for it.

To achieve any type of enduring success, we must ask ourselves two questions. First, "What do I really want from life?" And second, "What am I prepared to sacrifice to achieve my goals?" Life is made up of a series of choices. Wisdom is attained by asking oneself relevant questions. And then, one must be prepared to go down whatever rabbit hole one's answers bring one to.

Here I am reminded of Plato's famous allegory of the cave. Plato wrote about prisoners in a cave, watching shadows on the wall that they accept as real. One prisoner frees himself of his shackles, leaves the cave and sees the sun for the very first time. He then returns to the darkness, temporarily blinded by the sun's brilliance. He tells his fellow prisoners what he has witnessed and experienced. The other prisoners think he is crazy, yet he knows they live a life of illusion and denial that they are not ready to question. Knowing there is something much greater out there in the world, the freed prisoner is bound by his need to be a free man and to help others who are prepared to break free from their self-inflicted mental chains.

I believe that the moral of this allegory is that we all have the responsibility to speak our truths. We must be honest about our reality, no matter how uncomfortable or detrimental that may be. There will always be an audience for our truths. Remember, the game ends only when we are dead.

Weakness occurs when we look for quick fixes to fundamental problems. You wouldn't have embarked on your business venture at this stage of your life if you did not believe that adversity breeds self-reliance. Every great man has a need to search within himself for what he knows is just and right. This is the source of the kind of heroism that's needed to implement fundamental solutions to problems, for the greater good.

I passionately believe that it is our personal responsibility to find a way out of our self-created hell. Hell is believing that someone or some great power outside ourselves is going to lift us out of our misery. That's not going to happen. Instead, what we need to do is find what we are most compelled to do. We have free will because we have the choice to listen to what our lives are telling us we are meant to do. We exercise our free will when we pay attention to what we are drawn towards naturally. Alternatively, we can fight it-and suffer the consequences. To exercise our free will, we must make the commitment to move towards what we love to do; we must move towards what we are meant to contribute to this world.

Self-mastery comes about only after we take total responsibility for our own lives and understand that there is no such thing as a failure, that there is only feedback. Everything in life is a learning experience to be cherished. We must be willing to spend the time to discover, learn and then earn life's wisdom.

For everything that we lose, we will also gain something, and for everything we gain, we will also lose something. Only through our experiences will we learn how to navigate the ups and down of our lives. Only through living can a man achieve a richer and more fulfilling life, a life worth living. An experience can never be lost or taken away; indeed, experiences are the only things in the universe that are truly our own. Everything else is rented, transient.

Everything is an illusion. The ideal is to master the illusions of what we perceive as our reality. This is an aim worthy of each of us to pursue, obtain and self-master. In my humble opinion, this opens the gateway for a man to become the conscious creator of his own reality, to chart his own destiny.

The gifts we find in overcoming the illusions we face is what makes living a truly worthwhile endeavor. Nothing ever turns out as we first dreamed it would be. If it did, wouldn't our lives be boring? It's the journey of self-discovery that makes life worth living. Wisdom is understanding that life is not work. Instead, it's the most exciting game in the universe. Each of us has been invited to play. It is the only game worth playing.

Self-mastery is about becoming mentally, emotionally and spiritually better. Each experience should empower us to meet bigger challenges, thereby helping us to master the game of life. I have come to see my life-indeed, all life-as part of an awakened dream, where we can take control of it at any moment, where we can choose to take control of our destiny. We can direct our perception of our reality at any time.

I have also come to understand that as long as I

have breath in my lungs and a spring in my step, the game continues. The point of the game is to continue the play and to expand it by inviting ever more players to take part in it. The aim is not to win but to enjoy the play so that at the end of your life trip you can say to yourself that your only regrets are the things you did not do, not the things you did do.

When your vision is clear and it is right for you, the universe will conspire to help you experience more of its secrets. The only thing stopping you from having mastery of what you love is yourself. Avoid at all cost the luxury of feeling sorry for yourself. Go out and make the commitment to live out a full and complete life, one with no regrets!

Michael, every man has a burning desire to prove himself, whether it's to his community, to his partner, to a friend or to a family member. Yet remember, all you really need to do is prove yourself to the toughest critic of them all: yourself. To truly win in life, a man needs to stretch himself as he reaches for the stars. Then he has to work at 100 percent of his capacity to create something of value, something that will stand the test of time. The hardest game we ever play, the one most worthy of our playing, is the one we play against ourselves, every single moment of our day.

So, to answer the question "What should I do?", the simple answer is: it's your question, it's your life; go out and answer it yourself. All external issues force us to confront our internal goals. Everything that happens is for the purpose of learning and growing. Do what you find yourself passionately drawn towards doing. Your answer is only as simple or as complex as you need it to be.

The time is now! It is your moment to take the

quantum leap in your life and in your career. People are frightened of change because they feel that they're not in control. Remember, you are the producer of your life; you pick the projects, finance them and choose the directors, writers and actors. You are the one and only unifying thing on your journey.

For the time being, I will honor your wishes and step back from your life. I will be watching the risks you take, the challenges you overcome and the growth you experience, all the while staying in the shadows. When needed, I will be looking out for your interests by providing an invisible helping hand. I will be applauding your accomplishments, watching you develop into the man you are meant to be. I am in your corner—even if you can't see me there.

Our acts and words have the power to change our world. I am no more intelligent than you, but I have been on the path a little longer. I am sure that you will go farther down your trail than I have been able to go down mine, if you have the desire, the determination and patience. There's nothing more that I look forward to than the day when I become your eager student.

I will close here with an ancient Chinese proverb for you to keep in mind as you go forward in life: " A journey of a thousand miles begins with a single step."

The best place to begin your journey is where you are right now. From the sturdiest foundations, the tallest structures are built.

Now, go climb your mountain; it awaits you. I wait for you on the other side.

—Harold

CHAPTER 25

—⟫⟪—

THE DINER

ICHAEL ARRIVED AT the diner bright and early. He ordered coffee and breakfast, and waited for his former mentor to arrive. As he looked around the room, the image of him storming out on Harold more than 20 years earlier popped into his head. How foolish he had been, he thought. He had been given advanced instruction in life, but his youthful stubbornness blinded him from fully appreciating the priceless gift. Back then *he couldn't* fully comprehend how valuable Harold's lessons would be as he ventured through life.

Although Michael hadn't sat down with Harold for more than two decades, he had learned how to apply many of his teachings when navigating and negotiating business and his other life adventures. Harold's advice had helped him become a mature, well-adjusted man. As he sat there waiting for Harold, Michael thought about how this reunion was long overdue. He had many regrets as he thought back to his last breakfast with Harold; he wished he had not left as he had. But now he was being given a second chance, a chance to make things right, and he was determined to make amends.

Harold entered the diner. Michael quietly waved him over to the table—the same one they had always sat at.

"Your coffee, sir, just the way you like it—black," Michael greeted Harold, sliding a cup towards him as he sat down. "Good morning, Harold. I took the liberty of ordering your 'usual'—scrambled eggs and dry toast."

"Thank you, Michael, and knock off the 'sir' stuff."

Michael laughed. Harold hadn't lost any of his bite; he was as vibrant as ever. The two didn't say much of any significance at first. It was mostly small talk, safe conversations about things like California's winter sunshine—"Nice move, Michael," Harold had said approvingly.

Finally, though, the conversation turned serious. Harold leaned in towards Michael and said, "I owe you an apology."

Michael was taken aback. Why would Harold owe him an apology? Shouldn't it be the other way around?

"It's me who owes you an apology, Harold," he exclaimed.

"I was so young back then, and I should never have thundered out of here like I did. I regret my behavior—I was cocky and impatient. There have been so many days since then that I wished I had acted differently. And one of the most important lessons I have learned is the harm an untamed ego can do. I had been using it to mask my insecurities and fears, and it was killing my spirit. I want you to know that I am no longer the same man who burst out of here all those years ago."

Harold looked at the man he had affectionately called "kiddo."

"Thank you, Michael. I'm deeply touched. I really appreciate that. There is no need to call you 'kiddo' anymore. Look at you. I am now sitting across from a seasoned man, a peer. You are no longer the student you were when we first met. You have become a wise teacher in your own right and on your own terms."

Harold gazed out the window for a moment, then continued.

"Have I ever told you about the strained relationship that I had with my late father for much of my life?" he asked.

"No, I don't think you ever mentioned anything to me about your father."

"Mendel Bloom," Harold said in a lowered tone.

"My father—Dr. Mendel Bloom—was once a promising young doctor and researcher in Germany. Between the two world wars, he was one of the brightest minds in medicine and was being groomed by Dr. Otto Heinrich Warburg. Are you familiar with the contributions to humanity Dr. Warburg made?"

Michael shook his head as he listened intently.

"Dr. Otto Warburg won the 1931 Nobel Prize in Physiology or Medicine for his pioneering research into cancer. And he chose my father as his protégé. But all my father's dreams came crashing down with the rise of the Nazis. Any hope he had of following his chosen career path—any desire that he had of making a mark on medicine and on humanity—ended when he escaped Germany with his family in 1938, in the days immediately following Kristallnacht, the Night of Broken Glass. It was the only way to avoid certain death, and that's what we faced if we stayed in Europe. I was just six years old.

"My father never recovered from that. You could say that he died spiritually. After he arrived in the United States, he was never able to hit his stride or find a sense of place. Here in America, a land of great opportunity, he failed to obtain a medical license. My father was never able to practice what he loved to do most. He lived the rest of his days as a shell of his former self. Knowing that he would never reach his full potential was very difficult for him to deal with. My father became a detached and broken man."

Harold told Michael about how he had felt when he had been young, and how he had believed he was his father's greatest disappointment. Unlike his father, Harold hadn't excelled at academics; basically, he had been a terrible student. He had spent more time getting into trouble or hanging around his Uncle Max and his buddies at Manny's Deli and at his uncle's scrap yard than he had ever done in class.

"My older brother, David—he was another story," Harold continued. "He was an excellent student, just like my father had been. He went off to Harvard after serving in the Second World War and became a respected heart surgeon in New York City. I never saw my father happier and prouder than when David graduated from medical school. He had earned our father's open admiration and respect. When it came to me, all I ever 'heard' coming from my father was silence."

The younger Harold had tried to convince himself that he did not need his father's approval. He told Michael that he had dropped out of high school. As soon as he had turned 18, he had gone straight to the recruiting office to enlist in the US Marines.

"But I believe that every son wants the approval of his father," Harold said. "I observed this need being acted out again and again in the civil unrest that accompanied the Vietnam War. Hundreds of thousands of young men from across this nation poured into the streets to protest. Their protests were actually against their fathers, even if they didn't know it.

"I saw in their actions the same unconscious motivations that drove me in my reaction to my father. What they were saying to their fathers, to their fathers' entire generation, was 'Dad, look at me. Pay attention to me. Listen to me. Respect me. If you don't, I will burn down everything you value in this world until you do.'"

Harold admitted that he had spent much of his life unaware that he had been seeking out his father's approval. He had felt that anything that he accomplished, whether in business or his personal life, would never earn his father's respect. He had believed he would always be his father's biggest disappointment.

"I believed that I could never measure up to my father," Harold said. "When he was young, he was working on finding a cure for cancer. At the same age, I was off selling discounted baby diapers and cheap toothpaste. To compensate, I tried to add as many ones and zeros to my bank account, and to acquire as many tangible assets, as possible. I thought this would fill the void left by his lack of approval. Now I can see how misdirected my behavior was."

Harold told Michael that, in his father's later years, shortly before he had passed away, his father had asked for Harold. They talked—really talked—for the first time that Harold could remember. And for the very first time, father and son saw each other as individual men on their own unique journeys, seeking out their own answers to life's big questions.

"We had a heartfelt conversation that day. I will always remember what he said to me. He told me he had been frightened of the choices I had made. His fears had more to do with his own insecurities about not being a good father than with what I was doing or not doing. He told me that his greatest regret in life was not expressing to me that he knew that I had found my purpose and had followed the path that I was meant to be on. He told me that he loved me and that he was very proud of me, even though he hadn't been able to express it until then," he said.

"That day, my father shared those feelings with me. I understood my father and his pain—a pain that, unfortunately, many men carry with them to their graves. I appreciated my father that day for all he had accomplished and sacrificed for me and my family. He did what he could with what he had been given. Michael, these were the greatest gifts a father could ever give his son—the gifts of acknowledgment and respect."

Harold looked Michael in the eye, his demeanor still solemn.

"I should have said this over 20 years ago while we sat in this same place. I was just too damn stubborn. But it's never too late. Michael, you are a real mensch, a genuine and good person. Michael, I am proud of everything you have achieved despite all the obstacles in your way. I am proud of the man you have chosen to become. It is important that you hear this from me. I need you to know this."

Once Harold's words had sunk in, Michael understood why, so long ago, he had chosen Harold to be his mentor.

"I will treasure this moment for the rest of my life," he said. "Our relationship has always been important to me. Your words are precious to me. Harold, in many ways, you have stepped into the role that I had hoped my father would have if he had lived."

The two men locked eyes for a moment. Then Harold smiled and gave a warm nod.

"I still have a question," Michael said, leaning forward. "Is this what you meant at Mitch's funeral when you said that you had something to ask of me but there wasn't much time?"

"Partly. Do you remember what I said to you the last time we met here?" asked Harold.

"Yes. I'll never forget. It's like it happened just yesterday. You said that regarding the decisions I needed to make in my business, at that stage in my life, I wouldn't and shouldn't listen to whatever you could tell me. That I was not yet ready to understand. I needed to go out into the world and fall flat on my face—a lot. If I had what it took to get back up, only then would I be able to come back with an open mind, ready to really listen to what you had to tell me."

"Yes. Old age gives us, through experience, insights that are beyond the ability of youth to fully appreciate. The young deny their weaknesses; the old need to learn to accept them. What I wanted to share with you back then was that, when you have lived life long enough and you have experienced enough, you too will realize what is truly important in life. But this truth is not 'real' unless your experience of it is planted deep in your muscles. To discover your own truths, which one learns are actually universal truths, you needed to go out and make your own way first," said Harold.

"I believe I've come to understand what you were trying to tell me back then," said Michael. "In the first half of my life, my focus was on building up my identity and looking outside myself for validation and self-worth. Back then I was not able to listen because I had a great need to feed my ego's never-ending hunger for power over my environment. Over the past several years, my concern with the custodianship of society has grown, and I find myself needing to address that issue. I have discovered that when we harvest our lives—when we find wisdom from our experiences and knowledge—we receive returns on our investment in the form of inner riches that were unimaginable during our youth."

"The universe is the greatest teacher, if you live long enough," Harold said. "You have grown wise. The real goal of the second half of life, I have come to believe, is to become a healthy, well-adjusted elder. In youth, we go out into the world to make our mark, and pursue personal wealth and meaningless trinkets. In the last half of life, to be healthy, we need to go within ourselves and harvest our experiences and accumulated knowledge so that we may turn it into wisdom that can be shared. When we first met, you did not have enough experience to understand this."

"No instruction on my part could have taught you this. Any words of wisdom then would have been a poor substitute for you going out on your own into the world and learning these truths for yourself."

Harold paused, but Michael sensed there was something more that he wanted to tell him. "What else, Harold?" he asked. "There's something you're not telling me."

Harold nodded. "That's right," he said. "You have always been perceptive. There is something I haven't told you. It has to do with my health."

Michael felt his stomach sink.

"There is not much time left," Harold said. "I asked you to meet me today because I am dying. I have stage-four cancer—leukemia. The doctors are telling me I don't have much time."

Michael had always wanted to believe that Harold would always be there. Even during the past two decades of detachment when they were not speaking to each other, Michael was comforted in knowing that Harold was out there somewhere.

"Are you afraid of death?" Michael asked. "I'm sorry; it's an awkward question. I'm still trying to come to terms with Mitch's death. But my question goes to the heart of what we've been speaking about during our conversations at this diner all these years."

"I don't mind that you asked. I welcome it, Michael," Harold responded. "Only in the presence of death do we have a real appreciation for the life we have lived. It is more than all right that you asked. I lost my wife, Sara, my Chailee, my life for me, a few years ago, and it is a loss that will never heal. But I still find comfort in the fact that life needs to be experienced. This is the last leg of my journey, and I intend to finish it standing upright. My thoughts on my inevitable demise might best be summed up in a short tale."

Harold proceeded to tell the story of two waves in the ocean that were moving quickly towards the coastline. One wave noticed what was happening to the waves ahead of them, the ones closer to the shore. The wave began to cry. The wave beside him asked why he was crying. The crying wave answered, "Look at the waves in front of us; they are all crashing on the rocks and are ceasing to be waves. Can't you see? That's the same fate that awaits us when we hit those same rocks. I don't want to die."

The second wave remained calm and spoke in a reassuring voice. "You shouldn't be afraid. Those rocks, yes, we will hit them and then cease to be waves. But we will still be part of the ocean, which is vast and beyond our comprehension right now because we are just waves."

Harold gave Michael a comforting smile. "I don't know where we go when our bodies no longer have breath," he said. "I would like to believe that we return to the whole. It was here before us and it will be here long after our present forms are gone."

Michael sat back. He could not believe the direction the conversation had taken. But he also began to feel comfort in the decision he had made to sell his business and chart a new future.

"Now it's time for me to ask you a question," Harold said. "How do you plan to spend your remaining days, before you eventually meet your final hours?"

Michael told Harold that he had been speaking to Mitch about transitioning out of his company. "I was supposed to meet with him to start the process, but I found myself delivering his eulogy that day instead," he said.

"Have you changed your mind about making that transition?" Harold asked.

"No, I told Adam Boson from Mitch's firm that I plan to go ahead with transitioning out," Michael replied.

Harold had two more questions.

"Are you going to pass your company onto your children?" he asked.

"No," Michael answered without hesitation. "I believe that would handcuff them to *my* dreams and aspirations. I am very proud that my children are all independent and want to seek out their own destinies. I don't want to put them in a trap where they feel they have to fulfill mine."

"So, you are going to sell your business to that private equity lender that has been backing you all these years?" Harold asked.

All of a sudden a light bulb went off in Michael's head. He replayed Harold's question in his mind. Everything started to make sense to him now. The anonymous investor, the favorable lending terms he had received when he had begun his expansion all those years ago—no other lender had even come close to offering those terms. The strange conditions in the loan agreements that the lender had required. And the cryptic message at the end of the letter Harold had given Michael after Mitch's funeral. "When needed, I will be looking out for your interests by providing an invisible helping hand," it read.

Michael wondered how he could have missed the fact that it was Harold who had been behind the anonymous investor and that private equity fund all this time. It was now so obvious.

"It was you," he blurted out. "It was always you who was guiding me, investing in me and helping my business—in the background, out of sight."

Harold nodded yes, and then took a sip of his coffee.

CHAPTER 26

---≫≫≪≪---

THE REVELATION

MICHAEL WAS STILL in a state of shock. He collected his thoughts and took a deep breath, but he could utter only one word: "Why?"

"This will take another cup of coffee," Harold said, beckoning to the waitress.

"I can explain it best with a story. Believe me, Michael, there was no malice in my motives. To explain the intent behind my actions, I must tell you the backstory. It may be a long story but it's a good one and worth listening to."

Harold explained to Michael that he found it useful to look at business models through the lens of modern physics. Physicists tell us that the observable universe of matter makes up only 3 percent of the entire universe. The other 97 percent is outside our five-sense awareness. This 97 percent, we are told, is made up of both dark matter and dark energy. What we observe of a business owner's success is usually only his bottom line—what he sells and what he buys, his profits and losses—the 3 percent, so to speak. What can't be seen is the successful business owner's ability to deal with, overcome and manage ever-increasing levels of complexities—the other 97 percent.

"Have you ever noticed that 'evil' spelled backwards is 'live'?" Harold asked.

Michael shrugged his shoulders. "Okay."

Harold smiled as the waitress refilled his coffee. "True evil is when a human being is allowed to waste his talents," he said. "You were given natural gifts and endowments. My intent was to support them. I believe that if a man is not fully living up to his potential, his soul will die a slow and painful death. If a man who has the ability to prevent this from happening to another man chooses to watch and do nothing, well, this inaction is one of the greatest crimes a man can perpetrate on another."

The goal of all mature individuals, Harold said, is to assist the next generation in living out their true purpose. They can achieve this by (1) providing a supportive structure that promotes that individual's personal growth; (2) giving the freedom to the protégé to find his own answer to why he needs to grow as an individual; and (3) becoming a mentor when called upon to be one.

"I knew it would have been the wrong course of action if I overtly assisted you," Harold said. "You were too proud, and I did not want to stunt your growth. You would not have become the man you are today if I had stepped out of the shadows too early."

Learning how to deal with the ever-increasing levels of complexity in life is the mental, emotional and spiritual challenge that a successful business owner must overcome in order to manifest his success in the physical world, in the world of things that can be seen and counted. Our society confers high status on superficial things such as professional titles, whether earned or not earned, large corner offices, luxurious homes, expensive cars, and money in the bank. Yet the unseen is infinitely of more importance.

Those with a trained eye have invested the time and energy necessary to develop the skills for uncovering the true worth of a man. This is where the real treasure lies—it is an individual's intrinsic value that will be judged above all else.

Harold told Michael that his intrinsic value had increased through the many challenges he had taken upon himself. Over the years, Harold had witnessed Michael overcome many hurdles, to build a life on his own terms.

"A man's true worth can never be found in his financial statements," Harold said. "You needed to learn this for yourself. I could not tell you—you needed experience, to find this out for yourself."

When an important truth is unseen because it is unnamed, *Harold explained,* you may have to find a name for it so that it can be made visible. He believed that today's arrogant society teaches us to believe that the modern world is more advanced than all previous generations. There's a belief that we hold the corner on universal truths, whereas past generations were ignorant of them. This could not be farther from the truth.

"In fact, the most powerful word that ever originated on the Ancient Indian subcontinent about 3,500 years ago," he said, "is the word *maya*. It is derived from ancient Sanskrit, and it basically says everything that needs to be understood about our perception of reality."

Harold explained that *maya* has two meanings. First, it refers to how everything that we call our reality is actually an illusion—nothing we perceive as being real is as we think it is. Harold asked Michael to think about this notion for a moment.

"Nothing that we believe is real is actually real," he said. "Everything is a hologram created by our senses and interpreted by our mind to support our belief system—our beliefs about what we think reality is. Most hold their beliefs, whether they have tested them out or not. What we call reality is just a grand illusion to protect us from the truth, which is that we each create our perceptions of reality, moment by moment."

The second meaning of *maya* is to measure, Harold explained, and this is directly related to the first meaning. If everything is an illusion, then any measurement we make comparing ourselves with anything or anyone else just feeds our perception of what we believe reality is. *Maya* tells us that what we perceive really does not exist in the first place. What can be counted does not count, and what can't be counted does count. Reality is only how we choose to interpret what our senses are permitted to feed our minds, and this "reality" is filtered through our personal belief systems, a system that *most* in our society unconsciously leave unquestioned, thus allowing these unquestioned beliefs to filter our meaning and perceptions of reality.

Michael still had a nagging question. "You still haven't told me why you sat silently in the background, supporting my dream of creating a successful business," he said.

"As I said earlier, I am only human. I have all the frailties that come with that, and not everything occurred exactly as I would have wished. But in the end, everything turned out the way it was meant to. We are here—where we are supposed to be."

Harold told Michael that he finally began listening to his inner voice in 1984, at the age of 52.

"I made the conscious decision then and there to embark on a new journey, seeking out greater meaning and purpose for the rest of my life," he said. "I realized that I was my father's son, something I had denied up until then. I knew that to get out of the immediate world of the five senses—the world that most people are stuck in thinking is important—I had to do my part to make the world better than how I had found it. I had this responsibility to future generations who will inherit this world long after I am gone. Improving the world was the worthy goal my father had aspired to achieve in his lifetime. It was now my turn to consciously choose to take up the torch, and to carry this torch as far as I could before it was my turn to hand it to the next generation. It was *my* time to work towards making the world a better place. With age, I knew that seeking this ultimate goal would be the only way to heal my soul before I took my last breath and met my maker."

Harold paused for a moment, then continued.

"I have long agreed that material wealth is not a crime; it's a blessing," he said. "We humans are born to toil, and to reap what we sow. I am always mindful that one can't keep what one hasn't rightfully earned. When a person invests effort, he earns his reward. When he doesn't invest effort, he gains nothing and has squandered an opportunity to learn from his experience."

Harold went on to note a truism in Psalm 49. *"People, despite their wealth, do not endure; they are like the beasts that perish,"* he said, reciting the line.

"On the other hand, all our accumulated experiences, our friendships and the love we give to others while we inhabit this temporal plane of existence do endure," he said.

Harold then told Michael that he realized that the most dangerous competitor he had ever come up against was his own ego. "At age 52, I walked into Richard's office. Did you know Richard was my brother-in-law?" he abruptly asked, interrupting his own thought.

Michael shook his head. This was a day full of surprises.

"Anyway, he was my older sister Rachelle's husband. Rachelle had been like a second mother to me, always looking out for my well-being. So, for Richard, it was natural for him to treat me as his little brother from day one. I could always trust that he would put my best interests ahead of his own. When I was the black sheep of the family, it was Richard—and my Uncle Max—who would say, 'Let the kid find his own way. It doesn't matter if he learns his lessons on Monday morning or Friday afternoon. What is important is that he learns them, and learns them well.'"

Harold recalled the day he walked into Richard's office. He had delegated all his corporate structuring and financial acquisitions to Richard's firm over the years.

"I told Richard that I wanted out," Harold said bluntly.

Michael understood the feeling.

"I wanted to sell off all my business interests and simplify my life," his mentor continued. "I told Richard that I felt it did not matter anymore how much I had acquired. I knew that I could wear only one pair of shoes at a time, sleep in only one bed at a time, and be with only one woman, my Sara."

Harold explained that until that meeting with Richard, he had always been looking forward, never slowing down to look back and appreciate what he had accomplished and accumulated. His mindset had been focused on that next business deal, that next business acquisition, that next new store opening, that next real estate development.

"But the more I acquired, the more those things controlled and owned me," he said. "The problem was that nothing would ever be enough to feed my ever-growing ego. But there's also something else that I learned at that meeting with Richard: walking away isn't as easy as it sounds."

Michael was puzzled. Harold was the King of Main Street. He had earned the right to do whatever he pleased when it came to his business affairs.

"First of all, it was going to be very difficult to find out what I controlled and owned in the first place," he said. "I had set up sophisticated business, tax and estate plans and structures over the years, so that I could stay out of sight, be anonymous in the world. And I wanted to stay anonymous."

At their meeting that day, Richard told Harold that it would be a momentous undertaking just to determine Harold's net worth, and that it would be nearly impossible to do in secrecy. Richard said he and the firm were up to the task but that Harold would have to be patient. It took Richard six months to get everything in order, before he was ready to call Harold with the results.

"I remember the meeting like it was yesterday," Harold said. "Richard ushered me into his office, calling me 'little brother,' like he always did. He had a peculiar look on his face. I asked, 'What's that all about?' And do you know what he said?"

Michael shook his head.

"He just laughed and said, 'And to think you were the black sheep of the family, the one everyone was worried would never make anything of himself.' It turns out I was much wealthier financially than I could ever have imagined. I had been running so fast for so long that I had lost track of how far I had gone. Richard told me that I had my hand in almost every sector of the economy. I had actively participated in the greatest, the largest and the longest economic expansion that took place after the Second World War."

Michael wasn't surprised. But what Harold said next nearly floored him.

"Richard just said, 'So, here it is' and passed me a piece of paper with a number written on it. He then looked me straight in the eye and told me that if anyone ever got a hold of that number, I would be crowned the world's richest man, maybe even the wealthiest man who had ever lived."

Harold let out a big sigh.

"What did you say?" asked Michael.

"For the first few minutes, I said absolutely nothing. It was so much to take in. I knew that I was financially successful, but until that moment I didn't know how successful I had really been. I think I said, 'I guess I truly am the King of Main Street. I guess what's been written about me must be true.'"

Richard had told Harold that his plan to liquidate all his holdings at once was not an option unless his aim was to plunge the American economy into another deep recession or, even worse, start a global depression. There were not enough investors to buy him out. Richard feared that there would be too much supply and not enough demand for all of Harold's assets. If Harold had sold everything, he would end up breaking the confidence of the market, potentially with grave consequences.

"Richard knew me well enough to know that I needed time to digest the news of this gilded cage I had created for myself," Harold said. "All I felt back then was a sense of privilege to have earned so much and for being given the opportunity to give back and add to this world. It was my responsibility to wisely dispense with what I had earned so that it created the greatest good for the greatest number of people."

"But I had one lingering question," Harold said, leaning in to share one more thought with Michael.

"What was I going to do with all this wealth?"

CHAPTER 27

‒→≫≪←‒

RESPONSIBILITY

THE MORNING RUSH at the diner was subsiding. Michael looked up from his empty coffee cup and, seeing the other customers leaving for their offices, realized that he and Harold had been talking almost nonstop for the last two hours. It seemed like not a day had gone by since their previous meeting at the diner. No one could ever have guessed they had parted ways over 20 years ago.

"I believe we need more coffee," said Michael, beckoning the waitress.

"Nature is a funny thing," he then said. "It has a wisdom of its own. It won't give us what we want when we want it. And when we do get it, we usually no longer care to have it. Becoming rich doesn't change a man; it only shows the world who the man really is, who he has always been."

Michael wasn't surprised to learn that Harold was the richest man alive. That's why he had deservingly earned the nickname the King of Main Street. But Michael also had a few questions he wanted to ask Harold.

"Were you overwhelmed?" he asked as the waitress arrived with a pot of freshly brewed coffee to refill their cups. "That is, overwhelmed to learn the enormity of your net worth? What did you decide to do with it all?"

Harold took a moment before he replied.

"I wanted to give it all away, or at least as much of it as possible while I was alive," he said. "But how? The first voice I always listened to, ever since we met, was that of the true love of my life, my dear Sara. She had always been my support and my wisest counsel. Sara suggested that I look at what other men who had found themselves in my position had done. As always, she was right."

Harold had come to believe that what makes man different from all other animals is his ability to take another individual's experiences and learn from them, and apply that hard-earned wisdom in his own life. He believed in Sir *Isaac Newton's adage, "If I have seen further,* it is only by standing on the shoulders of giants."

"Sara was a voracious reader, like you are, Michael. She believed, after reading about many people who had earned great wealth in their lives, that they had found fulfillment and a sense of peace by consciously choosing to live philanthropic lives," Harold said.

"Richard helped guide me through the world of philanthropy, and I did my own research on Andrew Carnegie. He was a giant like no other man before him."

Harold recounted how he had found himself in a situation similar to that of Carnegie. Carnegie had risen from humble beginnings: he had arrived on the shores of the United States as a poor immigrant kid, and he had been the world's richest man by the time he had written his classical essay *The Gospel of Wealth*, in 1898. In this essay, he systematically laid out how he wanted to distribute his wealth, and he tackled many of the same issues that Harold was grappling with at the time.

A main tenet of Carnegie's well-articulated belief system was that it was important to give smartly while one was alive so that one could witness the social benefits created by one's wealth. Carnegie had believed that it is better to give with a warm hand than with a cold one, knowing that a wealthy miser and a fat steer are only of value to society when they are both dead. When Carnegie had contributed his money, time and resources to those in need, he had not believed that he was being generous or charitable. He had believed that he was doing what was right and just.

Like the great medieval philosopher Maimonides, also known as the Rambam, Carnegie had believed that the highest form of giving is supporting a fellow human being who can then himself rise up to help another individual, who will eventually do the same. Carnegie had believed that paying it forward took shape in many forms. A man could help another man by endowing him with a gift or a loan, by entering into a business partnership with him or by helping him find employment. That is, help came in many forms, always with the end goal of strengthening the receiver until he no longer needed the help and was not dependent on others. This healthy circle of life would thus continue generation after generation.

"No one can say Carnegie had failed to put his money where his mouth was," Harold said. "By the time of his death in 1919, he had strategically given away over 90 percent of his wealth."

Carnegie had honored his commitment to learning by funding scientific research and the establishment of a teachers' pension. He had always valued universal education because the generosity of others had allowed him to learn, develop and prosper. Before his death, he had financed over two thousand public libraries and countless schools. It was this same spirit that had led Carnegie to fund the building of the Peace Palace in The Hague, which today houses the International Court of Justice. Carnegie had believed that the highest value was that of universal justice and opportunity for all, based on merit.

Carnegie had believed that there are three modes in which surplus wealth can be distributed by the wealth creator: it can be left to the family of the deceased, it can be bequeathed for public purposes after his death or it can be administered for philanthropic purposes by the wealth creator—while he is alive to witness its benefits to society.

In the first mode—leaving one's fortune solely to family—Carnegie had observed that bequeathing great sums of wealth to children is more of a burden to those children than a gift, more of a curse than a blessing. He had said that doing so was "not in the welfare of the children, but was for family pride, which inspires these enormous legacies." He had believed that the aim of a parent should be to make their children healthy contributors to society. With this concept in mind, he had suggested that inheritances should be modest and provide only for unostentatious living, not extravagance. He had understood, however, that there must be different standards of inheritance for different conditions. For example, a disabled dependent child may need more inheritance than his sibling with a Harvard law degree who is a senior partner at a Wall Street firm.

Carnegie had not favored the second mode either—that of leaving great sums of wealth for public use after the wealth creator's death. He had felt that such bequests only create monuments for the dead. Even more pointedly, he had thought that they also proved the wealth creator's failure in life, because such bequests had not created any value while the wealth creator had been alive. According to Carnegie, "Men who leave vast sums in this way may fairly be thought men who would not have left it at all, had they been able to take it with them."

Carnegie had advocated for and lived by the third method for distributing great wealth. He had personally attended to the administration and distribution of his wealth to worthy causes. His goal had been to give it all away during his lifetime. He had emphasized that "the man who dies leaving behind many millions of available wealth, which was his to administer during life, will pass away 'unwept, unhonored, and unsung,' no matter to what uses he leaves the dross which he cannot take with him."

Carnegie had believed that the Pareto Principle, sometimes referred to as the 80/20 Rule, is always in play. That is, he had thought that the greatest concentration of wealth will always find its way into the hands of the few. Carnegie had understood that the few then had an opportunity for and the responsibility of mindful giving—they could, and should, choose to be a potent force for societal good. He had personally recommended that the main consideration of giving be "to help those who will help themselves. To provide part of the means by which those who desire to improve may do so." He had wanted giving to include the intent to do good by repairing the world and making it a better place for all.

Harold joked that that's why death taxes are so high: to compensate for what the financially rich but morally poor—those extremely wealthy individuals who didn't heed Andrew Carnegie's advice about honoring their life's fortunes by continuously distributing it worthily while they were alive—could have done but chose not to do.

Harold told Michael that there are people, both living and dead, who have accomplished what they wanted to realize in their lives, and that these individuals can become our teachers. They can help us achieve our goals. On the flipside, there are others who are looking for you to be *their* mentor.

"It's your choice to make the difference," he said.

"It's true, humans' evolution will be decided not by the strongest but by the wisest," said Michael.

"You've hit the nail on the head, Michael."

"It's not my observation; it's from Jonas Salk, the creator of the polio vaccine."

"It didn't take long for me to realize that I would need help distributing this great wealth," Harold said. "There was no way I could do it all by myself in this lifetime. The mission was too important. With great wealth comes great responsibility, and I took this very seriously back then, as I do today."

Harold recounted how he had gone back to Richard several weeks later to share with him how he would like to distribute his business interests. Harold had told Richard that he wanted to keep his anonymity the whole while. The intent behind his acts was not to signal to the world how great he was.

"The goal was infinitely more important than any one person, including me," he said. "I do not judge those who make it known to the recipients of their gifts who they are. Even if this public acknowledgment is what motivates them to give in the first place, the results are ultimately the same. But that did not appeal to me."

To accomplish his goal, Harold had decided he would refuse to take any tax deductions for the philanthropic work he had been about to embark on. He felt that it was important that the recipients of his gifts not know who their benefactor was. He didn't want his name on anything, choosing instead to adopt the Chinese philosophy set down by Lao Tzu in the *Tao Te Ching*:

A leader is best,

When people barely know he exists,

Of a good leader, who talks little,

When his work is done, his aim fulfilled,

They will say: we did it ourselves.

"Do you know what felt better than making my first million dollars?" asked Harold.

Michael shook his head.

"It was making the commitment to strategically give away a million times that amount. I wanted to create and oversee the process that would accomplish this. I wanted to have the satisfaction of knowing that future generations would bear the fruits of this worthy work."

Harold told Michael that after meeting Richard about his plan, he had embarked on his new life's mission. In the following years, he had looked for and invested in only worthwhile projects that supported this goal of empowering people to achieve the greatest good for humanity and the planet.

"I had tasked Richard to make the necessary legal arrangement for these gifts," he said. "But I said they had to be dispensed on the condition that the recipients not insist on knowing where the money came from."

Harold laughed.

"What's so funny?" Michael asked.

"Let me tell you, Richard had to reassure many recipients that these funds came from legal sources."

Harold noted how the money had been invested in schools, clean-water and air projects, disease control and prevention, sustainable environmental and community developments, and other forms of research. It was all for the betterment of people's health and the planet, and in support of democratic republican civic values. Harold had put his own spin on an observation made by Confucius and adopted it as his motto:

To be rich for a year, grow rice.

To be rich for ten years, grow trees.

To be rich for a lifetime and beyond, grow people.

And that's what Harold said he had aimed to do: invest in people. He told Michael that he had realized that he and Richard weren't young bucks anymore. So, they had spent many years discussing how Harold's patronage and philanthropic work would continue long after the two of them were gone. They had needed to develop a method to replace themselves, so that their work to better society would continue long after their deaths.

Together they had decided to revive the tradition of the patron and the protégé, the age-old student-teacher model, where wiser and older members of a society help their younger and novice counterparts mature and then take over. A patron is the teacher, the individual who uses his influence to help another fulfill his potential to take up his role in society. The protégé is guided and supported by his mentor, who is older, more experienced and a more influential person in the social order. As patrons, both Richard and Harold would make an active investment in their protégés' careers and success. Just to be clear, their motives had by no means been purely altruistic. They had believed that an investment in a protégé was an investment in their own long-term goal, which was to grow and continue Harold's legacy.

"We had learned that people between the ages of 15 and 35, and especially men, want to find a patron, someone to guide them through their professional and personal journeys," Harold said. "On the other hand, men start to feel the need to find a protégé when they enter late middle age. That's when their desire to pass on what they have learned on their life's journey is strongest; they want to create a lasting legacy."

At about the time he had turned 52, Harold had realized that what was lacking in society were patrons—individuals who believe in the young and are prepared to provide the air cover, so to speak, that protects them as they mature into contributing members of society.

"I was lucky that when I was growing up, I had my Uncle Max and also Richard, who was one of the greatest legal minds this country has ever produced," Harold said. "In the early days of my wholesale business, my Uncle Max introduced me to successful business owners in both his personal and business network, and he vouched for me. I was able to do business with these businesspeople thanks to his patronage.

"Richard guided me in a different way. His skills were in law, and they helped me through the never-ending maze of business structuring and acquisitions to ensure my business's growth and success."

Harold noted that Max and Richard had given him a primer on knowing how to find the right people to patronize. "Just by watching how the two of them conducted themselves, I learned what type of people mature into societal elders," he said.

"I find the subject of patrons very interesting," Michael said. "It was my need for a mentor that gave me the courage to first approach you in this diner."

Michael told Harold that long ago in tribal cultures, a father would bring his son, when he had reached a certain age, to a village elder to initiate him into the ways of the tribe—to become a responsible citizen and a contributing member of the community. When the time came, the son would take his rightful place as a tribal elder. This cycle continued generation after generation.

"Unfortunately, this cycle has broken down in our society," he said. "I have come to realize that my father could have never been my mentor, even if he had not died when I was 11. His role was that of a parent. But both the mentor and protégé need to feel comfortable enough to talk about personal indiscretions, something the protégé might not want to share with a parent. In a healthy mentorship relationship, the protégé will eventually become a peer of the patron. I'm reminded of the old saying that a society that forgets its past has no future."

"Yes, I couldn't agree more," Harold said. "The patron-protégé relationship is a dying tradition. And if it is not revived soon, and I mean in a big way, it will be the end of all that has made Western civilization the greatest achievement of human ingenuity ever."

It was fortunate for Richard, Harold said, that Mitch had shown up in his life when he had. Mitch had been an eager student. What patrons look for in a protégé is someone who delivers a standout performance and is extremely loyal and reliable. Someone seeking a patron shouldn't expect a handout—he needs to prove his value. Patronage is all about reciprocity. Protégés should pick their patrons wisely and vice versa.

"I took my responsibility of taking on the role of a modern-day elder seriously," Harold said. "I needed to find and nurture successors who would continue the important work I had begun. I had to make sure it would continue long after I'm gone. I sought out young people who had grit and a strong inner compass. At the same time, they had to be outwardly focused—on the world outside themselves. I wanted them to have the desire to make the world a better place."

Other characteristics Harold had looked for when selecting a protégé included competence, trustworthiness and discretion. The protégé was to birth unique skills to the world and would look out for the less fortunate in society. He would not forget his community responsibilities. A protégé would be both an individual and a team player, and feel a need to pass the tradition on to the next generation. Harold said he had searched for protégés who were up to the challenge. He had wanted individuals who were determined to live life on their own terms, through their own ingenuity. They would be men determined to make it on their own merit, rather than because of birthright or inheritance.

These individuals could be found almost anywhere if one trained his eyes to find them. Harold explained that they were often entrepreneurs, who constituted a unique group of people. Entrepreneurs are those people who strike out on their own and give themselves a great gift, that of the possibility to self-actualize. Harold's protégés were people who had created their own worlds. They knew what worked for them and what didn't, through years of experience with people and business. They knew what dedication meant. Any successful entrepreneur takes total responsibility for his life and business.

"Did Mitch know what you and Richard were up to?" Michael asked.

"Your friend knew you better than you think. He loved you and was your strongest advocate and ally."

"He knew?" Michael asked again.

"Do you remember that morning you first saw me, picking up trash near Daley Plaza? You were rushing off with Mitch to meet Richard for the first time."

"Yes, that was the first lesson I learned from you, and it was learned just by observing you," Michael answered. "The lesson was not to rush to judgment but to question underlining assumptions. Things are not always as they appear."

"Our first encounter was not by accident. Richard had taken Mitch into our confidence and was educating him on the ways of our mission. At the time, he was being groomed to one day take over from Richard and the important work we were doing. When Richard and I were discussing who might eventually take over for me, Mitch claimed that you were the ideal person for the job. He told us of how, in college, you did good without any desire for recognition. But you were rough, and it took a lot of guidance and some grooming to get you ready and up to the challenge," said Harold.

Michael just sat and listened. Everything was starting to fall into place.

"At first, Richard and I were unsure about Mitch's recommendation of you," Harold said. "I was a bit concerned by your reaction to me picking up that trash. I thought perhaps you were what I term a 'surface dweller,' a person who relies only on their five senses and does not dig deeper to find where the real buried treasures lie. Doing the digging requires a commitment to introspection, and its work. But when you approached me that afternoon at this very spot, determined to learn more about the unseen and where to find true value, I realized that you might be the one.

"I witness it every day, people who walk by millions of opportunities and don't stop to question whether it is an opportunity that can change the course of their lives. They just keep walking, as if what they had come across was nothing of value. There are so many undiscovered treasures. There is no such thing as luck, Michael—something you have learned through living out your purpose. But if there *were* such a thing as luck, it would be when an individual's preparation meets with the right opportunity, and that individual takes hold of it and does something of value with it.

"Well, before we met in person, I knew as much about your story as anyone could. How it had not been easy for you growing up. That you had lost your father when you were young. That you had held countless jobs from the time you were 12 years old, to help support your mother and sisters. The college scholarship you had received. I must admit, it was an inspiring essay you wrote for the selection committee," said Harold.

"You read it?" asked Michael.

"Yes," Harold replied. "I research everything I can before getting involved in any investment that requires me to devote a considerable amount of time to nourishing. I was especially impressed with the man you aspired to become. You were asking some really big questions about life back then; they were very advanced for your age. Your character spoke to me, especially the promise you had made. You had said you took your responsibilities for your citizenship seriously and had pledged to earn your rights and privileges. You had wanted to make your way through a free, democratic, republican society by honoring your obligations to protect that same society that had blessed you with the opportunity to fully express your individuality."

Harold explained that it had been clear from the essay Michael had written that he understood that in no other culture had so much been given to the individual, and for that same reason, these rights and privileges needed to be protected by each and every one of its citizens.

In the course of his investigation, Harold had learned that Michael's retirement and senior care facilities were different from others in the marketplace. The old model, in which the elderly were not recognized as wanting or even needing some level of independence, had been turned upside down by Michael. The old model just didn't work, and it resulted in a great loss for society when it came to gaining wisdom from its elders.

More than ever now, generations of youth were being neglected, growing to maturity without being initiated into adulthood by the guiding hand of elders. Michael's facilities were different. He understood that the seniors in his care were the bearers of human culture. It was a part of his company's mission to integrate these men and women into the community so that they could share their wisdom with future generations.

"I know you tried to hide this, but when I looked into your business, at first I found it strange that your profits were not as spectacular as they should have been. You ran a lean ship and had a keen eye for finding undervalued assets that others did not see; that is why your business was profitable," said Harold.

"I then understood why you had decided to go to lenders instead of selling off equity of your business to investors. You were secretly subsidizing close to 30 percent of your residents' housing, medical and healthcare expenses from profits. You knew that if you sold off ownership of your company, new partners would put an end to this practice. They would have put profits before people. How you had structured these subsidies showed that your motives were pure. You were doing what was right and just, not what was merely profitable. This is why I chose to quietly invest and lend you money, with the most favorable of terms.

I agreed with what you were doing, and I wanted to support this and to see if you would continue to do it. I wanted to witness what type of man you would mature into, especially once you had money."

Michael's face had gone white. "You were thorough in your research," he said. "I worked hard to keep that a secret. I hadn't even disclosed it to my wife. We've always had more than enough, and subsidizing the residents did not hamper our quality of life. I felt that I had to do what I could to provide dignity to those who had given their lives to our society and were now our elderly."

"Michael, I am telling you all this because I have one final request. It's a big one: I want you to take control of all my philanthropic ventures. I want you to take all the learning you have done over all these years. I want you to continue our work by creating a formal process that will ensure that the tradition of mentoring will be honored by future generations. As billions of youth transition into adulthood in the 21st century, we need more than ever for our society's elders to step up. We need more people to dedicate the second half of their lives to sharing their hard-won wisdom by giving their patronage wisely to the next generation. Are you willing to carry the baton?" Harold asked.

"As we age our responsibilities should not lessen but increase," Michael responded without hesitation. "I accept."

CHAPTER 28

—⟫⟪—

THE LEGACY

ICHAEL LEFT THE diner feeling reinvigorated. He had embraced this new calling for the last leg of his life. He felt the same youthful optimism and drive that he had felt when he had started his seniors' residence enterprise.

That would be the last time Michael and Harold would meet. The following week, Harold succumbed to his illness. Michael had never seen anything like Harold's funeral—thousands of people came from across the nation and around the globe to pay their respects. They wanted to show their love for a man who had at first reluctantly and then willingly accepted his duty in life, and who had succeeded at making the world a little better.

He was laid to rest at the Waldheim *Cemetery in* Forest Park, a suburb of Chicago. It was a place where countless generations of immigrants before him had been buried, years after venturing across the

Atlantic Ocean in search of the American Dream, as encapsulated by James Truslow Adams in his 1931 book *The Epic of America*, where he had written: "Life should be better and richer and fuller for everyone, with opportunity for each according to ability or achievement regardless of social class or circumstances of birth."

Beside Harold for eternity lay his loving and supportive wife, Sara. Nearby rested his brother, David, and his wife; his sister, Rachelle, and his brother-in-law, Richard; his Uncle Max and his wife; and his parents, Mendel and Ester Bloom.

After Harold's funeral and the seven-day mourning period that followed, Michael was ready to close a chapter of his life by merging his company into Harold's lasting gift to society, his private foundation. Michael was to guard the anonymity of the foundation, which, through its distribution of funds, would continue to be an instrument for creating good in the world.

A few months later, Michael entered the boardroom where Mitch and Richard had once schooled him in how to grow his business. The memory brought a smile to his face. Adam Boson greeted him and they got right to business. Waiting for Michael was a table covered with paperwork that would formally put Michael in charge to steward Harold's legacy. It was a mission that would honor those who had come before him. As he put pen to paper, signing the first of the many documents, he thought of Harold, Richard, Mitch, Uncle Max, Mendel Bloom and his father, Leslie Stevens. And there were so many others too who had helped get him to this stage, whose fulfillment of their responsibilities had made this moment possible.

After the last signature was inked, Adam turned to Michael and said, "Mitch tried to prepare me for the responsibility of taking over this important work that our firm has been entrusted to do. But I wish I were more ready and that Mitch was still with us."

"I miss Mitch as well. He saw something in you that is special, Adam—he had a gift for identifying hidden potential. I am fortunate that he saw it in me, and that he never gave up on me. I could not imagine what I would have missed out on in life if I hadn't had him as my friend and counsel. You will do well. I can feel it," said Michael.

"Before Harold became very sick, he came to see me here at the office," said Adam. "He told me that the young and old need to help each other fulfill their roles in society. The youth give the elders an opportunity to still be of value, while the elders gift tools that provide encouragement and empower the young to continue on their journey. Harold told me that I would do well to look to you for wise counsel and suggested that we meet regularly."

"It would be my honor to serve in any capacity you believe would be of value to you. Do you know that 1940s-style diner near Daley Plaza?" asked Michael.

"Yes. I pass it every day when I walk to the office."

"Great. It opens at 5:30 a.m. If you are up to it, let's meet there this Wednesday."

"I would like that very much. I'll be there bright and early," Adam said, smiling. "Oh, and one last thing. Harold gave me this envelope the last time I saw him. He wanted you to have it after you signed all the papers. He said you would know what to do with its contents."

Later that day, when Michael arrived at his hotel room, he opened the large envelope. It contained a notebook, in which was neatly listed hundreds of names plus contact information, in Harold's handwriting. Listed were all the people Harold had helped with his benevolent hand, either in person or by assisting in the background. There also was a note from Harold:

Dear Kiddo,

In the next 30 years, over $100 trillion will be transferred from one American generation to the next. This will be the greatest wealth transfer in human history. The healthiest and wealthiest generation the world has ever known is now entering its philanthropic primetime.

Everyone needs a little help. Here is a list of

people Mitch, Richard and I have been seeding, nurturing and assisting over the last three decades. All have shown their need and ability to give back to humanity. When you think they are ready, recruit them for our very important mission of paying it forward.

Please continue with their guided growth. Some on this list are already our active partners; others will eventually become valued allies. Your task also is to add to this list. As time goes on, those who are prepared to become societal elders will ultimately be ready to continue this chain of doing good. And always remember, Michael, that this chain was here long before us and will continue to grow long after we part.

See you on the other side.

Your friend and student forever, in this life and the next,

–Harold

EPILOGUE

THE RIDDLE REVISITED

TODAY WAS A rare milestone. It was Michael and Dawn's 60th wedding anniversary. They had once been young together and had borne witness to each other's lives. With each passing day of their union, their friendship and love grew stronger. Friends and family were flying in from around the globe to celebrate their diamond jubilee later that evening.

That morning as Michael reflected back on his life, he was proud that he had kept his pledge to his late mentor. He was following through on Harold's labor of love by providing mentorship to the next generation. Each day, he awoke with a renewed sense of youthful purpose, which *invigorated him*. Michael had rediscovered what ancient tribal societies had known. At night when the tribe gathered together around the communal fire, the elders would share stories that illuminated morals that would be of value to the youth. They helped them find their unique place within the tribe and the cosmos. Unfortunately, these skills of telling and listening have been mostly forgotten in modern society. Michael in his small way was helping to revive this healing and bonding tradition.

Very few among us truly comprehend the power of story. At its core, at its most significant level of meaning, story is transpersonal. It lies beyond rationality. When told right, it takes one to a higher level of understanding. It has the potential to illuminate our existence at more profound levels than any logical reasoning alone could ever achieve. Shared cultural stories are what bind one generation to the next and enable us to honor the past while looking towards a shared and empowered future. *Proverbs 29 tells us that* "where there is no vision, the people perish."

Michael began his task of manifesting his new calling. Using the list of names Harold had left for him, he continued to seed, nurture and assist young entrepreneurs and successful business owners. He helped them grow their enterprises, observing them mature into individuals who knew what it meant to be true citizens of their community, their country and the world. They demonstrated through their actions that they valued their responsibilities and obligations to society. They knew that each right and freedom they enjoyed needed to be earned, respected and appreciated every day of their lives.

Much of Michael's work was done in the background, without fanfare. This was the way he wanted it—and how Harold would have wanted it too. Once the individual had matured—and passed a pivotal test set for him and was ready—Michael made his presence known. That person would then be invited to be initiated into the Elders Lodge. Here he would begin his transition into his last of life and take on his most important role, that of a societal elder. Over time, others would join Michael in this mission. He would eventually pass on the baton so that others would take over the recruitment and management of the Elders Lodge and its mission. The lodge was structured in such a way as to eliminate hierarchy and traditional group boundaries. At the Elders Lodge, everyone was equal. Nestled in the deep woods of the Niagara Peninsula, it was purposely located far from the distractions of daily life.

It was turning into a beautiful summer day as Michael entered a lecture room on the lodge's grounds to greet the newest inductees, who had arrived just the night before. Looking into their eyes, Michael saw the future.

"Good morning, my name is Michael Stevens," he introduced himself to the small, intimate group, made up of some of the most accomplished individuals who had ever lived. "Some of you already know me, and some of you are meeting me for the very first time in person. I am thrilled to be here to speak with you today as you embark on the next stage of your life's journey. I would like to begin by sharing some reflections and a short story of how this place came to be. I also want to discuss with you how we intend to continue, together, the important mission of this lodge."

Michael spoke about how, over the past several decades, society had witnessed money dematerialize from paper into electrical pulses of ones and zeros. Trillions of dollars were swirling around the globe every second of the day. Unfortunately, the vast majority of it had no worthy purpose guiding its use. He spoke about how they were living in the most exciting moment in human history. Yet it was also challenging.

"There are so many incredible possibilities to look forward to, yet there is so much at stake," he said. "Right now, there are many environmental, social and economic crises, along with extreme political, racial and religious tensions. The roots of these crises do not lie outside ourselves but within us as a culture. It has been our craving for dominance, our love of the mighty dollar and our materialism, and our fears of each other that have led us to many of these societal woes we collectively face."

Michael shared with the group that he had been very much like them when he was a younger man and busy running a successful business. He had spent his career building his company, always looking to take it to the next level. But his inner voice had kept whispering that there was a greater purpose for him to seek out. He told the group about their journey ahead as well, noting that now that he was in his mid-80s, he found himself reflecting more and more on the journey his life had taken him.

"At your stage in life, I was beginning to ask myself important life questions, questions like 'Where have I been?'" He looked in turn at each person in the group.

"I wanted to fully understand where I was," he said. "What will my legacy be? Who have I met on my journey, and what value did I add to his life? Did I gain value from my professional relationships other than dollars? What about from my personal relationships? Who were my mentors? And most importantly, looking forward, who would I mentor?"

Michael told the group that every now and then we meet an individual who, when we study his life's story, offers us insight on what motivates a person to create, contribute to society and stand above the crowd. "I believe these are insights that, when applied, can enhance our own journey through life," he said.

"On March 21, 2014, almost 30 years ago, at age 82, a great man—and friend—left us," he continued. "The first time I met him in person was at a diner in downtown Chicago. Before that day, I had only known of him through his many achievements, and the whispers about who he was. His name was Harold Bloom—you would have known him as the King of Main Street—the man behind the Bargain Harold's shopping empire. I was fortunate that he became one of my great mentors. After hearing of his passing, the US president at the time wrote of him: "One of our nation's most notable citizens, this remarkable man will be mourned and missed not just for his business acumen but also for his generosity, which knew no bounds."

Harold's story was an inspiring rags-to-riches tale, Michael said. He had made America his home after immigrating here with his family just before the Second World War, fleeing from persecution in Nazi Germany. He had grown up in a neighborhood north of Chicago.

"What he had lacked in material wealth he sure had made up for with his vision and chutzpah," Michael told the group. "He would say,

'I started at the bottom when I came to this country. I needed to prove to myself that I was worthy of the challenges life put in front of me. I was hungry to find my success on my own terms.'"

Every so often, Michael would look intently into the eyes of those in the audience, as if he was peering into their souls. They were hanging on to his every word.

"I was privileged to have known him personally. But not because of his wealth or the accolades he received. I knew him as a great American, as a citizen of the world and as a wise teacher. We all have had these types of individuals enter our lives—those people who make an important contribution to who we become. We then carry a piece of them for the rest of our lives. Harold was just one of those rare individuals whose experiences, wisdom and legacy we can learn from."

Michael continued by sharing that everyone was there that day because of Harold's enduring vision, which had resulted in the creation of the Elders Lodge. Seasoned entrepreneurs and business titans came to the lodge from around the world to join together and also take a break from their hectic lives. Stepping back to gain perspective allowed them to then plan how they wished to transition out of their working lives. At this special place, others who had already made this transition successfully assisted them in transitioning into their last role, that of a societal elder. Here they would begin to formulate how they would choose to best use the considerable wealth, resources, knowledge, and wisdom they had accumulated during their lives, to assist the next generation in reaching its full potential and life goals, in preparation for when today's youth would in turn be ready to step into their role as stewards of the earth. So the circle of mentorship would continue, braving the test of time.

Michael then recalled Ernest Hemingway's novel *The Old Man and the Sea*.

"It's not just the story of an old fisherman who decided to venture out into the ocean farther than he ever had before, to catch a prized 1,800-pound marlin," he told the group.

"*The Old Man and the Sea* is a story of determination and

perseverance, of how one should never let go without a good fight. That was a key lesson for the old fisherman's young apprentice, who watched his mentor take on the elements and succeed despite horrible mental, physical, emotional and spiritual pain. Like the fisherman, Harold was a hero, a seasoned warrior who chose to attack accepted dogma wherever and whenever he found it. He believed, like Robert Kennedy echoing George Bernard Shaw, that 'some men see things as they are and say, "why?"'; he dreamed of things that never were and said, 'why not?'"

Michael recalled Harold's modest start, how he had scraped together the seed money to open his first store. He noted how he had suffered many setbacks in his life, but had endured and kept setting his sights on ever greater goals so that he would always be testing himself, pushing himself.

"He changed the way we shop," Michael said. "Harold made his mark on both wholesale and retail, on real estate development and investing. But he made his most significant impact on people's lives. One of Harold's greatest strengths was his belief in the value of investing time and energy into people, to help them find their purpose so that they could then make a meaningful contribution to society.

"In the early 1990s, Harold chose to invest his time and energy in me. The greatest lesson I ever learned from Harold, one that was far more valuable than any material object, I learned back in 1992. I had arrived at our usual spot, that diner in downtown Chicago, to find Harold looking a little puzzled."

Earlier, just before meeting there, Harold had talked with an able-bodied man who was panhandling on the street. He had since been asking himself how this man's life could have turned out that way—this man who had told him he had been born in this country, which Harold considered "the best country in the whole wide world," and who had been offered so many opportunities.

Harold had shared with Michael that he had been asking himself this question because he felt that even though he had come to this country not speaking the language, he had been able to make a good life for himself. Why had so many others not taken the opportunities presented to them to make something of themselves?

Harold would often share his gratitude for America by saying, "I came to this country with nothing and it gave me everything—it gave me freedom; it gave me my life." It was the same question that Harold had asked himself that had led Michael to become the eager student of a man who had lived such a complete life.

As they had talked, Michael had asked Harold a seemingly innocent question: What, when he was a little boy, had he dreamed of doing with his life? Harold had told Michael that he had dreamed of building a world-class business that would revolutionize how business was done.

Then Harold had joked that in his father's family, nonprofessionals were not considered "real" men. According to his father, "real" men became lawyers and doctors. But Harold had decided that he was going to chart his own destiny and become a business entrepreneur, realizing his youthful inner calling to build a revolutionary business.

Every great visionary needs his own muse, and Harold's was his wife, Sara, who had been the love of his life and who he had often referred to as "Chailee"—or "life for me." After Harold had returned from the Korean War, he had embarked with Sara on their journey, enjoying what life had in store for them. Most importantly, Harold had felt a great inner need to give back and to help the next generation make its unique contributions to society.

He had accomplished this by creating a private foundation as a vehicle for much of his charitable work, in America and abroad. He had made considerable endowments, funding causes he had passionately believed in. His aim had been to make the world better than he had found it. He had done this with total anonymity.

"As we finished our conversation that day, I asked Harold if he had felt that he had accomplished his vision, the one he had had when he was young. Harold smiled and then said, 'Yes. But there is a new vision. It is much bigger, bolder and more important than the first. It involves individuals like you if it is going to be realized. I'm going to need help. It can't be done just by me alone.'

"I turned to him and said, 'Thank you. You have given me a great gift today by sharing your insights on why you've achieved so much. You had a great vision that you felt driven to achieve, and you were very fortunate to have found a life partner to enjoy and experience your journey with.'"

That is what made all the difference when it came to having an ordinary life versus an extraordinary one. Michael shared with the group that he had always felt honored that Harold had chosen to spend countless hours with him, sharing his insights gained from a life well lived.

"That day, Harold taught me a valuable life lesson, which is that if you value something, you will be inclined to direct your energies towards it. If you don't, you won't," Michael said.

"He taught through example that one's only concern should be what one has in one's pockets, not what others have in theirs. One should always be proud of and satisfied with what one has, and not to begrudge others for having more or less. The grass of other people's yards might look greener, but those lawns need to be manicured by those who have been made the custodians of those green yards. What one does doesn't define who one is; it is what one gives that does. The world is a looking glass for the self; what one puts before it is what is reflected back. If life serves you up lemons, make lemonade."

At this comment, laughter broke out in the room. As the audience settled down, Michael continued.

"Most importantly, it is our responsibility and obligation to take care of that which we love, and to enjoy the best life possible while helping, or at least certainly not harming, others.

"Harold's story tells us that victory is not a prerequisite for honor. Rather, honor comes from having the fortitude to see a struggle through to the end, regardless of the outcome. Even if he did not always have the optimal result in every one of his business ventures, or in the task he's set for us, he knew that he had given it his all, and that he and others would improve during their next challenge. Glory and honor come not from the battle itself but from a determination to fight and always fall forward and upward.

"Harold was a citizen in every sense of the word; he understood his obligations to make this world a better place. Through his mentorship, I saw my world through a greatly enlarged and improved lens. Our society has so few wise men and women to be positive role models for the next generation. With Harold's passing, there is one less. But he will not be the last. I am thankful that you have all joined with me to continue the example Harold set.

"Before we wrap up for today, I would like to share with you one last story. Whenever Harold met someone who he saw might potentially help him realize his vision, he asked him a riddle. He told this person that how he chose to answer would reflect how he chose to approach life. The last time I met with Harold, I asked what his answer to this riddle was. I would like to share with you the riddle and the answer he gave me that day.

"If you are all alone in an ancient redwood forest and the largest tree cracks and falls right in front of you, taking down with it several other large neighboring trees, does it make a noise?

"Harold's answer was: 'Who cares? You're all alone. The purpose of receiving is to share.'"

ONE LITTLE FAVOR

If you enjoyed *The King of Main Street* and found it of value, I have one little favor to ask of you. If you could take a few moments out of your day to write a review about this book on Amazon.com, I would be very appreciative. Your feedback will be invaluable as I write this book's sequel.

Thank you,
Peter J. Merrick

KEYNOTE SPEAKER/INCOME AND CAPITAL ENHANCEMENT CONSULTING

Peter J. Merrick is a sought-after speaker, consultant and author on business succession, estate planning, and income and capital enhancement solutions. He brings pioneering insights and work experience in the areas of mentorship, financial succession and philanthropic planning. His public speaking appearances, consulting services and seminars are fully customized, and his unique research process is rich in practical content that can be put into practice immediately.

For further information on how to book Peter J. Merrick, please contact:

Info@TheKingofMainStreet.com or www.TheKingofMainStreet.com

ABOUT THE AUTHOR

Peter J. Merrick is an income and capital enhancement consultant, speaker and author. Since the early 1990s, Peter's career in business succession consulting and post-secondary financial education has been unparalleled in terms of depth and experience. He is considered one of the leading experts in succession planning, risk management, estates and trusts, US-Canada cross-border planning, and executive benefits and pensions across North America. Peter is a sought-after keynote speaker with expertise in project management for business succession. He is also one of the foremost experts in tax minimization planning solutions for some of North America's largest public and privately held businesses, property owners, financial institutions, and accounting and legal firms.

Peter is the author of three successful textbooks: *ASK: Advisors Seeking Knowledge: A Comprehensive Guide to Succession and Estate Planning*; *The TASK: The Trusted Advisor's Survival Kit*; and *The Essential*

Individual Pension Plan Handbook. All are considered seminal resources on tax minimization, business succession, estate planning and executive benefits. They have been referred to as "The Dr. Spock" references for succession planning experts, CPAs, CFPs, and wealth and risk management communities. Peter is also a professional financial writer, with over seven hundred published articles.

After being in the financial services industry for more than a quarter of a century, Peter has now written his first novel, *The King of Main Street.* His hope is that it will help readers understand the financial solutions and core values currently known primarily by experts. He wishes to pass on new and innovative ideas, along with successful strategies, to the seasoned business leader and aspiring entrepreneur alike. He believes the best business succession planning is done through the mentoring of our next generation of societal leaders.